Refusing the Favor

----- Refusing the Favor --------------------

The Spanish-Mexican Women
of Santa Fe, 1820–1880

DEENA J. GONZÁLEZ

New York   Oxford

Oxford University Press

1999

Oxford University Press

Oxford   New York
Athens   Auckland   Bangkok   Bogotá   Buenos Aires   Calcutta
Cape Town   Chennai   Dar es Salaam   Delhi   Florence   Hong Kong   Istanbul
Karachi   Kuala Lumpur   Madrid   Melbourne   Mexico City   Mumbai
Nairobi   Paris   São Paulo   Singapore   Taipei   Tokyo   Toronto   Warsaw

and associated companies in
Berlin   Ibadan

Published by Oxford University Press, Inc.
198 Madison Avenue, New York, New York 10016

Oxford is a registered trademark of Oxford University Press

Library of Congress Cataloging-in-Publication Data
González, Deena J., 1952–
    Refusing the favor: the Spanish-Mexican women of Santa Fe, 1820–1880
    Deena J. González.
       p.   cm.
    Includes bibliographical references and index.
    ISBN 0-19-507890-X
    1. Mexican American women—New Mexico—Santa Fe—History—19th
century.   2. Mexican American women—New Mexico—Santa Fe—Social
conditions—19th century.   3. Colonization—New Mexico—Santa Fe—
History—19th century.   4. Santa Fe (N.M.)—Ethnic relations.
5. Santa Fe (N.M.)—Social conditions.   I. Title.
F804.S29M54   1999
978.9'560046872073—dc21   98-49560

1 3 5 7 9 8 6 4 2

Printed in the United States of America
on acid-free paper

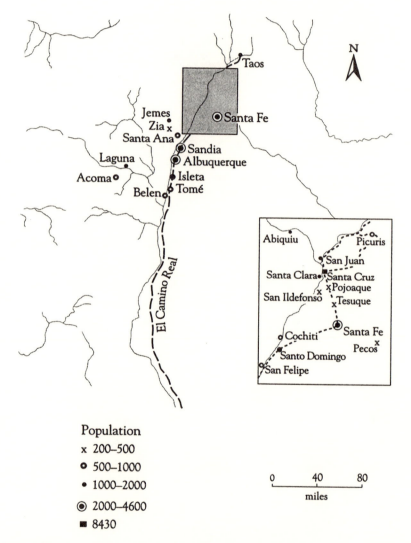

N

Taos

Jemes
Zia x
Santa Ana o
Laguna
Acoma o
Belen o
Sandia
Albuquerque
Isleta
Tomé
Santa Fe

El Camino Real

Abiquiu
Picuris
San Juan
Santa Clara
Santa Cruz
x Pojoaque
San Ildefonso x
x Tesuque
Cochiti o
Santa Fe
Pecos x
Santo Domingo
San Felipe

Population

x 200–500

o 500–1000

• 1000–2000

◎ 2000–4600

■ 8430

0   40   80
miles

Principal Towns and Road—1800. From Warren A. Beck & Ynez D. Haase, *Historical Atlas of New Mexico*, 1969. Courtesy of the University of Oklahoma Press.

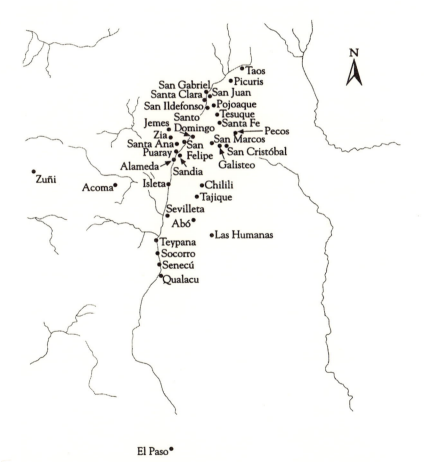

N

Taos
Picuris
San Gabriel
Santa Clara
San Juan
San Ildefonso
Pojoaque
Tesuque
Santo
Santa Fe
Jemes
Domingo
Pecos
Zia
Santa Ana
San
San Marcos
Puaray
Felipe
San Cristóbal
Alameda
Galisteo
Sandia
Zuñi
Isleta
Chilili
Acoma
Tajique
Sevilleta
Abó
Las Humanas
Teypana
Socorro
Senecú
Qualacu

El Paso

First Towns Established by the Spanish. From Warren A. Beck & Ynez D. Haase,
Historical Atlas of New Mexico, 1969. Courtesy of the University of Oklahoma Press.

PREFACE

This book examines a type of history by unraveling New Mexican women's experiences. I wish to understand nineteenth-century social and cultural history as much as I want to illuminate Chicanas' historical experiences. I wrote the book about a period in U.S. history for which disciplines are beginning to be reconfigured, from the inside: I have been, and still am, a participant in a process in which approaches to the study of history seek to disconnect, to reconstruct, and to reevaluate the past from multiple locations and across theoretical perspectives.

My understanding and sense of doing history has been formulated not only in an era of postdisciplinary movements, but also when as a child I knew intimately—without words or a vocabulary—the processes of colonization and conquest. I shared, with other 1950s baby boomers of New Mexico, some well-documented "truths." I was supposed to "know" that I was Spanish, but not Mexican; was of Spanish-speaking descent, but not Native. I "knew" that church, family, and community organized life for me and my generation of cousins, as it had for our aunts, uncles, and grandparents. I "knew" that education was important and that the more of it we "received," the better off we would be. I also "knew" that Mexicans were people from "the other side" and that we did not speak the same language, eat the same foods, or approach life in the same way, despite the fact that at home, grandparents and great-aunts and great-uncles insisted that we speak "Mexicano"; they meant "Spanish," the language, but they did not refer to themselves as "Spanish," in the way my parents' generation had begun doing sometime after World War II.

These self-designations were part of a *constructed* history, a culturally specific, historical reality, built on a highly selective memory that immortalized the Spanish (Hispanos) at the expense of Native inheritance and preferred institutional life over all forms of autonomous action or reaction, Spain over México. It omitted the fact that the frontier regions of New Spain for a brief moment existed independently from Spain and, for two decades, "belonged" to México. Before long, however, before México could determine its own political future, it went to war with the United States. Invaded in 1846, nearly bankrupt, and forced to give up nearly one-half of its lands in 1848, México bent under pressure from the giant to the north. These facts were rarely discussed in our history books and would have gone a long way toward explaining the cultural dynamics embedded in our decisions about what to name ourselves. More to the point, omissions overlooked the fact that migration and immigration from the Mexican interior provinces was steady and constant; in other words, not even New Mexicans, according to every available census, were isolated from other Spanish-speakers, or from México proper.

The folkloric past I had been taught, at home and in school, through many books and stories detailing a fantasy heritage termed "Anglo, Spanish, and Indian"—and always in that order—contained knowledge constructed to suit any number of political agendas. To ignore it here would be to diminish history's power and to undermine its effects. My intention is to use old and new facts, to understand and convey the multiple possibilities embedded in multilayered histories, and, yes, to position women I have come to know through the documents, women who intimately understood their oppression and sought reconciliation and survival. With responses ranging from defiance toward authority to deference in the face of survival, Spanish-Mexican women crafted lives of beauty and significance, power and revival; I watched this within my extended family.

What I formally learned in New Mexico's schools in the 1950s and 1960s contained inaccurate renditions of Spanish-Mexican history or of New Mexican history, but my experiences, familial and cultural, were real and did not always square with textbook knowledge of the sort that ignored women's presence or suggested that Spanish-Mexican women were illiterate or only saloon-keepers. Sketches in chapter 2 appeared in the very popular journal of the time, *Harper's Monthly*, in April 1854. Luckily, the writer, George Brewerton, was accompanied by an artist who left us images of roadsides, as well as saloons and gambling halls. Unfortunately, the same sketches convey misrepresentations that continue to this day and are still taught in history books.

Aspects of my heritage and of those who attended rural, New Mexican schools suggested that national history—the pilgrims moving ever westward, the cowboys their agents or heirs—and our own brand of regional history did not square, either. I knew that we had not come to the United States—it had come to us. I was/am a colonial subject, a colonized person claiming U.S. citizenship. "We," that is, my family, were not immigrants, but rather fourteenth-generation New Mexicans. Countries moved borders around us, and we "became" U.S. citizens through geography's slight. These "truths" shape the history I tell in these pages as much as their revisioning in my adult and academic life organizes my ideas about race, ethnicity, class, and sexuality.

I describe the background I bring to this work not because I am egotistical—on the contrary, I was raised to believe that speaking of myself was a mark of bad manners—but because the life of colonized people in the United States rarely gets equal attention and the lives of colonized women of color are even less known. My hope is that people will read this book with a mind toward learning something about the Spanish-Mexican women of the 1800s in the way some of them might have wanted it known or documented. Not all of these women would agree with my findings, any more than all Latinos of the present day might agree on a ballot proposition; nearly all, I suspect, would agree that their perspectives and ideas were, and are, overlooked and that the oversight impoverishes history and the broader society. My dream and recommendation through the example of this book, then, is for an embellished, richly textured and delineated, history of New Mexicans and of Chicanas.

Of the latter I can say that demographically they/we will constitute the largest "minority group" at the turn of the century. Among all Latinos, Chicanos (or Mexican-origin people) form the largest group, and within that ethnicity, women form the majority. Chicanas in the next century will constitute the largest "minority" population in this society. All the more reason, then, to focus our eye on their histories and to let those guide us into a new century.

Claremont, California   D. J. G.
March 1999

ACKNOWLEDGMENTS

The work and the ideas upon which this study are based originated outside libraries and derive to a great extent from many sources—published books and scholarly articles, conversations, conferences, and oral reports and interviews. Many people helped and encouraged me. While I was a graduate student at Berkeley, Professors Gunther Barth, Jim Kettner, and Alan Dundes were inspiring teachers and supportive mentors. They were each agents of my acculturation to the academy, and social and cultural critics—in their own work—of the nineteenth century. Ellen Schaelstrate, administrator of the Graduate Minority Program, and its directors, Professors Juan Martínez and Clara Sue Kidwell, were always friendly and were supportive of my many petitions and requests for money. A group in northern California, Mujeres Activas en Letras y Cambio Social (MALCS), provided friendship and support during years and across arenas in which we needed desperately to work collectively. The librarians at the Bancroft Library, at the New Mexico State Records Center, at the Coronado Collection at the University of New Mexico, and at the Huntington Library, as well as those at Claremont, were helpful, courteous, and efficient. Finally, members of the Sena family and a private, anonymous collector in Denver came to the rescue when I needed assistance with unarchived sources, and they shared with me their family collections after hearing me speak in Pueblo and in Albuquerque. I thank professionals and amateurs alike for their interest in this project.

Fellowships from a number of people and agencies have also helped this work. Betty M. LaFetra, an alumnus of Pomona College (Claremont,

California), gave the history department at Pomona College numerous grants to help defray my research costs. A Ford Foundation/National Research Council Fellowship in 1987–1988 allowed me to take a sabbatical and continue writing with a minimum of interruption. The Research Committee at Pomona College and the Tomás Rivera Center in Claremont have also been generous in their grants and in their providing of computer experts, while slide curator Susan Thalmann helped me clarify images for reproduction. I thank each for the support. The Chicano Studies Department at Claremont, the second oldest of its kind in the country, provided student research assistants—and I thank, especially, Joe Ayala, Virginia Aguilar, Alicia García, Maricela Ponce, Julie Amador, Maythee Rojas, and Brenda García, as well as graduate students Antonia Villaseñor, Alice Hom, and Tammy Ho. During my fifteen years at Claremont, while they were working in the Department of Chicano/a Studies as well as in their "home" departments, Professors Ray Buriel, Homer García, Héctor Calderón, Harry Pachón, Gilbert Cadena, Guillermo Villareal, José Calderón, Vicki Ruiz, Miguel Tinker Salas, Eva Valle, Alicia Gaspar de Alba, Rita Alcalá, Patricia Prado-Olmos, and Lourdes Argüelles have been among the finest colleagues anyone could imagine, sharp critics and instructive as well through their scholarship. Similarly, Pomona College's Department of History has provided great support and steady friendship. Friends in Santa Fe and the environs, Patricia and Mario Durán and Carol Taschek, have fed my spirits over the many years of visits, calls, and friendship. In Austin, Cynthia Pérez and Dina and Flores Almita have been good friends. I am grateful to all of these people for their willingness to tolerate and challenge my thinking and scholarly activism.

Many historians provided feedback along the way. Historians Antonia Castañeda, Emma Pérez, Ramón Gutiérrez, Albert Camarillo, and Sid Lemelle read portions of this work and lent insightful suggestions for its improvement, as did Dorinne Kondo in the field of anthropology. In the field of western American history, Patricia Limerick, in her own work and in her comments, led me into areas I would not otherwise have explored. Camille Guerin-Gonzales and Susan Johnson offered venues and ideas when my energy lagged, and their work inspires me, as does—in American Studies viewpoints—the scholarship of Alicia Gaspar de Alba. I thank them for their support and assistance. My editors at Oxford University Press—from inception, Sheldon Meyer, now retired, and then Susan Ferber, Thomas Le Bien, and Cynthia Garver these past years—have been more than helpful and efficient. Finally, Peggy Pascoe spent many hours on my manuscript and clarified each of its chapters; she has been consistently helpful and insightful with this project, unceasing in her devotion to western women's history.

Several workers at Pomona College and in my home also helped me complete the book: Helen Young, Corinne Dearborn, Obdulia Contreras, Alicia Plasencia, and Connie López took messages or cleaned my house or office, and I owe them a special debt because they were consistently patient and helpful. Amalia Cabezas, friend and roommate during her time in Claremont, helped me understand much about this matter of colonization. Dr. Leslie Jackson's wise counsel also never failed me.

Finally, the members of my family, all fifty-six first cousins and thirty aunts and uncles, across several generations, including godparents, plus my parents and grandparents, great-aunts and -uncles, brother and sister, have sustained this work when I thought it would never end. My mother, Vidal, whose love of history grew strong in "the old days," when she matriculated at the University of New Mexico during the period of the "great Borderlands historians," has never tired of either supporting my academic endeavors or of telling and retelling stories. My father, Santiago, has underwritten trips from one archive to another and has cheerfully supplied birthday cakes and gasoline as they were needed. My sister, Rita, is accustomed to receiving phone calls from me at odd hours and has helped me get to and from airports with no complaints. My brother, Benjamín, has impressed upon me the need to get this work done. My grandparents, Tomás y Juanita Trujillo, provided refuge, sensibility, and laughter, as well as good food and, always, debate; they helped me understand the nineteenth century better than most history textbooks could and served as conduits between the periods. I miss them terribly, but feel blessed to have known them as long as I did. Writer and scholar Alicia Gaspar de Alba dropped into my life at a moment when this work was languishing, at a juncture when a problem with word processors and source notes proved nearly insurmountable, and she decided to remain close to me and the project. Seven years later, I thank her for her poetry, short stories, and ability to unclutter my soul and make room in our home for history and literature, as well as for cats and a new puppy.

I am unable to adhere to the Spanish-Mexican custom of purchasing copies of this book for all of my close relatives, but I hope they recognize in it stories of our family and can decipher the lesson I seek to impart about the trauma, but also about the hope and dream, involved in overcoming colonization and fighting oppression.

CONTENTS

NOTE ON TERMINOLOGY

The words I use in this book to identify persons or groups living in the past frequently convey powerful ahistorical messages. For that reason, in the ensuing discussion, I term individuals, ethnic groups, and communities according to their preferred nomenclature, and have sought to devise a historically appropriate vocabulary. When the distinctions seem unclear, I have considered other factors, as in the case of Irish-born migrants to Santa Fe who might be properly termed immigrants (to the United States) but who here are included with all Euro-Americans. I have avoided using the inaccurate but popular "Anglo."

SPANISH-MEXICAN   This word is hyphenated to indicate that the persons were Spanish-speaking and, beginning in 1821, lived under the Mexican flag; they sometimes considered themselves "españoles" (Spaniards), although the majority were not Spanish, but mestizos.

MESTIZO   Generally, a person of mixed ancestry; it refers here to a person of Native/indigenous and Spanish heritage.

MEXICAN   A Spanish-speaking or indigenous person residing south of the boundary established between the Republic of Mexico and the United States in 1848/1853; most Mexicans were mestizos. This word, although Hispanicized, dates to the Aztec period.

NATIVE/INDIAN   "Native" is used when the point being made concerns indigenous customs and cultures. At times, "Indian" is used in reference to Native peoples but as a Spanish-Mexican would employ it, and not as a Native would, because Native Americans named themselves by community or by culture of origin. For example, the "Navajo" were/are Diné. Many Native communities surrounded Santa Fe, but Native residents of Santa Fe were not always distinguished in the documents by their community of origin.

EURO-AMERICAN   A person of any European origin, except Spanish, including the Irish-, Prussian-, and English-born migrants to Santa Fe. A Euro-American might have belonged to several ethnic (but not racial) groups, whereas a Spanish-Mexican was of two "races," Native and Caucasian.

MIGRANTS   Refers most often to male Euro-Americans who migrated to Santa Fe after 1821, and also after 1848, when parts of the Mexican North were formally ceded to the United States.

RESIDENT   Refers to the Spanish-Mexican and Native people living in New Mexico before and after the conquest, to distinguish the local population from arriving migrants.

AMERICAN/AMERICANIZATION   An American is, and was, a person living in the Americas. In this study, the words follow a contemporary convention; they refer to the U.S. conquest of New Mexico and the gradual imposition of U.S. institutions, values, or concepts. They refer implicitly as well to the century in which U.S. citizens began to think of themselves as the only true Americans, although in fact New Mexicans referred to Euro-Americans as *norteamericanos*.

Refusing the Favor

Prologue

This work revolves around a simple question that is posed by New Mexican
history: How did the lives of the women of Santa Fe change when the
United States colonized the former Mexican North? This seemingly straight-
forward query led to several discoveries about the way Spanish-Mexican
women lived during the past century, about what they valued and believed, and
about how they reconstructed their daily routines after they were besieged by
strangers from the United States.

For much of the twentieth century, historians believed that the conquest of
New Mexico by Euro-Americans in the period between 1820 and 1880 had been
relatively painless. According to the prevailing interpretation, it involved only
minor skirmishes, shed little blood, and was facilitated by the Spanish-Mexican
upper class. When Stephen Watts Kearny and his soldiers marched into Santa
Fe in 1846, they met no resistance; without a fight, they substituted the U.S. flag
for the Mexican one. On the town plaza that day, Kearny promised prosperity to
the people of Santa Fe, saying, "We come to better your condition."

This story, with its emphasis on cooperation between Spanish-Mexican
elites and Euro-American conquerors, was an appealing one, partly because it
assumed that the U.S. flag's unfurling led to social and economic improvement
for all. But the tale is simply untrue. Conquest and colonization impoverished
the majority of the residents of Santa Fe and perhaps much of the New
Mexican north. It disempowered women, who had previously exercised certain
rights guaranteed by Spanish law. And it made most Spanish-Mexicans dependent on wages, earned in jobs controlled by Euro-Americans.[1]

3

In hindsight, when I began this work, my organizing questions had been based on opinions about the nature of social change that were nearly as positivistic—and erroneous—as those advanced by early Borderlands historians. Such scholars as Ralph Emerson Twitchell and Howard Roberts Lamar had argued in their early works that the condition of Spanish-Mexicans gradually improved over time or implied that conquest was not impoverishing. Many historians accepted the prevailing assumption that the United States' takeover signified economic, political, and social advancement. The evidence in this case study suggests otherwise.

Change, most social scientists say (and historians of the nineteenth century would agree) implies the reformation of the social order, and this was the case in Santa Fe. Wealthy traders, merchants, and, later, lawyers entered the town of several thousand residents and installed a new economic and political order. That change, however, did not necessarily improve the conditions of life for anyone, including women and children.

Reform and intrusion cause personal, psychological trauma; the experiences of the nineteenth-century women of Santa Fe were not exceptional in that regard. They changed their methods of coping and their strategies for surviving, as they began to accept the presence of literally thousands of new men, Euro-Americans, and to accommodate such different institutions as a rearranged court system and formal schooling.

Their style of dealing with the intruders did not follow a top-down pattern. Only as I looked more deeply into Santa Fe's history did I come to grapple extensively with colonization's multiple, unplotted directions, with the responses of women to events and to conquerors, and with their responses circumventing the outsiders. My logic initially told me that change, even change initiated by merchant capitalists, brought rewards as it created the hostilities that the conquered always vent against their conquerors and that invaders always promulgate against racial or cultural "others." Implicit in my original and optimistic notions about Santa Fe's large population of women was a sense that, because as a group they had survived the United States' takeover, they were special; at worst, they had weathered the crisis, and, at best, they had surmounted it.

Santa Fe was, however, the center of a complex, multiethnic frontier, and little of its 390-year history is simple. The Pueblo Indians of New Mexico had, for centuries, called Santa Fe—which was situated at the base of the Spanish-named Sangre de Cristo Mountains—the Dancing Ground of the Sun. Had the sun ever danced, it surely would have danced there. When the Spanish began crossing the valley in the 1540s, during Francisco Vásquez de Coronado's expedition, they remarked that the area's crisp air and changing shadows elicited special feelings. Coming upon the site from higher ground on the north, and looking downward, they were awed by the magnificent beauty of the "bowl," balanced easily by the surrounding hills and mountains. Moving away but still on the plateau and glimpsing back, they saw peaks jutting thirteen thousand feet into the clear air. The mountains framed the eastern side. Descending to level ground, the explorers observed the ruins of an ancient

Indian town, still visible beneath sagebrush and piñon trees. The unusually still, clean air at six thousand feet above sea level often left the newcomers gasping. Almost seventy years later, they built Santa Fe on this site. Two hundred years after that, Euro-Americans began traversing the Dancing Ground.

Always, the mobile Comanches, Apaches, and Navajos, as well as the Pueblo Indians living in concentrated villages all around the Dancing Ground, continued to cross the conquered terrain, sometimes trading with Spanish-Mexicans; at other times, raiding fields and taking hostages; and even, at times, marrying the Spanish-speakers. In the two centuries before the United States had an interest in the northern outposts of the Spanish Empire, Spanish-Mexicans and the Indians of New Mexico had developed a uniquely regional, culturally mixed way of life. From the Pueblos, the Spanish had borrowed food preparation skills, if not their actual cuisine. In turn, from the Spanish, the Pueblos borrowed the cultivation of more varieties of corn, to support the larger population, and the mixing of chile spices brought northward and incorporated into their diet. The adaptability of food on both sides proved easier than other developments.

In fact, racial mixture throughout the Spanish Empire proved a consequence of conflict. Contact and conquest, some studies have argued, induce conflict followed by accommodation.[2] In practice, they extract a heavier toll from their victims. Through interracial and intercultural relationships, Native and Spanish-Mexican women on the Dancing Ground and elsewhere bore children of mixed European, African, and Native ancestry. For those women, contact and conquest held a meaning that stretched beyond struggles to control institutions or to retain religion. They straddled two worlds (and later, when the United States invaded northern Mexico, three). For them, intercultural contact was a fact of everyday life, and they saw daily reminders of its consequences in the faces of their children.

Like those of many social historians, the assumptions that guided my earlier work on these topics were tempered by specific thoughts about the great power that economic intervention holds over a community, particularly when the original inhabitants are poor, but subsisting. Altogether, these sets of assumptions—those concerning social change as essentially positive, race mixture as an example of the "meetings" of cultures and those regarding the harsher reality of economic interference—were greatly modified as a result of this study. I am now, more than ever, impressed and discouraged by the disruptive role that economic colonization plays in the lives of ordinary, working-class people; in this case, the takeover of New Mexico by the United States impoverished the majority of women, even the tiny 5 percent of the population that, I estimate, belonged to the upper class in those decades. Ultimately, this story carries a distinctively sad message because it is, in fact, the history of the women who survived the conquest, but who, as a result, emerged financially poorer than when it began, and their descendants remain there today. In that sense, their accommodation to Euro-American ways can be depicted as a linear descent into poverty. That their economic condition did not improve greatly then—and has not done so since—only makes it more difficult to conclude their story.

The research from which this book derived also revised my notions about how the Spanish-Mexican women fared when the United States conquered the region. At first, I had conceived of the women—who numbered over two thousand at any given time during the period from 1820 to 1880—as both struggling survivors and active accommodators. This conceptualization proved to be like the proverbial double-edged sword. Their colonial past, I knew, portended women's survival. They were, after all, hardy frontierswomen far removed from the Mexican centers of sociopolitical and religious governance (Mexico City, in the case of the Spanish Empire, and Durango, in the case of the Roman Catholic archdiocese). Culturally and racially, they were of mixed ancestry: mestizas descended from both the Spanish and the Indians. Their numbers were rising in this period, perhaps doubling since the mid-eighteenth century as more native peoples "became" Spanish-Mexican and as more migrants from México's interior moved northward.[3]

Demographic shifts could not disentangle institutional barriers. Women lived within an oppressive class-delineated society and under harsh patriarchal conditions; the community's anchors—the political offices of the Mexican governance system, the church and its directors, and the extended family networks many centuries old—held women in place and placed women at the bottom of many hierarchies. Women had survived marginalization of this type, and much more.

It turned out that the other side of their story proved to be equally significant. By 1820 women constituted over half of the adult population and appeared in the historical record as people who had acquired or retained basic rights by virtue of their previous citizenship in the Spanish Empire. Among these were the right to be heard in a court of law and the right to sue and be sued. As parishioners in the Catholic Church in towns on the frontier, women also exercised a degree of autonomy and controlled key ceremonies essential to the rites of the church: they cleaned its altars, plastered its walls, and taught children how to become good Catholics. Thus they emerged, from that perspective, as independent characters capable of carving out a life in what was then the Mexican hinterlands.

Their *mestizaje* (mixed racial origins), like their mixed, variable status within the institutional apparatus of their society, also contributed to a far more complex, indeed contradictory, portrait than the one I painted previously in other essays. Women were, in fact, central to the survival of Spanish-Mexican culture and, although financially impoverished in the nineteenth century as a result of Euro-American contact and conquest, they managed to resist aspects of their colonization.

To unravel the mysteries of cultural survival and of adaptation to change, and to understand the complex ways in which the economy shaped this conquest, I have divided this book into three sections. Each underscores a theme that is either symptomatic of or that derives from colonization; each profiles, around that theme, types of women or individual characters. Entrepreneurs, rebels, accommodators, widows, and will-makers thus form the cast of characters, while a chronological arrangement highlights broader currents of social and political turmoil; my alternating between the specific and the general also highlights what I see as the most important methodological contributions of this work. In linking the specific contestations that involved women against colonization—and nineteenth-century New Mexico was a contested zone—and in examining their inversions of particular rituals, such as will-making, I describe how these Spanish-Mexican women did so much more than survive colonization. They refused its basic premise, which aimed at integrating them, at its lowest rungs, into a nineteenth-century economy and society that was being transplanted from the midwestern and eastern United States.

Like the pre-1820 patriarchal and archaic system that told women they were either "good" (virginal, maternal) or "bad" (sexual, transgressive), the world after 1820 began sending, or having to send, women different messages. Santa Fe's women played against the Euro-Americans who were migrating there and, in some cases, even managed to dupe a few along the way. I have sought to focus, then, on women's ways of resisting, by using the thousands of archival documents available to us in Spanish, which emphatically convey their values, worldviews, and self-esteem; I have focused on a few individuals whose uncovered, or discovered, lives suggest alternatives to the dilemmas a violent takeover imposes—to go or stay, to abide or resist, to accept or challenge.

The issues involved in using the approach I have outlined here are at the crux of what forms women's history—that is, what makes this new field exciting and challenging to male and Western conceptualizations of the larger discipline of history. It might seem that this book has no theoretical base because I do not explicitly subscribe—as these women also did not—to a durable form of internal colonialism or to verifying constantly outward colonization. However, the interpretive stories I tell of these women's lives are in fact informed by many theories basic to social and feminist history, including, but not restricted to, political economy and domestic economy as well as to theories exploring racism, sexism, and heterosexism.

An excellent example lies in my discussions of widowhood. Widows are frequently described as wives without husbands. I instead view them as unmarried women, women unpartnered with men; and I place them in the context of generally being unmarried, which was a far more important condition in frontier New Mexico than we have been led to believe. Most adult women spent their lives in a state of unmarriedness, either never having married or been partnered with men, or having outlived their husbands. If we focus on their relationship primarily to husbands or to other men, we miss some crucial elements of their existence. Women were indeed bound in marriage and as residents by the full-fledged compilation of laws that had come northward with Spanish-Mexican officials, and were embodied in a heavy and vexing legal code recorded and compiled in texts and on official documents; women also managed to disavow marriages, to obtain annulments, and, in many cases, to outlive husbands and never remarry.[4]

The cases defying the theories, or, as I call them in subsequent chapters, the idioms (of race, sex, gender, class, or location), sustain my focus on women's lives throughout the period beginning with Mexican independence and going up to 1880. In discussing politics, sex, race, ethnicity or economics, I refer frequently to the secondary literature on those subjects, especially that written by Chicano/a scholars, because I do not want to lose the thread of the women's stories or subsume them in a "race for theory," which engages and enrages so many scholars across the diverse fields of cultural studies, feminist literary criticism, and philosophy.[5] These newer theories were constantly before me, as stories emerged from the massive documentation available on women. I decided to focus on how women, who were sometimes far removed from decision-making settings, experienced or might have experienced the turmoil induced by the changes men initiated. It therefore seemed appropriate to devise a new methodology that, from the inside out, or the bottom up, helped document women's oppression and resistance, especially when the records I used avoided tracing the development of women's ideas, while simultaneously focusing on the turmoil in their lives. It would have been easier to sort out only social or economic patterns, to trace these historically, and to leave behind the work of scouring literally hundreds of thousands of documents in the church archives and in the government's records. The wealth of evidence about both women's oppression and resistance, about the ideology of the situation and the reality, spoke loudly for a different approach.

Equally significant to the structure of my interpretations is thematic unity, which remains important but in the background, like theory. Purposely, I lifted personalities out of the historical record that I found interesting, and I sometimes refer to them across decades to show that change and continuity do not always work progressively toward improvement. Women were constrained by patriarchy and by Roman Catholicism across the six decades studied, but they also subverted these and manipulated powerful men to achieve a measure of autonomy for themselves.

The story of María del Refugio Herrera in 1824 provides a case in point. Although the local cura (priest) was angry at her for refusing to marry Juan de Jesus Rivera, she insisted that she no longer wanted to marry him. The priest requested that she be disciplined for breaking her "promise" to marry him, but this evidently did not change her mind. In the census records of the 1840s, the same woman is included in a household with another male adult and children, suggesting that she indeed went her own way and eventually married someone else.[6]

Such practices of refusal and examples of independent spirit suggest that we must begin rewriting New Mexican women's history to incorporate what those of us from that part of the country generally believe to be the case—contemporarily and historically, women have as much as possible, forged their own destinies, despite cultural and economic confinement and limitations of the sort that bind parties contractually in practices like matrimonial promises or a legal arrangement, but that are fraught with fractures. The historical record can be silent on the matter of personal agony in such key decisions as marriage choices for women, but it is equally silent on their *lack* of agonizing. In such instances of silence, as I illustrated with the case of María Herrera, I have sought instead to allude, to suggest, as the data or records allow.

To focus on, or isolate, such individuals as María del Refugio Herrera might seem to undermine the cultural, political, and social complexity that I said existed on this racial, cultural, and sexual frontier. How historians decide to highlight an individual at the expense of a community provides fuel for one of the biggest debates running through the profession of history. Texts that are written mostly by men and that focus exclusively on men are increasingly being criticized for overlooking the majority of the population, who were women. In fact, I fully acknowledge that stretching one theme or set of themes across time and concentrating on a small group of "representative" women who are peculiar, because they have entered the written record, might seem exaggerated or, worse, might lean too much in the direction of fictionalizing or of neglecting the interdependent totalities of the lives of women, men, and children. I have chosen this approach, however, because the social history of the southwestern United States continues to suffer from a traditionalism that makes heroes of men and heroines of one or two women, while ignoring the many different ways women and men *can* be studied. My sense of the historiographical contribution of this approach to the history of the Spanish borderlands or the U.S. West outweighs stricter concerns for order, chronology, or tidy theoretical formulations.[7]

Thus, organizational and methodological issues reflect broad historiographical ones and are important for the simple reason that problems continue to plague ethnohistory, western American history, and women's history as well. Historians generally shy away from distending or even isolating trends, themes, events, and characters, precisely because they dislike overgeneralizing. We tend to fret more about accurately defining "how life was" than about the possibilities for building multidimensional, even symbolic, portrayals. Authors, folklorists, and even artists and movie producers have been left to cast and remold our historical figures into believable or unbelievable personalities, in whatever way they see fit. History is left the duller, while literature, folklore, and art—although suffering perhaps the accusation of ahistoricism—are enriched. They still seem capable, far more than history, of making people come to life.

The task of focusing on people's lives, and the assumption upon which it rests—that stories are crucial to history—inform my narrative throughout this book. Thus I examine the lives of Santa Fe's women by placing them at the forefront of unending colonization, while keeping their humanity in sight— they were human beings who had their own contradictory needs, desires, and ideas. Sometimes, the evidence is too scant to "tell it like it happened"; at other times, it is too fragmented to support biographical composites. I have sought instead a middle route, embellishing with details from the historical record, if necessary, and omitting entire scenes when my own imagination begins to skew history. Many portions of this book revise previously held assumptions about how race, class, gender, and sexuality operated on the Spanish-Mexican frontier, and the book as a whole testifies that women undergoing colonization are not merely "acted upon"; nor are they entirely victims.

This book ends during the year in which the railroad approached Santa Fe, a new jail was constructed on the town plaza, and the unprecedented Euro-

American migration to Santa Fe was ending. The cutoff point proved difficult to enforce because, as is the case with many stories of the so-called western frontier, the iron horse, the jailhouse, and the wave of Euro-Americans bearing cash are symbolic.

These developments in the lives of women pointed to a new, larger, and perhaps graver, situation. Ensconced in a sort of "iron cage," as Max Weber, Ronald Takaki, and others have argued, the Spanish-Mexican women of Santa Fe participated unwittingly in their own colonization, becoming dependent on wages in a phenomenon they shared with many, including those who immigrated to the United States. Why they labored for the lowest wages, why they were poorer even than many immigrant groups, and why they continue to occupy that place in the economic hierarchy today are important questions to ask in regard to this period and the one following it.[8]

The conclusion that the colonized women of Santa Fe became poorer by 1880 is inescapable when one charts their relative wealth and poverty beside that of the Euro-Americans moving into Santa Fe, when one looks beyond 1880 and notices that the jail records contain primarily the names of Spanish-surnamed people, and when one closely examines the records of land and property transactions and realizes that the exchanges worked principally to the advantage of the incoming white or Euro-American migrants: 90 percent of resident Spanish-Mexicans lost their lands to the colonizers.[9]

The travails of colonization, and the reconstruction efforts that followed the land takeovers and property losses after the U.S. war with Mexico, remain primary lessons in this story. By 1880, few residents of Santa Fe could escape the tentacles of Americanization in any arena. In their churches, schools, and courts, women resisted the worst of these intrusions; the strategies they invoked paralleled those found in enslaved African American communities; those of indigenous, reservation people; and those of immigrants brought to the United States to lay railroad tracks or, later, to lift crops from the fields.[10]

The Spanish-Mexican women's survival and accommodation to change resemble the history of several other nineteenth-century American ethnic groups. They share the dominant feature of institutionalized oppression that was experienced in the 1800s by diverse groups such as African Americans, Native Americans, and Asian Americans. But again, the New Mexico case offers some interesting contrasts. In New Mexico, after 1848, the courts and church offices fell into Euro-American hands, and fewer women turned to them to resolve conflicts; after 1848, the majority of women labored for wages and remained bound to the lowest places in the economic hierarchy. After 1848, larger numbers lost their lands and property to the enterprising Euro-Americans.[11]

Still, the Spanish-Mexican women clung to, and even embellished, particular cultural traditions, which distinguished them as well from other ethnic groups of the nineteenth century. They gambled, smoked cigarettes, and danced in public, as before; they gathered annually to climb ladders and plaster adobe walls in their villages and towns, defying Euro-American and Victorian conventions. They bequeathed property and inheritances in testimonials recited before scribes or magistrates, as they had done before. Other demographic data reinforce elements of continuity between past and present.

In the main, the Spanish-Mexican women were a resident population and not an immigrant or a migrant one; perhaps 5 to 8 percent of the total population had recently migrated from other parts of Mexico, but most retained a legacy several generations, and in some cases many generations, old, and lived in the same region as their ancestors had lived. They did not emigrate to the United States; the United States came to them. Racially, they were also distinctive. Although the majority spoke Spanish and were Catholic, many could have claimed mixed Spanish-Indian heritage and some later also claimed Irish-Spanish inheritance. In their diet, dress, and appearance, they were a mestiza, or mixed-race, population, and this mestizaje formed their own identity as much as their long association with a particular geographic locale even as they refused to deploy that term itself. Usually, they referred to themselves in "official" contexts as *vecinas* (residents), a legal term signifying residency, place, and stability.[12]

Despite many adaptive strategies—such as learning English and electing officials—the region Spanish-Mexicans claimed as their home became like a minicolony of the United States, and its subsequent colonization distinguishes the locals from many other ethnic minority groups now residing in this country who were either forced to come here through enslavement; put on reservations or relocated, as Indians were (I mean the legal definition of the term "Indian" here, as invoked by the invading Euro-Americans); or who were displaced to the United States by global market conditions. That feature also sets the Spanish-Mexican women apart from other ethnic minority groups of the nineteenth century, who, except for those who were indigenous or who arrived as slaves or as children of slaves, came as immigrants eager to absorb themselves into American society.

Historians know that no matter how strong the urge to assimilate, few groups in the last century or in this one were allowed, institutionally, politically, and economically, to achieve that goal. Assimilation works, social scientists remind us, when the host society agrees to accept others. In the United States, especially during the nineteenth century, that was neither possible nor allowable for many groups; exclusion acts, segregated facilities, and lynchings testify to this sorry chapter in U.S. racial history.

Moreover, colonialism on the former Mexican northern frontier affected all classes and both sexes. Even the upper-crust Spanish-Mexicans suffered as they watched their wealth decline and their class status being constantly redefined by strict regulations on trade with Chihuahua in the colonial period; by even stricter ones under the newly independent Mexican state and later when Euro-American merchants were granted licenses to trade with Mexicans in the 1820s; and finally, under American capitalism, through territorial political structures established after the U.S.-Mexican War. This book traces those social details as well and invites a glance at territorial policies as they affected a local, resident population.

Given my focus, this book does not intend to mythologize either the hardy women residents of a region under conquest or the machinations of the powerful United States, bent on acquiring Mexico's northern lands. Rather, by examining the experiences of Spanish-Mexican women and placing them against the backdrop of extensive colonization, it seeks to unravel this group's infinite perseverance and to probe the methods of its resistance and adaptation to change. The more vociferous actors—the traders, soldiers, merchants, politicians, and missionaries—cannot be ignored, but neither do they have to occupy center stage. The evidence about women's lives abounds and deserves our attention.

This is not to overlook the fact that women and men were equally affected by the slow trade caravans winding their way into Santa Fe in the 1820s. When Mexico declared its independence from Spain in 1821, the enterprising Missouri traders joined with the merchants of Santa Fe and unleashed a social revolution as well as an economic one. The earliest phase of the trade began transforming local markets and interfered in politics by introducing manufactured items and retailers to a community that had known fewer of these before. Trading began to alter family and community life by making scarce articles desirable and necessary. Take the example of farming tools: Until the late 1820s, handles and some implements were fashioned by hand. After the manufactured hoe became more available, evidently by the late 1830s, women began willing these implements to heirs, which suggests their importance.[13]

The Dancing Ground of the Sun displayed a form and style of border economics unknown in other nineteenth-century locales. Initially, one border itself had been drawn centuries earlier under the Spanish *provincia*, or departmental, system (1590s). Then, at the time of Mexico's independence in 1821, centralists opposed federalists and replayed the old pro–Spanish Empire or anti-Empire stances of previous decades. A border between a governing center and a ruled frontier existed not merely as a geographic or cultural division separating Nuevo México, a provincia (department), from Durango, Zacatecas, or Mexico City—government centers; it also existed as a politically measured basis for financial arrangements. A tribute was paid to move goods from provinces to the treasury's coffers southward. Mexico City's financial and political institutions were marked by many imprecise financial agreements. Independence in 1821 signified their realignment.

But the trade developing between Mexico and the United States also set in motion the machinery that brought Euro-Americans to Santa Fe, and it laid the foundation for extended social relations. Its organizers not only found customers but also began to push Spanish-Mexicans in new directions. Conflicts arose between the traders and the locals. But merchandising continued at a methodical pace. The horse-drawn wagons rumbled slowly into town and then departed southward for Chihuahua. Their steady pace and visible tracks reiterated the manner in which institutions and people from the United States began affecting Santa Fe.

The gradual introduction of such new items as tools by a different people undid the work of even the loudest anti-Euro-Americans, a small group of locals who abhorred the inroads the newcomers made. But material goods, even the cheapest, like calico cloth, helped squash strong objections to the trade and

allowed commodities and providers to make a place for themselves in Santa
Fe. Perhaps the buyers and receivers had not understood how economic change
would alter their lives; or perhaps they had also envisioned an improvement.
Perhaps they did not regard what was at first a careful venture, of only a few
traders, as a step toward full-fledged conquest. In any case, the factors leading
to the eventual takeover of the Mexican north by the United States are not as
important to this study as the impact of economic colonization on ordinary
women and their daily lives.

Interestingly and importantly, the border zone's economic gain, like its political gain, was loaded with meaning for women. Women participated in the
economy, sometimes as traders, sometimes as widows preserving their dead husbands' property. They were as interested in the edicts emanating out of México
as anyone else. Arguments made in the local courts transfixed the entire community, I argue in this book, not only because women were at the center of local debate, but because in fact they existed in the middle of broader, national
and international debates. In other words, a dispute as it appears here might
seem to carry significance of only a local or specific nature, but it was replete
with implications for other arrangements that were once constructed as men's
terrain in the international theater or were diplomatic in character. The pre-
ponderance of evidence conveyed by the many examples around which I organized this study suggests that political and diplomatic history must also focus on women.

At the outset, colonizers from the United States wove a financial web whose
threads entangled everyone, and especially women. Poor women, the most vulnerable members of the community, experienced the harshest effects of conquest as they went to work for the traders, and later the soldiers, in Santa Fe.
The censuses after 1848, when New Mexico became a territory of the United
States, list women as working primarily as laundresses, seamstresses, and cooks.
While "storms brewed in other men's worlds," between the old capital of
Mexico City and the new one, Washington, D.C., these women's way of life
might have survived, but it also changed.[14]

In the courts, women demonstrated the ways in which Euro-Americans began interfering in the life of the community, and although they argued about,
and resisted, the encroachments of traders, they also became entangled in business ethics and the new economy of the prewar years. Manuela Baca was such
a figure and is introduced here in the first chapter. Married to a wealthy local
man, and well-off through her own inheritance, Baca stood before the courts
to answer charges of financial mismanagement. She persevered in an exciting
twist involving the complainant. Another group in this period began adapting
to the U.S. method of conducting business by marrying some of the newcomers
or running successful operations on their own, including the infamous Doña
Maria Gertrudis Barceló. Neither the intermarrying group nor the women
entrepreneurs comprised a substantial proportion of the female population
(less than 10 percent for the former, fewer than 20 women for the latter), but
their activities represented alternatives to the gender ideology of traditional
Spanish-Mexican culture and of the nineteenth-century United States be-

cause both specified a public sphere for men, a private one for women. After the war, the shifting position of women in Santa Fe was evident; more women, for example, began writing wills and conveying property to elder sons than before; more appeared to be searching for remedies to rectify the problem of an imposed, displacing economic structure, which had dispossessed women and men of their land and properties.

It is crucial to remember that economic and political spheres were gendered arenas, just as the Catholic Church, the parish, and the courtroom were spaces detailing the significance of sex and gender during a period of conquest and colonization. Let us take the example of women who married Euro-Americans in the 1820s and 1830s. We could say that they facilitated the transition of men from another culture and we might label them a "greeting" generation. To configure them primarily in that capacity defies history because history suggests that they should be known to us in one role, as intermarrying women—that is, only as wives and sexual partners. Many resisted the encroachments of strangers and their political resistance is crucial to both a gendered analysis and a sex-based one—examining women as assistants to colonization, or in regard to decisions about marriage, for example; and to a political one—women as defiers of the Euro-American takeover. Examining the last categorization requires that we think of Spanish-Mexican and indigenous women of Santa Fe as legal residents and that we look upon Euro-Americans in the era before the war of 1846 as illegal conquerors or undocumented settlers. Sometimes westering men were in fact certified by the Mexican government or officials to travel and trade in the northern territories, but at other times they were not. Some interactions between the greeting generation and the migrating one, then, were friendly; others, decidedly unfriendly.

The point of this book, of this reversal of traditional categories, is not to ascribe blame (to portray good Spanish-Mexican women and bad Euro-American men), but to unravel the complex nature of cultural and racial interaction by removing it from the standard, nineteenth-century categories of deficiency theory. Common to deficiency models is the sense that Spanish-Mexicans in this era were victims, or less superior, incapable, and inept in matters of entrepreneurship, capitalist venturing, or military might. Women were indeed drawn into conflicts around some of these issues, but they were also shapers of conflicts and choreographers of the outcome.

Another guidepost in my conceptual framework, and one drawn from the stories I seek to tell here, relies on the great capacity of women to remain in constant dialogue with men—creating an active exchange even as their situation declined economically and socially. A binding feature of the bits and pieces gathered here from hundreds of scattered and uncatalogued sources resides in the ideas and ideologies women often advanced through their refusals. Manuela Baca and Juana Lopes, discussed in chapter 1; La Tules, in chapter 2; and the widow Chaves, in chapter 3—all asserted their rights forcefully; when they yielded the courtroom and their struggles to men and retreated, their absence sometimes assured the desired outcome. Few of their actions can be read as passive or unconscious. Wealthy or poor, these women's dilemmas suggest a linked historical fate, a series of shared purposes designed to achieve some victory over adversity even when they were forced to suspend their personal or political interests.

The many personalities that I have discovered and rediscovered in the archives of New Mexico, and that I describe in this book, support the conclusion that not all of the Spanish-Mexican women of Santa Fe can be held inflexibly to one method of resistance or of survival; nor can they be drawn into one category (woman) and not others (saloon owners, will-makers). Across the pages of their histories, their daily lives require that we examine them in multiple categories, just as the colonizers are identified as trappers or traders, politicians or lawyers, migrants or immigrants. Spanish-Mexican women were intermarriers, gamblers, widows, merchants, saloonkeepers, peddlers, laundresses, and seamstresses. Their economies, personal and public, were as much in a state of flux as their titles, interests, and statuses. Their political practices also centered sometimes on separatism or separation—an activism of spirit and determination where they retreated from the stage to insist on a particular outcome. At the end of this period, I group them into one category of impoverishment or poverty, but I surmise, from and through my own arguments with traditional history, that the actual structural impositions of colonization did not overdetermine their lives. The evidence suggests we carefully craft several readings of women who could just as easily be shown locked into poverty or moving against tradition. I have tried to do both things here in order to lend the example of broader readings and of reinterpretations.

By 1880, many were financially impoverished but culturally rich, and the majority of women seemed to have staved off complete colonization. Their resistance efforts were not always visible to the newcomers who wrote about them, nor are they visible to contemporary historians who continue today to interpret these events without giving attention to women. What follows is one depiction of their lives, a slice across a relatively short span of time, but of crucial significance if we are to understand how this region came under U.S. domination and how a group of Spanish-Mexican women survived, and sometimes refused, that favor.[15]

Women in the Courts

*Conformity and Dissonance
before the War, 1821–1846*

Compared with many of her Spanish-Mexican relatives and friends, Manuela Baca was a wealthy woman. She owned several properties in and around Santa Fe. With her husband, the well-known Miguel Sena, she controlled an indeterminable, but large, portion of Santa Fe's developing merchant economy. The partners owned three homes and pasture outside the town; they were active in the trading market between Missouri and Chihuahua, Mexico, which had made Santa Fe its nucleus. Sena made his money by buying property with cash raised from selling livestock, trading with the surrounding Indian communities, and operating a mercantile store in town. Despite her upper-middle-class position, however, Baca's life was far from idyllic. From April 6 through September 13, 1832, she appeared in court on several occasions to answer charges brought against her by a Euro-American merchant, Alexander (or Alejandro, as he was referred to in the court documents) Le Grand. During that period, her wealth or status provided her little consolation and, indeed, was the source of her vexing troubles.[1]

Le Grand charged Manuela Baca with failure to pay a bill of over one thousand pesos for food and goods she had purchased from his store. According to his inventory, Baca had bought on credit six yards of calico for three pesos; a padlock, worth two pesos; two yards of flannel for nine pesos; and thread and fifteen yards of velour, costing thirteen pesos. All of the items were sold in the space of a few weeks and were included among lists of food and whiskey. Le Grand contended that Baca had also bought goods for her neighbors, and that her bill was significant.[2]

When Le Grand began presenting more-detailed lists of groceries and luxury items, Baca's husband stepped forward and produced his own bill, which also totaled over one thousand pesos. Sena's list contained different items, however, and his brothers appeared before the local magistrate to support his claims about the inaccuracy of Le Grand's list. Assuming control as his wife was seated nearby, Sena ended a lengthy speech by saying, "Pues es [b]ien publico que estos individuos no saben el castellano" (It is well established that these individuals do not speak Spanish). To his mind, that fact proved decisively that Baca had incurred the debt and fully intended to pay it, but that men who could not speak Spanish were suspect, as was their inventory.

Eventually, the debt debated in this case was adjusted and the matter laid to rest. It raises, however, many issues having to do with class, gender, race, and culture in the towns along a Spanish-Mexican frontier. As one among nearly forty similar cases contained in the court records between 1820 and 1848, it deserves special attention.[3]

The first unusual aspect of this case is that it took five months to settle the dispute. Clearly, these were not ordinary charges of merchant against client. Another curious feature was Baca's intermittent appearance in the courtroom itself. As the case dragged on and more witnesses, including brothers, cousins, and uncles, came before the alcalde (magistrate), Baca receded into the background. In the final days of hearings, she appeared not at all. Rather, men seemed to be dealing with men. The woman who launched the case seemed almost peripheral to the matter at hand once the case got under way.

The courtroom drama was permeated, or so it seemed at first, with an air of formality and ritual; in this case, the drama was that of men defending a woman's honorable intentions. The case certainly demonstrated a notion of honor and how honorable actions affected both men and women. The courtroom provided, in that regard, the credit-happy woman a public means of deferring to her husband and relatives, and allowed her and them to restore her honor. Her honor is as much a part of this story as the honor of her family and husband. All recognized the debt repeatedly, but persisted in doubting Le Grand's intentions, which they felt were less than honorable.

A prior confrontation may have exacerbated relations between the parties. A few months earlier, Le Grand was accused of pointing a pistol at Sena's chest. Le Grand charged that his arrest while the matter was being investigated was unjust, and complained of mistreatment and unfairness. He admitted that he had approached Sena brandishing guns, but insisted that Sena and his brothers were also carrying weapons.[4]

Accumulated resentments thus contributed to the debt case. Baca's enormous bill provided a ready vehicle for Le Grand to express his animosity. Because he was new to New Mexico, having come from the eastern United States, he probably did not imagine that his concerns about a mounting debt would become so entangled with feelings about relatives, family pride, honor, and principle. While the men dealt with the outward manifestations of the problem at hand, Baca's name disappeared from the court documents. She seemed to have choreographed the affair around men, whom she then allowed to settle the case. The event clearly stipulated the roles set for men and those for women. They differed, and no matter how many times women sued or came to court, men easily relegated women's arguments to the background when they chose to do so.

This analysis of Sena's and Baca's concern for family honor and individual reputations could end here, but one more piece of evidence, found in folders containing miscellany, adds a decidedly different twist to the story of Baca's day in court. A bill from a customs house, filed one year after the case ended, charged that Miguel Sena and Manuela Baca owed additional taxes for items sold to the Navajos and the Pueblo Indians. The listing corresponds neatly with Le Grand's original inventory.[5] Suddenly, the husband's and wife's concerns take on a different meaning. The partners were carrying on a lucrative trade on the side and profiting from a business venture in a quasi-underground market because it was removed from the watchful eyes of relatives or appointed officials.

Mexican law allowed, but strictly regulated, commerce between the Indians and Spanish-Mexicans.[6] Local and federal officials worried about the sale of guns and munitions to Apaches, Comanches, and Navajos. The Comanches were especially successful dealers in arms; they traveled as far as Louisiana and Arizona to sell weapons to other Indians. Illegal trading, conducted by both Spanish-Mexicans and competing Euro-Americans, continued in the 1830s. Sena's and Baca's motives in contesting Le Grand's list was to protect their profits. The longer Sena was able to keep authorities from probing that aspect of their financial affairs, the better. Both manipulated not just ascribed gender roles—she retreated as he defended her honor—but also the economic, cultural, and social idioms of the day. Casting doubt on Le Grand as an outside Euro-American entrepreneur directed the judge's attention away from their illicit activity and masked their motives as efforts to retain their class position in the developing trade economy.

This tactic would have been helpful, if swaying the judge's opinions had been important to winning the case. It is unclear from the documents whether the judge was of junior status (alcalde ordinario de segundo voto), or of senior status (alcalde de primer voto), which would make his concerns difficult to pinpoint. His level was, however, important in his final decision to make Baca pay her bill. Chosen by distant officials, but always a leader in the community and usually a person engaged in business as well, the alcalde probably shared the same class privileges as Baca and Sena shared and might have favored the defendants on that basis. From the scanty evidence, it is impossible to determine which side, if any, he supported. He could have been involved in trading ventures with the Euro-Americans. His own prejudices, and those of the magistrates who generally presided in these sorts of cases, are not necessarily central to understanding the rhetoric deployed or the symbolic oratory displayed in the testimonials or speeches given in the courtroom. No jury sat in judgment on these local matters, either, so Miguel Sena probably did not give his lengthy speech to seek social redemption. Discussions of honor, scholars have suggested, are frequently linked to social redemption.[7] The Baca-Sena parties knew they could appeal to a higher court, but the time and expense involved made such an appeal unlikely. Because the judge was already predisposed to accept the word of locals over that of foreigners, the final arguments in this case were probably not made to convince the judge, nor to serve any clear purpose, such as clearing the family's reputation or defending the woman's honor. Sena's concluding speech about honor and reputation, like the references to integrity recorded in many other court testimonies during this period, added a final flourish to a chivalrous defense that was based on honor and involved pride, on a superficial level, and money and security of status, on a deeper one.

By 1832, with such cases still coming before sympathetic alcaldes, the Santa Fe Trade was over a decade old. Merchants from Missouri and the eastern United States had gained the upper hand over local merchants in the trade itself, if not in local governance.[8] The ricos of Santa Fe, as persons of the upper class identified themselves, were plagued by worries and frustrations over taxes, which the central government in Mexico insisted on collecting. That, and their rivalry with the encroaching Euro-Americans, whom the government in Mexico City encouraged in the trade, placed the upper crust merchants in a precarious political position. Sena and Baca, as members of that group, were treading on shifting ground. Understandably, they were attempting to preserve economic advantages while they competed with Le Grand.

Le Grand had capital and the backing of the Mexican government, but he had several disadvantages as well. The governors who granted him license were far away, and he came from a tradition built on the notion of the store as the site of purchasing activities. This was a decisive handicap in a region with no decent public roads or navigable waterways. Spanish-Mexican merchants retained their devotion to peddling merchandise, which was well suited to the mountainous terrain and the great distances between villages and towns. If purchasers could not come to Santa Fe, merchants traveled to make the sale. In the late summer, Spanish-Mexican buyers who had fruit or produce to trade came from the surrounding villas and communities to buy goods and to act as middlemen for the outlying areas. As the largest settlement west of the Mississippi River until 1848, Santa Fe easily attracted these customers. Other peddlers sold firewood or chickens to store owners in exchange for flour or tools, which they bartered with other villagers or with the mobile Apaches, Comanches, and Navajos. By controlling the trade in this way, the upper class retained its rank over the local poor, the Indians, and the encroaching Euro-American merchants.[9]

Sometimes, however, men and women controlled the local economy more tightly than they could a courtroom, where contentious or feuding parties often vented issues unrelated to financial disputes. In June of 1845, Ana María Rendón and Juana González battled in court over the rental of two rooms in Rendón's residence. Leasing rooms was common in the years before the war, particularly among widows and poor women. Renting yielded extra money for the landlords, but sometimes produced problems as well. Rendón never specified the nature of her tenant's objectionable activities, but she did state that noise permeated the house and that she was distressed by the number of people confined to González's rooms, which were next to hers, and by the tenant's overall neglect of her lodgings. Misuse and abuse of a contract drove Rendón to court and the magistrate ruled in her favor by requiring González to honor her agreement and live alone and quietly in the rented space.[10]

Before hostilities erupted into the war between the United States and Mexico in 1846, women filed at least forty of these types of suits in the civil courts; men filed over one hundred. The number may not seem unduly large, but given the lack of diaries, letters, or memoirs written by either women or men, the women's cases constitute an important body of material that details their experiences. The court documents exhibit common characteristics. Poor women tended to file grievances as often as the wealthy. Women *and* men brought disputes jointly before the court. The gender of the litigating parties does not seem to have unduly influenced the outcomes, nor do the documents suggest how often the orders of the court were obeyed. Most probably complied, since to ignore the court invited scandal and problems. Women who did not follow the advice or recommendations of the local authorities tended to return to face the same charges. Men sued by women also appeared to have complied with the judges' orders and to have avoided recidivism. Because local civil courts heard few cases that involved the more serious crimes of rape or murder, and many cases of theft, assault, adultery, forgery, and indebtedness, the judge's admonishments were often heeded. The proceedings and the courtroom itself thus describe an arena frequented by women and not necessarily prejudiced against them.

In most of the suits or grievances presented by women, particularly suits involving families, men initially commanded the courtroom, established a context, especially for their daughters and wives, and then retreated. Women frequently won their grievances, and they employed various tactics to do so. One case illustrates how they accomplished this and how women's autonomy and resistance were perhaps less important to winning a case than their traditional observance of decorum, respect, and deference.

During the summer of 1822, Juan Pablo Pacheco claimed that his son-in-law, José Antonio Trujillo, had assaulted his daughter, María Ramona. The father stepped in, he said, to defend his daughter's honor when Trujillo accused her of adultery. Grave and sincere, the father asked that the marriage of one year be dissolved. María Ramona began her testimony by thanking her parents for their help. She then asked for her husband's respect, hoping "that my husband respects me as I do my parents."[11] Respect anchored the values of María Ramona and her family, and not only parent-child but also husband-wife relations were its embodiment. The judge ruled in favor of the daughter and specified that Trujillo not bother her. In addition, he required alimony payments "for a number of years."

The daughter might not have wanted to bring the matter to court, but the father's insistence—and his support—induced her to go before the judge. "We are at a loss about what to do," the father explained, indicating that the court was their final resort. Once the matter was in the judge's and others' hands, the father stepped back and let the authorities do their job. For María Ramona, appearing in the courtroom at her father's behest reinforced the strong cultural message that women should let men resolve their problems. A judge, if accorded deference, was likely to render a judgment in favor of the plaintiff; if a father was present to monitor the proceedings, all the better. The judgment favoring the Pachecos showed how a well-behaved woman could wield influence by simply testifying carefully, while an affronted parent, or spouse, hovered nearby.[12]

The women in these cases, the defendant Manuela Baca and the plaintiffs Ana María Rendón and María Ramona Pacheco Trujillo, were manipulating—and bound by—the prevailing gender prescriptions that their society embedded in the orders and regulations of the civil court system. Under Spanish family law, established in the Laws of Toro of 1369 and in use by the early sixteenth century, women were granted the right to defend their inheritances, property, and goods brought to or acquired during their marriage. Over the centuries, different regions of the Spanish Empire used these and other laws that were ecclesiastical in origin to more precisely define women's rights in civil court. Both church and state reinforced the decisions taken.[13]

In New Mexico, one of the northernmost provinces of New Spain, women had the right to sue and be sued in a court of law and to retain their family names, when they desired or when matters of property or inheritance required it. The historical record indicates that these rights were not only granted but frequently tested. Over 10 percent of the cases listed in the indexes of the judicial court proceedings, as local adjudications are classified in the archives, involved women.[14] The general pattern of those cases suggests that women used the legal structures to act both independently of men and in consort with them. This is not to ignore, however, the basic fact that women derived benefits or privileges from a system that had been established primarily to "protect" women who "belonged" to a family headed by a man. Although women did not surrender their property in marriage—the same laws protected dowries, as well as property jointly accumulated in marriage—property was defined and protected in the context of a relationship sanctioned by the church and the state, a relationship, in other words, that served men.[15] This protected and limited women's rights.

Going to court or appearing before a magistrate were not unusual for women in Santa Fe in the two decades preceding the U.S.–Mexican War of 1846–1848. And not all cases concerned strictly the protection of property. The archives of the period are filled with remonstrances, complaints, charges, and countercharges made by one party against another. Bickering among friends or neighbors occurred regularly and frequently, and the local court was the place to resolve such conflicts. In 1828, Santiago Armijo reportedly stole a rope from María Josefa Anaya. The entire community knew this because Anaya accused the thief during an evening promenade on the plaza. Armijo reversed the matter by going to court and attempting to sue Anaya for defamation of character and insulting him viciously in public. In the end, Armijo was found guilty and was ordered to return the rope.[16]

The matters that appeared before the local courts, where women often litigated, tended to be resolved quickly. This was not the case elsewhere during the Mexican period, but on the frontier outposts magistrates often served the local populace in this way as the government's representatives. They were the arbiters designated by a government eager to make the law available to frontierspeople and to free the regional and federal courts of most local disputes. In an era during which the reforming of cumbersome political structures at the local level was in the air, the civil courts were among the first institutions to yield to the pressures of a new constitution, that of 1812, and to accept changes in the laws. In the late colonial period, most magistrates were appointed and approved by the governors of the province. The regional commandant general approved the selections. The process was refined up until independence. Local alcaldes (magistrates) had a junior or senior rank, and they ran the bureaucratic affairs of the community, including overseeing the correct application of the political, military, and economic rules of the government.[17] Because these appointed officials were burdened with multiple duties, local disputes had to be settled promptly. The Le Grand–Baca case was exceptional in that regard because it dragged on for months.

The Armijo–Anaya litigation, on the other hand, was rapidly resolved, and it typified most cases recorded in the dockets of the court. Humble parties, contentious litigants, and misunderstood plaintiffs all appeared in the courtroom, which consisted of two small rooms of an adobe building on the plaza; roughhewn benches, a rickety table, and a few chairs for witnesses or observers completed the simple surroundings in which arguments were heard and judgments dispensed.[18]

Seemingly mundane matters, like the loss of a rope, achieved extraordinary significance in this setting because they raised questions central to understanding the lives of most women, rich and poor alike, in the years before the war. The first had to do with honor, reputation, and modesty, serious matters in a community of nearly four thousand, where people tended to know one another well, where intermarriages among the same families prevailed over generations, where the concerns of one became the concerns of many. Manuela Baca, her husband, and his brothers, in responding to Le Grand's complaints, neither disputed the debt nor apologized for its size. Rather, they refused to trust Le Grand's word. While the magistrate's scribe Hispanicized Le Grand's first name, and perhaps with that gesture made him more familiar, Baca and Sena stood before the magistrate and rejected such familiarity. Sena's statement about linguistic facility thus embodied more than a notion of superiority— Spanish-Mexican over non-Spanish-Mexican; local merchant over foreign trader. Until the end, Sena, his wife, and his brothers questioned Le Grand's motives. Raising the issue of honor and promoting it with the security of their solid, upper-class status sent a strong message warning interlopers and future litigants to be wary of tangling with any one of them. In that sense, this tactic preserved their integrity.

Reputation, for persons of the upper class, embodied more than a particular set of reflexive reactions to a situation. It dictated instead a way to live and to continue living. Preserving the family's wealth in the future depended, for Baca and Sena, on acting aggressively in the present. Preserving individual reputations, as Armijo demonstrated, was vital to many local residents as well. For working-class women such as the poor María Josefa Anaya and the battered

María Ramona Pacheco Trujillo, the ideology of respect, or family honor, was resurrected perhaps not to enhance economic security, but to at least retain the little that existed. Burglaries and physical abuse presented severe hardships for women who lacked resources other than respect. And indeed the majority of Santa Fe's women, a group constituting an average of 52 percent of the population in any given year, did not own stores or benefit directly from the trafficking in merchandise that began after 1821. They were poor mestizas, barely surviving.

Barbara Roybal was typical of the majority. She appeared in 1839 before the magistrate to complain about her husband's affairs and his refusal to settle debts. She did not know how she would feed her children that winter.[19] She, too, was "protecting" her reputation as she sought remedial action from the court.

In many of the cases cited so far, a regard for modesty is evident in the language women used and in the resolutions they sought. Pacheco Trujillo demonstrated the concept by appearing reluctant to step before the judge and then suggesting shyly that her concerns had less to do with money than with the respect she thought her husband owed her. These steps were, to be sure, decorous and necessary in leaving a bad marriage, but they reveal so much more than their superficial purpose. Women like Pacheco Trujillo adjusted their behavior to achieve the results they desired. Whether they were consciously or unconsciously manipulating powerful structures or the men who controlled them is unclear, but in the majority of cases in which women appear as plaintiffs or defendants, both women and men repeatedly resurrected the notions of modesty, honor, and reputation. In this way, women codified their behavior to suggest the resolutions they desired. More often than not, women who acted like Pacheco Trujillo got what they wanted from the courts.

Linguists tell us, however, that language manipulation and language forms signify many things.[20] The goal of preserving reputations or solidifying one's standing in the community is one possible explanation of what words in testimonials meant. In some cases, the words Spanish-Mexican women employed and the resolutions sought by litigants shed light on family and community structures and say a great deal about women's search for power and their general disempowerment within the institutional framework of the society. "Quisiera no decir," literally meaning, "I would rather not have to say," appeared in no fewer than ten of the civil cases recorded, but this phrase did not always signify that the woman did not *want* to say—for that, she could or would have remained at home. It referred to the social idiom, that complex set of received notions about a woman's proper role in society, including, among Roman Catholics, ideas about deference, humility, and unobtrusiveness. In court, women were, if not ignoring the requirements imposed by the idiom, then certainly suspending their allegiance to or concern for them.

Even more demonstrative of the extent to which women lacked autonomous power was their reliance on fathers or husbands as witnesses, which suggests that women had to include men to validate their cases. Women never fully controlled the structures established to resolve disputes, either in the courtroom or in most other arenas.

Other equally important issues linking these court cases were the scarcity of material items and the economic problems in general. In a town hungry for manufactured goods, the loss of Anaya's rope, for example, could have caused severe hardship. If an animal was lost or wandered into a neighbor's garden, negligence was bound to be discussed in court as seriously as other complaints and to be resolved as speedily. The Santa Fe trade between Missouri and Chihuahua had introduced articles like ropes, padlocks, and hoes, but these remained expensive and scarce. Residents of Santa Fe like María Josefa Anaya safeguarded their tools for good reasons; their theft or any dispute about the ownership of articles also led residents into the dusty courtroom.[21]

These cases were resolved in civil court, but many others also made their way into the ecclesiastical courts, where the social pressure to adhere to proper roles was even more pronounced. Perhaps the reasons had to do with the demise of the mission system on Mexico's northern frontier, a fact that further reinforced the need for conformity. Disintegration of the missions occurred in Texas, New Mexico, and California at different paces, but by the 1830s, the missions were deserted, the buildings had collapsed, and general disarray gripped the entire system on the frontier. The economies of the missions lay as fallow as their fields, especially in the decade preceding independence, when achieving freedom from Spain became increasingly urgent. The missions provided relief for the weary and the poor and respite for troops during the fight for independence; they had been established both to offer hospitable resting spots to travelers on the roads leading northward and to continue converting Indians and harnessing their labor.

The missions quickly caved in to the pressures of bankrupt treasuries and of government officials who robbed them of their products and self-sufficiency. In Alta California, the Franciscans supplied both the military and the provincial authorities, only to find themselves bankrupt, and without revenue or assistance from the interior during the struggle for independence.[22]

In addition, the independence movement itself questioned the central purpose of the mission system, which, as noted, was to convert Indians and channel their labor for the benefit of the state. Now, according to the philosophy promulgated under the Plan de Iguala of 1821, Spaniards, Indians, and mestizos were to be dealt with equally. Some leaders of the independence movements wanted to do away entirely with racial and ethnic distinctions. Not all federal leaders accepted this doctrine. Twenty years later, conservative President Antonio López de Santa Ana reverted to earlier policies by proposing that the Jesuits return to the Americas and reestablish missions on the northern frontier to help control the mobile, fighting Apaches and Navajos. His plan failed, but it illustrates the problems plaguing the missions of the north, including those of New Mexico. New ideas, an economy sanctioning foreign trade, and a loosening of the entire ecclesiopolitical structure contributed to the development of a different religious climate.[23]

The demise of the missions followed a natural course in New Mexico, where by the 1820s few Franciscans resided anyway. An 1834 federal decree secularized all missions—that is, removed them from the control of the regular clergy, like the Franciscans, and placed them under parish-supported priests (curas).

By 1830's, mission
priest declive

Secular priests were by then in great demand, and the number of regular priests declined dramatically throughout Mexico; the Spanish-born were expelled, and the number of bishops who could ordain priests also declined. By 1832, of the fifteen missions remaining in New Mexico, only five had resident priests.[24]

Another persistent problem nagged at whatever authority the church-appointed officials retained: The line between civil and ecclesiastical matters had never been clearly drawn. Technically, civil governors represented, in the colonial period, the king and the pope, that is, the state *and* the church. Nowhere is this fact more obvious than in the way people used both types of authorities—priests and civil officers—to adjudicate their disputes. It is not clear from the court and church cases selected for this study whether civilians sometimes attempted to play one official against the other, just as it is not always clear whose interests, if any, the judges or priests sought to protect. From what is known about church affairs in this period, seeking a resolution in both arenas clearly could not hurt. For one thing, the few priests who were sent to the frontier regarded the assignment as punishment; the minority who wanted to reside in the area, because they preferred the climate or wanted to retain their independence within the church—the frontier was one place to do that—made many of their decisions without consulting with the bishop or higher, regional authorities. This might have made the curas' decisions appear, to parishioners, as arbitrary or indisputable. Thus, litigants were safer if they filed some complaints with both the priest and the magistrate.[25]

Because the suits filed in the ecclesiastical courts are more difficult to categorize than those presented before the civil authorities—over one thousand exist in the church documents in the decade preceding independence and the two following it—my analysis is restricted to a sample of cases selected randomly from twenty rolls of microfilm containing the "loose documents of the diocese" and those classified for the Villa of Santa Fe.[26] Some of the suits were actually filed before the ecclesiastical court and the alcalde, particularly when the situation being adjudicated required a priest. In 1830, for example, a resident of Albuquerque sent the parish in Santa Fe a note describing a corpse he had found in the river. The man described how he had administered extreme unction (the last Catholic rite) and the place where he had buried the body. He said he had already informed the church—so priests sometimes received information before the civil authorities did.[27]

Although New Mexico was in ecclesiastical disrepair, Spanish-Mexicans, like the man who dragged the body out of the Rio Grande, remained pious and devout. Their devotion extended beyond worship and Sunday observance and was often expressed within the traditional colonial framework that had bound civil and religious governance. For the authorities, the affairs of one were necessarily the affairs of the other, and although tensions frequently marred the uneasy marriage of church and state, frontierspeople sometimes had no choice but to go to the curas and the alcaldes with the same problem.[28]

Luckily, the church records are full of details that allow historians to decipher the values and concerns women carried into both the church and civil courts. Catholic law required detailed recordings of life's events, from baptism through confirmation, marriage, and death. Some parishioners went beyond the explicit laws and filed suits affirming appropriate standards of behavior, and some did so without caring whether they received compensation for damages or not. Appearing before the ecclesiastical court in 1815, Doña Ursula Chávez, a large property owner and the wife of a man of considerable wealth, sued her neighbor for failure to live up to a contract whereby the neighbor was to care for her sheep. Chávez opened her testimony with a standard, and lengthy, proclamation to God and the Virgin Mary. "At God's mercy," she began a paragraph detailing the verbal agreement. She continued to outline her concerns about the neglect her animals had suffered. The outcome of her case is unknown, but some years later she was back in court, alleging that a priest had misappropriated church money; she began to describe that grievance with another long prayer to the Virgin Mary. Both times, Chávez decried misconduct and seemed more concerned with righting people's behavior than with extracting any retribution. In the first, she perceived an abuse of a verbal contract; in the second, a misuse of ecclesiastical power and the theft of something that belonged to God.[29]

Grave worries about morality motivated Chávez's complaints. In the first lawsuit, she was upset that her animals were faring so poorly because of a "lazy" shepherd. In her second suit, seventeen years later, she was worried about the defalcation of church funds and the way the priest was overstepping the boundaries of her goodwill. She abhorred theft, she said, but especially if the thievery took something that she considered belonged to the church. The second, in particular, also concerned money and power. Many New Mexicans during this period were upset about constant tithing designed to support the clergy, and a woman of means, like Chávez, would undoubtedly be upset by the priest's abuse of an already burdensome system. Tithing became voluntary in 1833, and the priests complained constantly of neglect after that time. New Mexicans like Chávez had grown reluctant to give away their cash—what little they had—only to see it wasted, stolen, or sent to the faraway diocese in Durango.

In this setting, conflict and resolution took on several meanings in the affairs of women. For women, the union of family, neighborhood, church, and court spelled methods of control as firmly entrenched as any prevailing attitudes about women's capabilities or rights. The records decisively sketch the subordination of women in these overlapping spheres, but reveal as frequently the distinctive pattern of options they exercised along a changing frontier. Although all residents in so tightly woven a community as Santa Fe understood the implicit problems of greed and disruption, the court and church cases detail a society giving women choices, especially when they argued before officials, with each other, or with people who aggravated them. The rights they enjoyed under Spanish law did not necessarily grant them total freedom, but women did not always seek freedom. Those who did faced social ostracism.

Some women went into court unwillingly and were often dragged there to justify their actions. Manuela Baca, María Ramona Pacheco Trujillo, and Ursula Chávez may have been more typical of the litigating group, but reluctant parties also ended up in civil court. Juana Lopes was such a person. Her

Euro-American husband, John Scolly (his name was Hispanicized as Juan Escobe), appeared before the magistrate in the mid-1840s to complain about his wife's adulterous behavior. He claimed that he could no longer control her and wanted a divorce; but, he continued, because they had been married for so long and were raising children, he found it nearly impossible to imagine how they would get along without her.

In his statements, which the court's Spanish-Mexican clerk translated into Spanish, he noted: "In my very house, I have heard said adulterers knock on the window when they want my wife to go out."[30] Several witnesses testified that Lopes was indeed unfaithful. Not surprisingly, other witnesses appeared to testify that they had been with Lopes in her house; a neighbor swore that she saw many strange men and foreigners leaving Lopes's home. When Juana stood before the judge, she neither admitted nor denied the charges. She maintained, as the judge explained, that "it was her ass, she controlled it, and she would give it to whomever she wanted."

Juana's unrepentant declaration shows that not all women acted deferentially when they entered the courtroom. Defiant women remained the exceptions, however, and those who drew attention to themselves were bound to arouse suspicions. In the case of Juana Lopes, these suspicions were not unfounded, at least if the parade of witnesses can be trusted. Lopes's case is unusual, too, in that it appears in the record at all; few examples of wayward, mischievous, or marginal women are contained in the documents, but the anomaly, in this case, is meaningful. Lopes clearly had no intention of being ruled by the court.

The judge could do no more than enjoin Juana to stop "roving" and reconcile with her family. The judge might have been wiser than first appears. In this period, no court's punishment equaled the wrath of a family or neighbors. The pressures to conform were many; the penalties for transgressions, severe. The magistrates imposed their authority and admonished both sexes to comply. When this failed, other social restrictions came into play.

They extended, in some cases, to charges of witchcraft. Accusations of witchcraft were not confined to women: The marginal, the deviant, the eccentric of both sexes were vulnerable.[31] In a society pushing gradually toward merchant capitalism and plagued by serious problems of governance in ecclesiastical and civil affairs, women were often powerless before the worst of these charges, and their behavior was strictly circumscribed. They were peculiarly susceptible to suspicions of witchcraft or adultery and to banishment from the town if they were deemed guilty.

Sociologists and psychologists tell us that in societies or cultures founded on strict notions of conformity, transgressions can frequently take extreme forms. It is impossible to determine exactly where Santa Fe or Spanish-Mexican communities on the northern Mexican frontier would rank on an imaginary scale plotting conformity, but it is clear that throughout the colonial period and in many regions of New Spain, going against the grain was not unusual, but neither was it condoned. Spanish-Mexicans in Santa Fe did not tolerate violations easily and frequently relied on the collective will of the community to secure cooperation.[32]

But other, practical concerns, having less to do with violating social dicta, might explain Juana Lopes's behavior. She was not radically different from most women who appeared in court except that she was married to a Euro-American in a decade when intermarriages with the newcomers were still uncommon. John Scolly worked as a day laborer when he first arrived in Santa Fe, and only later became a wealthier merchant. Lopes was from a poorer family, and her marriage to Scolly enabled her parents, with his assistance, to purchase some land north of Santa Fe. Women like Lopes usually worked at home and did not have the option of marrying someone who would improve their class status. Instead, they raised children, tended gardens, and, by the 1830s, began to take in laundry or to work for the incoming Euro-American merchants. In that way, they shaped the family economy and did more than make a "contribution." In the case of the independent Lopes, the ability to work for wages clearly had one benefit because it signified that she was not dependent on Scolly. It is possible that what was mistaken for adulterous behavior had more to do with a family's poverty than with an indivdual's morals, and to judge such women by contemporary, U.S., or Protestant values proves limiting. Some women took in boarders and were later charged with cohabitation, a charge that caused scandal but was rarely punishable by a fine or an arrest.[33]

Juana Lopes was not judged to be a threat to the social fabric, but the records simply do not lend themselves to painting a complete picture of her predicament. Other cases—many dealing with abuse, battery, or adultery—are more richly textured and allow better glimpses of women's daily lives and the multiple difficulties with which they contended.

In the late 1820s, Juan González of Pojoaque, a small community ten miles north of Santa Fe, argued before the magistrate in the capital that his niece, María Francisca Martínez, had been unfairly criticized, unjustly scrutinized, and falsely accused. Without a trial, he claimed, she was being forced to leave the area by an accuser whose name she did not even know. According to the uncle, Martínez had suffered tremendously: "Even now she does not know who is maligning her and spreading prejudices that do not allow her to marry for the scandal that has ensued and [is] without a legal basis in fact."[34] The exile, in this case, seemed self-imposed and was not the result of a judgment against her. Rather, the assault on her character and reputation, following the uncle's logic, prohibited marriage and forced her to seek a mate elsewhere.

The records never gave the niece's testimony; she probably never testified because her uncle's testimony sufficed and may have been enough to aid her cause, which appears to be that of finding a suitable husband. In such cases, women who had men upon whom they could rely were infinitely better off than those who did not. Male support could derive from fathers, uncles, judges, and priests, as well as from husbands and brothers.

Sometimes, men also appeared in the courts to halt spousal abuse. For example, from September 2 through November 21, 1823, a magistrate in Santa Fe listened to complaints against José Antonio Girón, a wife beater. A priest, Juan Tomás Terrazas, brought the case to the civil court because he had witnessed Girón's beating of Micaela Ortiz. Vecinos (residents of the town who had established households) corroborated the priest's account and claimed that

Girón had a quick temper and a vicious disposition. They had often seen him beat Ortiz. The judge ordered Girón to leave Santa Fe because, given the multiple charges against him, he was unlikely to mend his ways and the woman was therefore in danger of a further assault.[35]

Not all women were so lucky. In December 1844, proceedings began against Rafael Montoya of Corrales (a town near Albuquerque), who was charged with the murder of his wife. Twice in the 1830s, she had gone before the magistrate in Santa Fe to say that she feared her husband.[36] This is one of the few cases demonstrating that wife beaters did not necessarily heed the court's advice. A woman's relatives could not always prevent further abuse. In the earlier case, Girón had been beaten by Ortiz's brother and challenged to a fight by her uncle. Indeed, the possibility of angering a woman's family did not always restrain men and perhaps even worsened the situation for some women. Similarly, women living without men, or women whose male relatives lived far away, appear in these few documents to have been susceptible to abuse and battery. Given the number of widows in the nineteenth-century Southwest in general—in some communities, they made up 20 percent of the adult population—many women lived in households without men. Historians must exercise caution when concluding that married women or women with consanguine relatives were somehow less likely to be attacked.[37]

Sometimes women took up the problem of assault with priests in the ecclesiastical courts before going to magistrates in the judicial courts. María Loreta García of Bernalillo (a town just north of Albuquerque) complained that her husband of two years treated her cruelly, refused to work, and beat her and the children. She said, "How can I continue to live securely by his side? He tires me and mistreats me, hitting me, and I am tired of suffering."[38] García brought the case to the cura in Santa Fe because she wanted to initiate a divorce and an annulment through the church. So urgent was her complaint, she stipulated, that she could not continue living with a man who was so inhumane and "like a wild lion." She said that if the divorce were not granted, she would rather live outside the church than be dead within it.

A sense of urgency permeated García's remonstrance, as it did the pleas of most battered wives. The judge and the priest could ultimately do little to aid a worsening marriage or to stop men's violence. In one case, relatives tried to resolve the difficulty by punishing the husband, but that seemed a temporary solution. In my convenience sample, wife-beating dominated the cases women brought before the ecclesiastical courts. The remedies are hard to pinpoint; their successes remain unknown. Divorces could be granted, although ecclesiastical divorce required many steps and months or years of paperwork and negotiation.[39] A priest could initiate the process, which took so long to reach the archdiocese's offices—for New Mexico, the first stop was Durango—that sometimes the parties died first. Annulments had to be presented in Mexico City and eventually in Rome. The more common form of "divorce" in nineteenth-century New Mexico was separation. Sometimes husbands and wives occupied the same house but did not share rooms. That still did not solve the hardship of a woman whose husband beat her, but, combined with the power that relatives, priests, or judges wielded in such matters, it often helped.

In each of the situations described—the women whose husbands beat them, the wife who had affairs with other men, the daughter whose father encouraged her to appear in court, and the woman who did not pay her store bill—a deeper problem emerged. Ultimately, these women depended on men or institutions and were needy nevertheless. In no case, their complaints suggest, could women rely solely on men or on a formal arena for resolving their problems. Ties between court, church, and family provided measures of relief or of restriction, but no single institution proved capable of solving an issue and laying it to rest, and certainly not to the satisfaction of everyone.

The most difficult of these cases also points to why the U.S. invasion, twenty years later, and the trader-merchant conquest before that, caused perceptible changes in the community of women. Santa Fe was a society with some disaffected members, and was divided, after 1820, as before, by class. The wealthiest members of the town seemed ready for a change; they were unhappy with the Mexican edicts flowing from Mexico City, as they had been displeased earlier with the way the interior governors sought to control the outposts on the frontier. That, plus the fact that they were the largest Spanish-Mexican settlement north of Chihuahua City, predisposed them toward trading with and encouraging the "norteamericanos," as they referred to Euro-Americans. Women, particularly those of the upper class, were important to the changing configurations of the cultural and economic landscape. Manuela Baca was not about to stop buying at Alexander Le Grand's store; and, as long as she and others kept their accounts, Le Grand profited and remained in Santa Fe.[40]

Other problems permeated Spanish-Mexican society, problems far more serious than disputes about bills and ropes: Jealousy and adultery plagued married life and arose as often as wifebeating and assault charges. Sometimes the two were linked. Barbara Roybal, residing in Galisteo, just outside of Santa Fe, appeared before the Santa Fe magistrate to complain of an assault. Her husband, she said, had "swatted her with a shoe and bruised her in the mouth." Her father, she said, was her sole source of support. Moreover, she had known about her husband's "friendship" (or affair) with another woman for a while. "I do not cry for him or about the friendship," the complainant lamented, but "for the children." Roybal wanted the husband banished and requested that he be required to pay alimony.[41]

Although raised to be deferential toward, and respectful of, parents and spouses, women had few qualms about petitioning for dissolution of marriages. Similarly, they regarded marriage as a relationship unlike blood relations, although they hoped it would approximate consanguinity. "I wish he would respect me as I do my parents," as María Ramona said. When their marriages soured, as they sometimes did, few women felt compunctions about removing themselves or their children from their husbands; and they asked judges to order men to assume financial responsibility for their offspring.

A frontier society, Santa Fe provided, though it might not have approved of, realistic solutions that closed the gap between what should be done and what was done. The town had a proverb—"Where one is born, one always knows; where one dies, one never knows"—that reiterated the message that kin and home were of prime importance. One's birthplace, relationship to one's parents, commitment to family, and enduring respect for relatives and spouse were the themes conveyed constantly in folkloric expressions. Underlying the instruction, however, was the cold, hard fact that not all of life's events could be predicted. Hence, the equally popular adage, "Better to have a good neighbor than a relative far away," carried down-to-earth advice. It indicated an acceptance that relatives sometimes moved far away and exerted pressure and guilt on kin to keep them from doing so.[42]

Family and community thus imposed a formidable order on women's actions. Numerous times, troubled couples attempted to reconcile—which was the solution preferred by judges and priests alike. Divorce required lengthy, convoluted procedures; even then, not all priests approved of it. Separation became the easier, more acceptable solution, but it imposed limitations as well. It was an uneasy middle position. Appearing before the judge again in 1839, Barbara Roybal demonstrated the problems that separations induced. By then, she had moved to Santa Fe and her husband was having another affair. He refused to pay for a cow and some sheep she wanted to pasture outside the town. "I am uncertain about how I will feed my children this winter, were it not for my parents."[43] On that gloomy note, Roybal ended her appeal.

Women's requests for maintenance took on added significance when they had to support children. For example, the inability to feed her children troubled Roybal. Relying on her parents probably did not offend her, but she seemed ashamed about having to ask them for assistance. For a family without means, the extra responsibility of caring for abandoned or neglected relatives often caused hardship. Because she was at the mercy of her parents and relatives, the woman with dependent children understood intimately how her situation affected others.

Daily, the most impoverished citizens, especially women and children, were reminded of who their best advocates were. The charity upon which they relied was offered within families, not by institutions. Generosity and sharing grew between friends and individuals. "My neighbor is practically giving us the animals because he feels so badly," Roybal pleaded before the judge.[44] Once again, the message conveyed the preeminence of family, the need for kin, and the importance of friendly neighbors. Women's wills from the same period suggest a deepening interdependence among the needy: Women continuously ordered payment from or toward the rental of pastures for keeping a cow or pig, or for putting out an animal to stud.[45]

In the face of a developing merchant economy, Roybal's version of interdependency persisted. Of course, Santa Fe in the 1820s and 1830s had become a busy trade center, a market-oriented town where Native entrepreneurs, Spanish-Mexican storekeepers, and Missouri's merchants met and exchanged or sold items.[46] By 1832, $95,000 in merchandise had flooded the capital. The town attracted many wayward and hungry people, and it made modest efforts to care for the indigent rather than send them on their way.

Not considered public charges, wanderers nevertheless tapped the collective consciousness of a town that was 222 years old and structured around related persons. "I feel sorry for these strangers who have nothing to eat," one woman told the priest.[47] He promptly wrote to the bishop of Durango, requesting guidance and inquiring about extra funds for feeding the poor and hungry. One transient who appeared before a judge was urged to look elsewhere for work, but he argued that he had no place to go. The judge called the priest, and they put the indigent man to work at the church.

Evidently, the number of such persons was noticeable, because in 1840 Bishop José Antonio Laureano de Zubíria of Durango, whose jurisdiction included the Santa Fe parishes, circulated Pope Gregory XVI's pastoral that reduced the holy days of obligation, when work was supposed to be suspended, and attached a lengthy statement to it about the care of the wayward. Bishop Zubíria included a discussion not only of persons who missed church but of the indigent and the migratory. The problem was evidently common to, and acknowledged throughout, the Republic of Mexico.[48]

Although families in Santa Fe assisted, through their networks of kin and friends, destitute members of the society, partnerships did not always work smoothly in an extended family. It is possible, by ignoring the dissonance between relatives and others, to gloss over the tensions that marred true interdependence. Marriage, as we have seen, was the relationship in which issues and dissension first arose between spouses who crossed the rigid lines of propriety. Often, transgressions bordered on the mundane, compared with the crimes of assault and battery. Discerning what was mundane to one person, and not to another, was problematic, however, particularly when the deed involved money. Doña Gregoria Quintana sued her husband for selling her grain mill without her permission—hardly an ordinary matter. Francisca Romero took her husband to court because he had gambled away her burro. The judge ordered that Quintana receive payments from the mill itself and that Romero's burro be returned to her. On the surface, Quintana's complaint appeared to be the most pressing; certainly, her mill was worth more than Romero's burro. If Romero's burro was her only property, however, its loss could hardly be termed insignificant.[49] Moreover, upper-class and poorer women commonly willed their burros to their heirs, which suggests that the animals were valued and perhaps valuable as well.[50] The carreta (cart) was the typical vehicle for moving goods, and the burro was the beast most suited to the task. In that sense, burros were extremely valuable.[51]

Wealthy and poor women shared concerns over property that drove them into court. Although it might be useful for historians to delve into the dissimilarities among the lawsuits women of different classes filed, such efforts are frustrated by incomplete records and record collection, which make drawing conclusions based on numbers nearly impossible. Equally distressing is the problem of how to determine the class origins of the litigating women. Quintana was a proprietor who, in her lawsuit, outlined a middle- or upper-class position. Romero went to court over the loss of one burro, but that does not necessarily mean she was poor or of the working class. The difficulty of correlating other sources with a woman's solitary appearance in the historical record, when portions of census records are incomplete or missing altogether, makes definitive statements about class—based on property—awkward.

limits of sources

√ 1

Colonial historians have theorized, however, that Santa Fe was a villa comprised of *ricos*, *pobres*, and *genízaros* (rich people, poor ones, and detribalized Indians), Pueblo women, slaves, and abandoned foundlings; the defining characteristics within these categories were race, ethnicity, and culture as well as financial circumstances. The period that began roughly at the turn of the century and continued through the Euro-American conquest defies such categorizations, however, because merchant capitalism made some old ricos poorer, while some previously classified as pobres became slightly better off. Genízaros and women remained invisible except when they appeared before institutions like the courts. Historians who view the Euro-American takeover as the event that finally clarified class categories have been criticized for not taking into account the presence of merchant capitalism before traders trekked into town. The criticism is legitimate. My effort previously was—rather than pinpointing origins—to take stock of the shifting ground once Euro-Americans began making inroads in Santa Fe's economy and their manufactured products became more available. However, the impending takeover should not be given undue weight, regarded as inevitable, or accepted unquestioningly as a marker in women's lives. For Manuela Baca and others, the presence of new men and their products *was* significant, but not all-determining, as the variety of women's lawsuits attests.

1820s merchant capitalists + traders

Another valid criticism brings the issue of class into sharp relief: People cannot be put into neat categories of rich or poor, top or bottom, insiders or outsiders. Class configuration on the Mexican frontier varied by region, with destitution, wealth, and production meaning different things among the residents. Merchant capitalism allowed some movement between classes. Widows, it appears, sometimes retained class privileges and sometimes lost them. A few shepherds became livestock owners or cattle foremen after the war; some Spanish-Mexican lawyers lost their practices because the Euro-American territorial system did not consider their legal training legitimate. Each of these examples says something about how class position affected all frontierspeople.

As if categorizing women's class position were not burdened enough by problematic sources, and by competing theories, another layer of differing interpretations exists. Chiefly, court records underscore societal discontent, and the class motives that guided lawsuits were naturally distended in the race to have judges weigh displeasure or grief. Conclusions relying only on lawsuits must be tempered with this recognition; hence, in the notes, I include references to similar situations documented outside the courts. There is also the problem of how or why the records were kept in the first place. Spanish and Mexican law required careful recording and filing but did not preserve or safeguard all of those documents. Many were lost, and historians cannot numerically reconstruct class configurations using them alone. Rather, they must be used with caution. The most one can say is that class, for litigating women—like race, culture, and gender concerns—exhibited itself in the documents and *might* mean, within a range of choices or decisions, such and such. Finally, because the court testimonials of women have not been used extensively by most nineteenth-century Chicano or Chicana historians or Borderlands scholars, conclusions drawn solely from them remain debatable.[52]

difft to make class diffs

These precautionary notes do not mean that other types of conclusions cannot be drawn. Discontent clearly characterized relations between persons living in Santa Fe, women included. Most women's cases were lodged against men, but a few were made against other women. The difficulties between the landlord Ana María Rendón and her tenant Juana González offer one example of lawsuits between women. Other lawsuits charged women with fornication in cases where two women were involved with the same men. Many of these women, like Juana Lopes, described their illicit sexual relations, and adolescents frequently conceded that they were involved in sexual relationships. Juan de Jesus Archuleta sued a man who had disfigured his daughter's face with a razor after finding her with another man—she was fourteen years old.[53] The disfigurement of women who committed adultery was not unusual; in the colonial period, the historian Ramón Gutiérrez has noted, the practice occurred among both Indians and Spanish-Mexicans. In this way, angry men or husbands "marked" wayward women and censured their behavior.[54]

The courts showed no reluctance to arbitrate cases charging illicit liaisons, and affairs were not easily tolerated by wives, especially poor wives. "I want only for him to leave her and give us his attention," stated one litigant who was worried because her husband, Juan Trujillo, had not paid their food bill.[55] His transgressions pained her, but far more immediate was the worry about food and sustenance. Likewise, men who acted irresponsibly toward their families were the subject of long, heated discussions. Witnesses for the plaintiff, or wife, usually were called to corroborate her testimonies. Because so many others could—and often did—become involved or were brought before an alcalde, these cases often reached the courtroom only as a final resort. In fact, extramarital affairs were rarely the central complaint in women's pleas; usually, the wandering husband and mistress were exposed only to demonstrate the gravity of the man's abandonment or neglect. Infidelity, such complaints suggest, was bad, but neglect was worse.

Men charged with adultery were sometimes banished or forbidden to see their mistresses. Juan Trujillo was presented with one of those options and told that if he chose to stay with his wife, the court might appoint a guardian to monitor his behavior. The solution he accepted is not known, but the serious charges plus the involvement of others in the "private" life of couples suggest that the orders of the court in this way encouraged changes in behavior. With the inclusion of other types of arbiters, the problem became a community matter.

By forcing individuals to keep a promise, or by making the punishment so severe that parties were likely to think twice about transgressing the rules, Santa Fe and the frontier communities surrounding it kept individuals aligned with the principal mores and ideals. The court and church records depict a society at once capable of upholding models of behavior and of harboring individuals who did not quite meet the standards deemed appropriate by the society at large. Catholicism enforced, in fact created, many of the values, and remained solidly in the forefront of debates over improper behavior.

Women lived with these and other pressures and also rebelled against them. For women, judges and relatives were often similar to modern-day arbiters because they could not always force men to behave differently. Several times, assaulted or affronted wives brought a matter before the court, but in particular, the case of Juana Lopes indicates another, equally important attitude. Even within the confines of a rigorously moral society, preoccupied both with how people behaved and how they treated each other, women could bend the rules without being completely ostracized. Belonging to an extended family helped in this regard. Few censuses found people living alone.[56] Almost without exception, marginal women—prostitutes, witches, the insane, and the retarded, for example—had families. Each individual member of Spanish-Mexican society knew that she or he had someone who could be called forward and would be willing to take sides. Such women as Juan de Jesus Archuleta's disfigured daughter, the impoverished Barbara Roybal, and the offended Manuela Baca attest to the importance of family as witnesses and for support. Plaintiffs and defendants alike appeared in court with relatives in tow.

Before the war, Santa Fe could be characterized as a town whose institutional structures urged women to conform. Not everyone accepted that uniformity all the time, and some rejected it entirely. The women who came to court were definitely reluctant—in this period of social, political, and economic transition—to move outside preferred structures or to stray far from basic norms. Without family, neighbors, and friends, women recognized their economic vulnerability. They did much more, however, than make the best of a bad situation. Many divorced, or separated from, their husbands; some twisted the situation so that their honor and reputation remained intact; others declared openly that they had no intention of changing or reforming.

In an era when the United States and Mexico were revamping their notions about how society should operate, and when political reform movements and race questions emerged squarely in the forefront of debates, Santa Fe's residents largely followed ways that differed markedly from Protestant or U.S.-driven traditions. As the United States undertook a revitalization campaign, devised institutions such as jails, poorhouses, and asylums to handle recalcitrant or marginal persons, and established a full-fledged reservation system to confine Native peoples, Spanish-Mexican frontier society continued to rely on kin and the church to handle its many social problems.[57] The forms of settling differences varied throughout the former Spanish Empire, making it impossible to draw definitive conclusions about whether Santa Fe was typical or not under the old system of governance. After independence, Mexicans attempted to retain some political and ecclesiastical structures and to reorder others. Political turmoil prevailed—between 1820 and 1840, the Republic was led by over twenty presidents—and therefore many frontier communities like Santa Fe suffered, but ignored, the many edicts issued from Mexico City to Chihuahua City and to Durango, and then to communities northward.

To Euro-Americans coming from cultures and an economic system that relied increasingly on institutions other than the family to handle deviance, Spanish-Mexicans seemed to be nonconformists, especially the women, as we shall see in the next chapter. Spanish-Mexican society continued to rely on traditional ways of mediating conflict, however; it drove out the worst offenders, arrested others, but in the main, attempted to resolve antagonisms quickly. These ways remained invisible to Euro-American eyes.[58]

Spanish-Mexican women were caught in the middle of national struggles and of economic, political, and social disarray. They were neither immune from, nor ignorant of, the changes at hand. In the 1820s, as many as one hundred Euro-American merchants resided in Santa Fe and by the 1830s, another hundred had arrived.[59] By then, Mexico was fully independent, and its treasury was bankrupt. Even far-removed communities like Santa Fe were affected by subsequent Mexican debates over federalism and centralism, which were central to resolving the mounting debt crisis. New Mexicans equated centralism with taxation and with unfair representation. Many despised the 1835 appointment of the centralist Col. Albino Pérez as governor and comandante of the militia; in 1837, a small group of rebels had beheaded the governor and elected a mestizo (half Pueblo Indian, half genízaro) as temporary governor.[60] The group then formed a junta popular, which ran aground when the wealthy, antitaxation forces from the area south of Albuquerque coalesced against the rebels.[61]

The primary motive behind these revolts was the same. The poorest sectors of the population were tired of military conscription, food shortages, and the lack of cash. The middle and upper classes were tired of the heavy burden of taxation and of the continuing problems with marauding Indians. The economy was in shambles. Rich and poor alike were looking to Mexico City to resolve political difficulties and to Euro-American merchant capitalists to aid the worsening economic situation.

During these two decades of rebellion and political crisis, women were plagued by other problems as well. Affairs, unhappy marriages, reticent spouses, and ignorant Euro-Americans, as well as more serious crimes in distant cities, contributed to women's growing unease. Not that their lives had ever been constant or static. But the flux that occurred before the U.S.-Mexican War had taken place in a familiar cultural arena, and the drama of life contained familiar players. In the 1840s, a decade marked by war with the United States over control of the Mexican North, women's lives changed even more rapidly. The results would prove more calamitous than they had been during the crisis over independence.

Quest.
Who was Barceló
why
how did she deal
w/ Euro.An merchant
class?
g gambling - a shock
Euro An Protest
how did g accommodate.
how did they acc. men?
how did Barceló acc?

Women under Siege

*Sexuality and the Gendered Economies
of Colonization, 1840–1852*

Gertrudis Barceló of Santa Fe was born in 1800 and lived through half a
century marked by growing economic and social disarray. In her lifetime,
the confusion surrounding women's lives intensified when dollars flooded the
marketplace, replacing pesos. Before she died in 1852, Barceló could reflect on
changes in the economy; on the ways in which, respectively, traders had replaced trappers, merchant-enterprisers had replaced the traders, and bureau-
crats the merchant-enterprisers. Barceló herself helped create a new world in
Santa Fe by building a prosperous gambling saloon that became a busy social
center for locals as well as for Euro-American traders and soldiers.

These men plied their trade at her establishment so frequently that the
Missouri–Santa Fe–Chihuahua Trail seemed to lead men from Missouri to
Barceló's gambling tables, then south to Chihuahua. Having participated in
card games, a vice they considered Santa Fe's worst sin, some men tried to ease
their consciences by writing about Barceló, her successes, and her society.
Their stories fabricated some details, omitted others, and exaggerated local customs. They criticized Barceló and embellished images of her with portraits of
other women to argue that Santa Fe's women were worthless. Nothing could
have been less true. Barceló grew wealthy on Euro-American money, yet Euro-
American men called her everything but what she was: a businesswoman.

Barceló's case did not represent that of all women of the era. The contrasting poverty in which so many lived, and which deepened after the U.S.-
Mexican War of 1846, points out how atypical Barceló was in exploiting the
economic opportunities created by merchant capitalists. Other women tried to

avoid the fate of continual impoverishment by marrying foreigners, men culturally different from them but usually of their own class and religion. Other women eased the transition of some Euro-American men in ways that Barceló did not, but both helped socialize them to Spanish-Mexican customs and to Santa Fe. This chapter surveys how a particular brand of <u>accommodation</u> worked for Spanish-Mexican women like Barceló; it relies on the travel literature of this period, on diaries and reminiscences of Euro-American conquerors, and on complaints filed in court to portray hardships and women's survival in the pre- and postwar periods.

Accommodation signified more than the active incorporation of new men into an old community because it operated in multiple directions. Cultural accommodation is rarely passive; it is more often a subtle and important consequence of resistance; in colonial situations, it has even been a characteristic form of resistance.[1] In the United States, scholars usually discuss cultural accommodation as being what people do within the confines of a difficult racial or cultural situation; in modern terms, it is used to describe immigrants who are adjusting to life in the United States and occasionally to examine how Euro-American communities adjust to new people. In the case of nineteenth-century Santa Fe, it signifies something else because the town was predominantly Spanish-Mexican and Euro-Americans were consistently considered "outsiders" by the Spanish-Mexican majority. (See Table 2.1.)

Because of women like Barceló, a few nineteenth-century Euro-American men adapted more easily to life in Santa Fe, becoming Hispanicized despite vast cultural differences; some, like Juana Lopes's husband, John Scolly, became

TABLE 2.1 Santa Fe's Changing Demography, 1850–1880

	1850	1860	1870	1880
Total Population	4,320	4,555	4,847	6,767
Female	2,166 (50%)	2,247 (49%)	2,488 (52%)	2,662 (38%)
Male	2,154 (50%)	2,308 (51%)	2,359 (49%)	4,105 (62%)
Ethnic Background				
Spanish-surnamed females	2,126 (49%)	2,160 (47%)	2,488 (52%)	2,662 (38%)
Spanish-surnamed males	1,915 (44%)	1,995 (44%)	1,803 (37%)	2,178 (32%)
Non-Spanish-surnamed females	40	87	50	130
Non-Spanish-surnamed males	239 (6%)	313 (9%)	556 (13%)	1,927 (30%)[a]
Female-Headed Households				
Total Households	930	879	1,216	1,461
Unmarried, Spanish-surnamed female heads of households	201 (22%)	253 (29%)	322 (26%)	183 (13%)[b]

Sources: United States Census Bureau, Original Schedules of the Seventh, Eighth, Ninth, and Tenth Censuses of Population, for Santa Fe (microfilm, NMSRC).

[a]Note the rise of non-Spanish-surnamed men between 1870 and 1880, +1,371.
[b]Only those enumerated as widows make up this number.

permanent residents when they married Spanish-Mexican women. But that type of accommodator was rare; most of them scorned women like Juana Lopes or denigrated the capabilities of women like Barceló.[2]

The early summer of 1846, when New Mexicans finally received word that Mexico and the United States had severed diplomatic relations over the annexation of Texas, was as chaotic for Barceló as for others doing business in Santa Fe. Local residents, in the two years before war was declared, had continued to be aggravated by President Santa Ana's calls for centralism and by his appointment of an outsider—not a New Mexican—Gen. Mariano Martínez, to the governorship. Martínez was spared the fate of the earlier centralist appointee, Governor Pérez, who had been assassinated by a group of rebels. Martínez returned instead to Mexico City after one grueling year during which provincial affairs fell into utter disrepair. The next fall, New Mexicans chose Manuel Armijo—a leader in one of several counterrebellions—to govern. In that way, they declared their independence from Mexico City and sent out a warning that they were interested in preserving their own political parties and advancing local interests over federal ones.[3]

The New Mexicans' propensity to chart their own political and economic course was not new. Tradition dictated a reticence to follow exactly the plans laid out by distant authorities, in civil and church matters.[4] This, perhaps as much as poverty and other hardships, contributed to the desire for change. With the ricos, Armijo's group, firmly in control of the political situation and of the militia, and with upwardly mobile women like Barceló eager to make a profit from the merchant-enterprisers whose numbers had doubled in the 1840s, Santa Fe seemed to be priming itself and ready for a takeover. When Gen. Stephen Watts Kearny and his bedraggled, exhausted troops arrived in Santa Fe in August 1846, the townspeople gathered on the plaza to observe the unfurling of the American flag. Sporadic resistance against the Euro-American troops flared in the surrounding areas throughout the ensuing two years, but overall, the Santa Feans Kearny assembled and others, including women, appeared as resigned to the change as many in the impoverished Mexican North.[5]

The reasons for the lack of visible military resistance, and for the seemingly quiet acceptance that greeted Kearny and his forces in Santa Fe, also had to do with the events of the previous decades and the manner in which merchant capitalism had accomplished its goals—opening up new markets; undermining older, established systems of interdependence; injecting new products into a depressed economy; and encouraging local people, with the cash generated and the capital invested, to begin working for wages—as well as with the growing social disarray of the 1830s exemplified by the lawsuits against even wealthy residents like Manuela Baca. She and others of her class defended in court their right to continue trading in the old manner, surreptitiously and without the meddling of federal authorities.[6]

In addition, merchant capitalism had relied on the ricos, like Armijo, and the merchants, like Baca and Barceló, to help reorient New Mexico away from Mexico and toward the United States for products and material goods. But it, and the overly needy Mexican treasury, had also had a share in displacing the

TABLE 2.2 Personal Income Index for Non-Spanish-Surnamed Males

Dollar Amounts	1860	1870
$1–$999	100[a]	50[b]
$1000–$999	28	80
$10,000–$14,999	6	6
$15,000–$19,999	5	5
$20,000–$39,000	11	7
Over $40,000	4	3

Sources: United States Census Bureau, Original Schedules of the Eighth and Ninth Censuses of Population, for Santa Fe (microfilms, NMSRC)

a. Includes 34 soldiers at Fort Marcy.
b. Includes 18 soldiers at Fort Marcy.

rich in the game for profit; in the decades following the war, even the wealthiest lost the struggle for local control of the New Mexican economy and its political system. If the upper crust of New Mexico, who never constituted more than 5 to 8 percent of the total population, expected Euro-Americanism to lead them out of the financial crises of previous decades, they were sadly disappointed by their displacement in the new economic order (see Table 2.2).[7]

Theoreticians of merchant capitalism and of its historical operation inform us that it exerts control in several distinct phases and on different levels, depending on the involvement of the state, the political structures in place or those installed by new governments, and the level of exploitation of workers.[8] In the first phase—corresponding in this case to the late eighteenth century and lasting into the late 1850s, when the Santa Fe trade between Missouri and Santa Fe first began to wane—merchant traders were concerned primarily with introducing and maintaining a steady flow of manufactured items. In the second phase, and as the trade began taking on the characteristics of industrial capitalism—which for Santa Fe possibly took place in the last decades of the nineteenth century—the primary motivation for the merchants and others in control resided in sustaining the production of goods and in exploiting the local workers. What ultimately distinguishes the phases is the matter of control; in the first phase, control was informal, and in the second, it was structured. But what underlies each worked to the same end: the struggle to control resources and workers was purposefully disruptive of the social order.[9]

In this chapter, I focus intermittently on the disruptions, on the social and cultural cleavages induced by merchant capitalism, with an aim toward positioning women's responses and strategies within a fluctuating economy increasingly shaped by merchant capitalism, in which gender was an underlying, but unacknowledged, issue. The reasons gender and women have been overlooked in traditional accounts of the takeover of Santa Fe by Euro-Americans are varied, but the evidence is clear on this point: Women were not merely affected by the merchant-capitalist occupation; women, in the memoirs of the colonizers, were spotlighted, examined, and described, and their activities were scrutinized. Barceló, in particular, received inordinate amounts of disagreeable attention in the literature. Poor women were portrayed negatively as well, but they were mentioned, which points to the importance and significance of all women and the centrality of gender in the works of memorialists and travelers.[10]

In addition to women's roles, other aspects of merchant capitalism were significant in the takeover. Some corresponded again, and not surprisingly, to the period when Santa Fe was shifting slowly away from a late-eighteenth-century and early-nineteenth-century merchant-trade economy to a merchant-capitalist one. A characteristic of the former was that the trade could afford to be unscrupulous, its agents not caring at all if they traded whiskey or guns to the Indians or to Spanish-Mexicans; a characteristic of the onset of merchant capitalism in the period when Barceló was setting up her gambling tables was that the agents were far more directly involved in production *and* consumption; hence, Barceló and the other ricos of New Mexico, as well as the Euro-American merchants, became interested and invested in the content of, and the rising profits derived from, their trade. Silk and satin cloth in place of calico, brandy in place of whiskey, and picks and axes in place of hoes and shovels began to be loaded on the caravans leaving Missouri. Merchant-bureaucrats, lawyers who were also investors, land speculators, and others who had aspirations to political office, accompanied the wagons into Santa Fe after the war to displace the first merchant traders and the New Mexican upper class, and they provided a clientele for the luxury items of the changing marketplace. Although a few women occupied this upper trading echelon, the majority took their place at the bottom of the new hierarchy, as servants to the businessmen—they became either domestics laboring for wages or street vendors peddling food and beverages.[11]

Although the wealthier New Mexican merchants suffered in the years after Kearny's soldiers took over the town, and in the period following 1848, when New Mexico was officially made a territory of the United States, their predicament seems a mild one as compared with the situation of most women, who remained poor and disenfranchised in the new economic and political structures of the war years and the postwar era. Women's primary occupations as they appeared in the censuses of 1823 and 1845 indicate the type of work done for wages. Servant, laundress, and ironer were the most frequent occupations; the vendor Barbara Baca listed laundress as her occupation, which indicates that some women held more than one job. During the decade before the war, women were increasingly employed by Euro-American men and their wives, and they were not well paid. In 1836, Chiquita Manuel de Anda sued her employer, María Brown, for her month's salary of twelve pesos, which had been withheld because the servant had broken a dish. Brown was ordered to pay the salary but to keep two pesos as compensation for the cup.[12]

In the First U.S. Census, of 1850, over 70 percent of the adult female population cited occupations such as laundress, domestic, and seamstress, indicating that within two years of the signing of the peace treaty ceding New Mexico to the United States, the largest percentage of the resident female population was locked in at the bottom of the economic structure. Wages were differentiated by race or ethnicity; "Mexicans," as Spanish-Mexican women were identified in the national censuses, received lower wages for the same jobs as "Americans." (See Table 2.1.) Moreover, the nature of the jobs suggests that women's labor was difficult and tedious, and the humble wages received portray the depressed economy and women's lowly position in it.[13]

Some travelers' accounts in newspapers and magazines of the time, after the war, portrayed idyllic scenes of burros burdened with wood bundles and of Mexicans resting on the roadside (Figure 2.1).[14] The interest of merchants was piqued as many wrote home about the opportunities awaiting them en route to California, and the goldfields, and during the westward trip in general. The impact of the influx was undeniable in that it may have meant women were employed, but it also signified a form of dependence on the steady stream of newcomers.

Ultimately, both merchant capitalism and Mexican authoritarianism could be faulted for the ongoing poverty of the majority population: Santa Fe's Spanish-Mexican women (see Table 2.3).[15] Many travelers and social commentators of the period described the supposed economic and cultural malaise that gripped the town and ignored the origins of scarcity and economic problems in general. The burro appearing in sketches seemed to stand for both, enchantment and servility. Sometimes the new employers, and also the resident upper classes, resorted to violence or brute force to enforce contracts and keep women in lowly positions. Maria Francisca Sena charged Don Benito Larragoita with exerting undue violence against her daughter, whom he had

FIGURE 2.1 Road Scene. Figures 2.1 through 2.7 from *Harper's Monthly*, April 1854.

TABLE 2.3 Wage Differences Based on Ethnicity and Gender, City of Santa Fe

| | Daily Wage | | | | | | % of Spanish-Surnamed Female Population age 15 | | |
| | Americans[a] | | | Mexicans[a] | | | | | |
Occupation	1860	1870	1880	1860	1870	1880	1860	1870	1880
Day Laborer, male	1.50	1.60	1.75	1.00	1.10	1.15	—	—	—
Domestic, female	1.50	1.75	2.00	.50	.55	.85	25	31	48
Laundress, female[b]	.20	.25	.25	.10	.15	.20	30	28	25
Seamstress, female[b]	.10	.15	.15	.05	.10	.10	20	21	15

Source: United States Census Bureau, Original Schedules, Social Statistics, Eighth, Ninth, and Tenth Censuses of Population, for Santa Fe County (microfilm, NMSRC, Santa Fe).

a. Enumerator's term.
b. Per item.

slapped while she was in his employ; Larragoita was ordered to pay the wages owed, and the girl, who was frail and ill at the time of the lawsuit, was ordered to uphold her contract and return to work as soon as possible.[16]

It was not uncommon for employers, both Spanish-Mexican and Euro-American, to discipline servants or withhold wages as punishment for wayward conduct; they were also not above whipping them or ordering their laundresses to rewash clothes. Sena and others who testified in court about their work and what was expected of them made it clear that they worked diligently at back-breaking jobs because they needed the money. But travelers and writers refused to see this. Women, one visitor remarked, simply "grind corn on a rock, make tortillas, and dance"; another stated unequivocally that Spanish-Mexican women worked very little.[17] Thus, male visitors to this frontier community cast their gaze upon local hard-working women and disparaged them without equanimity.

"The minds of the people are as barren as the land, with as little hope of being better cultivated," remarked W. W. H. Davis—a traveler, and later the acting governor of the territory of New Mexico—as if to reinforce some prevailing notion of the poverty of the place.[18] Barceló and her kind, however, hardly embodied the characteristics of desolation or idleness. Vendors, fruit peddlers, bakers, and gamblers—all occupational groups that included women—could be seen operating out of carts or stalls around the plaza.

Barceló, the town's leading businesswoman and owner of a gambling house and saloon situated one street away from the busiest corner of the plaza, exemplified an ingenious turnaround in the way she and other women began resolving the problem of the powerful Euro-American merchant, who by 1846 was lodged more firmly than ever in their midst.

By the time the sketches accompanying George Brewerton's articles arrived in New Orleans and then were sent on to the East Coast, locals and travelers alike were predisposed toward examining the contradictions before them. In the sketches, the steadfast burro remained on the town plaza, and women with

FIGURE 2.2 Grand Entrée into Santa Fé

rebozos were on the rooftops, but now the charro (Mexican cowboy) of rodeo fame, mounted on his trusty, if tortured, steed, also took his place on the chaotic plaza. Even the locals on the rooftops—depicted in "Grand Entrée into Santa Fé" (Figure 2.2)—seemed suspended both in time and in the face of the Zorro-like savior of Santa Feans, the man on the stallion.

This sketch vividly captured the town's energy. In Barceló's community of over four thousand, four hundred new men who were busily engaged in trading and selling, plus the additional soldiers Kearny left behind to keep New Mexico secure for the United States, made a difference.[19]

Indeed, merchants such as Alexander Le Grand, the famous Magoffin brothers—James and Samuel—and, in the next decades, the five prominent Spiegelberg brothers insinuated themselves into the developing economy and later into the territorial political structure. They owned the principal businesses and threw up new buildings to demonstrate their power. Other newcomers never stopped seizing opportunities to control trade and to describe the seemingly wanton behavior of Santa Fe's citizens, especially its women, and particularly Barceló.[20]

Acknowledging that these men had a culture and orientation that differed from those of the locals—as Miguel Sena and Manuela Baca had themselves done in court—does not entirely explain the reasons why they disparaged women. Closely examining their intentions in the context of changing patterns of merchant capitalism does not tell us why or how these particular men assisted the takeover of New Mexico. Nor does focusing on the derision they heaped on women fully explain the variety of responses women offered to the

FIGURE 2.3 View between Taos and Santa Fe

worst of these comments. Barceló, like Manuela Baca, established ingenious methods of dealing with the foreigners, but those methods remained imperceptible to arrogant commentators such as Davis. Not surprisingly, ignorance of Spanish and of Roman Catholicism did not stop him or other literate, mostly Protestant, outsiders from negatively describing New Mexico's women.[21]

Travel accounts of the nineteenth century generally were overtly conscious of the desires and proclivities of their readers and were written to reinforce what existed already in the popular journals and magazines of the time. Hence, the authors described the unsavory material conditions—Matt Field, for example, gazed upon the adobe buildings and labeled Santa Fe's houses a testament to "the power of mud"—while they noted the miserable conditions and distasteful activities of women because they thought such portraits would suit their largely anti-Catholic audience (see Figure 2.3). Scenes of crosses and hunched-over agrarians reinforced the same point. Except for one lonesome government official, Brantz Mayer, whose book indicted U.S. travelers by citing their prejudices against Mexicans, these images and accounts exhibited condescension and an implied, if not outspoken, sense of superiority.[22]

The uniform outlook is not the only characteristic binding the works of travelers and reporters, and suggesting their significance in the conquest. Many employed the logic of the traders Josiah Gregg, James Ohio Pattie, and others to pattern their books after previously published accounts. A particular format and duplication procedure usually guided the nineteenth-century travel account and was designed to encourage a consonant style; by extension, it produced a uniform vision. Travelers to New Mexico copied the style and content of Zebulon Pike's narrative of his reconnaissance trips in the early nineteenth century; long titles, lengthy introductions, and a concern for recording not only the minutiae of the topography, climate, flora, and fauna but also the customs of the local inhabitants, standardized the accounts. Later, traders and soldiers continued to record their daily experiences in New Mexico and devoted enormous energy to life's details. Tremendously popular, the stream of diaries and memoirs, like the slow but steady trade caravans, shifted the nation's attention westward and encouraged audiences to think of the reports as accurate and true.[23]

Some scholars, in an effort to contextualize the blatant racism and nineteenth-century cultural prejudices in the writings of visitors to New Mexico, overlook another critical feature of travelogues and memoirs. In this instance, the superficial social commentary of transients who later became territorial residents, such as W. W. H. Davis, became embedded in the national psyche, became part of the nationalist and race idioms of a country in a period of conquest. In other words, their remarks about adobe buildings or women's work did not merely embody race prejudice against Spanish-Mexicans, but they also actively promoted it throughout the country in the nineteenth century. Their legacy is as important to understand as the tenor and subjectivity of the accounts. The underlying purposes of the prejudicial treatment of women were as central to the methods of colonization as was unveiling a shifting merchant capitalism, for it was in their uses of women that merchant capitalists exposed their intentions and the intentions of the United States—to colonize a population and to assure it that status in perpetuity.

The commentaries did anything but portray life accurately. Underneath the remarks about immorality or about how New Mexicans "literally danced from the cradle to the grave" was cultural vibrancy, demonstrated in the passion for dancing and games. Barceló, or La Tules (Tules is the diminutive of Gertrudis), was its embodiment. She was an expert dealer at monte, the most popular card game on the northern Mexican frontier. The gambling hall she operated was a long room—mistaken by some historians for her apartment—that measured fifty feet by twenty feet; in fact, the hall was some distance from Barceló's home, although decorated in a similar style. Mattresses were folded against the wall and covered with Mexican woolen blankets; these became couches and chairs that were easily moved when the music began; soldiers described the numerous tables filling the sala (hall) and its rough-hewn furniture. Barceló was usually the dealer at the center gaming table; she was so expert with the cards that every visitor to her sala felt compelled to describe her nimble fingers and deft hands:

> A female was dealing (the famous Señora Toulous [Tules]) and had you looked in her countenance for any symptom by which to discover how the game stood, you would have turned away unsatisfied; for calm seriousness was alone discernible, and the cards fell from her fingers as steadily as though she were handling only a knitting needle.[24]

Matt Field, perceptive Irish observer and social commentator, witnessed the mountain of Mexican silver and gold coins piled high in the middle of the table and swept away when gamblers failed to match the cards dealt by Barceló with those already laid out in the corner. The game was based purely on chance, involving no strategy or cunning on the part of the participants. Barceló, however, had a strategy. After 1846, when Kearny's soldiers swarmed the town, the stakes grew ever higher as the game began to be played with American dollars; Barceló became more eager to embrace the strangers and find new ways to relieve them of their cash.[25]

Perhaps Barceló's response to the merchant takeover, to military intervention, and to a form of capitalism that began circulating a new currency in the town and developing a market economy, can be explained in another way. Even before 1821, individuals like Barceló had witnessed the activities of traders who entered their town and changed it. All along, local shopkeepers and vendors had been active in the developing marketplace. They had forged ahead, especially after independence, establishing partnerships with the adventurers, who brought new manufactured items to Santa Fe, while exporting the products of New Mexico, including minerals and equally valuable goods like wool, sheepskin, livestock, Navajo blankets, and handwoven rugs.[26] Although fined repeatedly by the Mexican government, gamblers continued their operations, much to the dismay of Euro-American travelers. Gregg explained that "the love of gaming also deserves to be noticed as a distinguishing propensity of these people," and he agreed with Frances Calderón de la Barca's comments regarding the passion for games, which, to their minds "is impregnated with the constitution—in man, woman, and child."[27] Appalled by the idea that even appointed officials gambled and danced at the saloon, the newcomers were bound to continue misunderstanding other social activities.

They attempted to make sense of some of these, but when they could not, litigation provided one method of resolving conflicts. Sometimes the troubles between resident business keepers and newcomers were well publicized, like Baca's and Sena's problems voiced in their courtroom drama of the 1820s against Le Grand; at other times, they were even more public and contentious. In the 1840s, Marcelo Pacheco, a businessman, successfully sued William Messervy for slander, calling the Euro-American merchant "a trespasser who thinks he owns everything."[28] Not surprisingly, uncooperative local partners exhibited a reticence reminiscent of the 1820s and 1830s when they refused to give up their control of the markets. Indeed, initial misgivings still manifested themselves in an ongoing distrust of Euro-American merchants. Few travelers reported the struggles between insiders and outsiders. Historians have relied on their memoirs and recollections and thus have subsequently ignored the evolving tensions. The evidence is striking, however, especially if the impact of the new merchandising is traced across time. Eventually, even the influential Pacheco's serious concerns about Euro-American encroachments yielded before the power of the dollar. By 1840, Euro-Americans monopolized trading on the town plaza and occupied three sides of the square, paying rents to one another as high as ten to twenty dollars a month.[29]

Curiously, at Barceló's gaming tables during the 1840s, the lack of confidence between newcomers and residents abated somewhat and yielded to a different, if uneasy, partnership. Initial criticisms about Barceló and her card games passed after many spent entertaining evenings at the gambling house.

In the spring of 1847, Lt. Alexander Dyer first visited the saloon. By June, his journal listed attendance at no fewer than forty fandangos and described numerous visits to La Tules's. Frequently, cryptic citations indicated his rush to abandon the journal for the card games: "At the Me. House tonight" meant a visit to the monte house, and this notation appeared dozens of times in any given month. His Mexican war journal leaves the distinct impression that a soldier's life, for those of his stripe, involved a constant round of entertainment; visits and parties at Barceló's hall were part of an officer's busy social life. Once they began going there, soldiers and others lingered and returned often.[30]

At the numerous tables that lined Barceló's establishment, men who could not speak Spanish, and people who did not understand English, learned a new language. Card games required the deciphering of gestures and facial expressions, but did not depend on any verbal communication. Soldiers new to Santa Fe, and travelers, understood, easily enough, what was important at the gaming table. Over cards, the men and women exchanged gold or currency in a ritual that emblazoned their meetings with new intentions. While drinking, cursing, and smoking, the soldiers and others unloaded their money at the table; if Barceló profited, they lost. But the games were such a diversion for the lonely troops that they hardly seemed to mind. The stakes grew larger at every turn, and many dropped out of the games to stand at the bar. Barceló's saloon took care of those who did not gamble as well as those who lost. Sometimes, a group of musicians arrived and played for the crowd. At other times, women—who, if not gambling, had been observing the scene—cleared a space in the long hall, and dancing began.[31]

Deeper-seated, anti-Mexican feelings and moralistic judgments were temporarily suspended in favor of the profits that awaited the wagerers if they won at monte or the pleasures that were to be savored each evening in Santa Fe, even if they lost. Barceló did more than accommodate men by inviting them to gamble. She furthered their adjustment to Santa Fe by bringing them into a lively setting that required their presence and money. At the saloon, the men were introduced to Spanish-Mexican music, habits, and humor. They could judge the locals firsthand and could observe a community's values and habits through a single activity. After a few drinks, their initial fears and prejudices yielded gradually to the relaxed, sociable atmosphere of the gambling hall. Her establishment took in lonely merchants and soldiers whose best hand among locals proved to be the cash they carried. The saloon also gave the community an opportunity to scrutinize the inclinations, drinking habits, and other characteristics of the newcomers.

Even continuous, visible socializing, however, did not keep Euro-Americans from depreciating Spanish-Mexican women, especially prominent ones like Barceló.[32] Matt Field described the women of Santa Fe as "dark complexioned, some of them [being] pretty, but many of them plain, and most of them ugly."[33] Zebulon Pike had, earlier, turned his judgmental eye on women, who, "with a few exceptions are taken up in music, dress, and the little blandishments of voluptuous dissipation."[34] George Wilkins Kendall, an adventurer who joined the 1841 Texas filibuster against New Mexico (known as the Texas–Santa Fe

Expedition), paid women a compliment by suggesting that they were kind and attentive, but only in contrast to the men, whom he found to be "a semi-civilized enemy—cruel, relentless, and treacherous," "[brutal] and cold-hearted."[35]

A few others concurred. George Douglass Brewerton, for example, also sympathized with New Mexico's women, whom he considered to be hard toilers and "slaves to the tyranny of their husbands."[36] His account of La Tules, with its accompanying sketch of an unjovial-looking, rather haggardly, "Lady Tules," repeated a leading refrain of the period between 1846—the time of the United States' first invasions of the territorial capital city—and 1854, when the sketch and the serialized reflections by Brewerton first appeared in *Harper's Magazine*. Puffs of smoke surrounded the depictions of women and priests, and the latter were shown in a Franciscan-like costume, with rosary crucifixes attached at the waistline or around the neck. On the other hand, La Tules, "in the language of Gregg," as Brewerton noted in his account, is encoded and "unmasked" in the nineteenth-century terminology reserved for prostitutes, her face appearing drawn, her off-the-shoulder cotton dress topped with a cross and a rosary, and above it, a smaller, "choker" necklace of beads (see Figure 2.4).

The reiteration of her proper title, first drawn by Brewerton from Josiah Gregg's immensely popular *Commerce of the Prairies*, "Señora Doña Gertrudes Barceló," or "Mrs. Gertrudes Barceló," then followed by his own caption, "Lady Tules," did more than outline Brewerton's propensity for exaggeration and sarcasm. The repetition served to reinforce his humorous regard for gambling and gamblers in Santa Fe, bearing witness, as he wrote, to that most ghastly of

FIGURE 2.4 Lady Tules *portrayed as prostitute*

sights, Catholic women and even children at the gaming tables. He linked up with, or at least relied on, the artist who had accompanied him during his "Incidents of Travel"; to juxtapose cigarettes, rosary beads, and a cross reinforced his feelings of anti-Catholicism. His pen and the sketch led readers as well to question just what sort of womanhood, what sort of femininity, what sort of femaleness was on display in the gambling halls of Santa Fe, while it focused attention on the most "infamous" woman of all, Lady Tules.

Beyond the fascination with Santa Fe's public displays lay other pressing socioeconomic issues in Tules's own time, and it would be a mistake to ignore their significance. In this period, the U.S. Congress was debating the annexation issue. Jane McManus Storms, a Washington letter writer, and others used similar material to argue that the annexation of Mexico would aid "Mexico's long-suffering and hardly-treated working classes."[37] These writers advocated the annexation of Mexico's northern territories and sought to defuse negative stereotypes in their efforts to justify a takeover, to lay claim to the land, if not the people who occupied it.

Other commentators persisted, however, in linking female licentiousness to the boisterous social scene and, unlike Storms, exhibited less confidence in the possibility of reforming the revelers. Thomas James recalled that, during the annual Catholic processions celebrating holy days, "the city exhibited a scene of universal carousing and revelry." "All classes," he continued, "abandoned themselves to the most reckless dissipation and profligacy. . . . I never saw a people so infatuated with the passion for gaming."[38] Brewerton puzzled over the festivities, saying that the saints, mostly "rude engravings," were "decked out by the females of the family with all sorts of tawdry ornaments."[39] Even supposedly religious occasions, according to these Protestants, afforded nothing more than an opportunity to revel in superstitions and drink and dance. Whether commemorating saints or gathering for entertainment and diversion, these observers suggested, Spanish-Mexicans were lascivious.

The writers did not restrict their comments to a "priest-ridden peasantry," to gambling, or to women's "dissipations."[40] Kendall described the women's dress, the cotton or linen chemise, as an "indelicacy" and "immodest."[41] Field described La Tules's "loose dress" as an affectation, "seeming to study negligence."[42] At other times, he called the card dealer the fashion empress of Santa Fe, who—when she deigned to appear at a fandango other than her own— wore "a blaze of rich jewelry and silk."[43] Dress itself, however, was not the only example of women's "loose habits." Many activities were similarly investigated, including the actions of priests, who also gambled. Brewerton, in his serialized "Incidents of Travel in New Mexico," would repeat the charge in the 1850s that Mexicans were hopelessly debased: "What better could you have expected. . . . when those whom they are taught to reverence and respect, and who should have been their prompters to better things, not only allow, but openly practice this and all other iniquities?"[44]

Josiah Gregg, in his massive and popular two-volume description of frontier trading, focused several pages on the shocking spectacle that he encountered in every Mexican community—women gambling. Puzzled by the apparent ease

FIGURE 2.5 The Padre Wins

with which farmers, priests, women, servants, and paupers gathered at the local gaming tables (Figure 2.5), he resolved the conundrum by linking the activity, as traders of his class might, to its potential for upward economic and social mobility. Gregg felt that gambling, although considered sinful by many
Euro-Americans, held out other possibilities for Spanish-Mexicans because it
illustrated "the purifying effects of wealth upon character."[45] Using rather
unusual and twisted logic—because Protestant Euro-Americans generally
equated gambling with undeserved wealth—Gregg nearly approved of New
Mexicans' efforts to improve their characters by making money at gambling.
La Tules, he postulated, had risen from poverty, and from being a woman of a
"shady character" and a "common prostitute, . . . a whore and a gambler," to
become prosperous and well received in the best circles by the 1840s. But it
was not the gambling alone that purified Barceló's soiled reputation, as far as
he was concerned. It was her inner strength and, in his reflections, her individual ability to do something with the money *saved*; in other words, she had
"earned" a better reputation through hard work, thrift, and diligence; gambling
was her means to improve herself, and this was a lesson he hoped would not be
lost on other Spanish-Mexicans.[46]

On a spectrum of attitudes, Gregg and Kendall were unusually optimistic
because many other observers had little faith in the ability of Mexicans to "up-
lift" themselves. Moralistic anti-Catholics of the United States could not yet
reconcile themselves to the sight of Mexicans who were gambling, smoking,
and drinking. The vast majority questioned how the nation would reform the
wagering Mexican populace, but they did so from a distance, usually after they

had returned to their newspapers and publishing houses in the East. While in residence in Santa Fe, the group of writers and observers was indeed hopelessly pessimistic. For that reason, too, La Tules's activities were legendary and were distorted in their accounts: She denoted for them the necessity for reform, but their call for it was tempered by a sense that the goal might not be easily accomplished.

The question remains, however, whether she or her moral character had actually changed or improved in the ways memorialists implied they had. Little is known of her birth and of several years in her life, but the established facts indicate nothing unusual in her upbringing. Some things about her past were atypical of other women in Santa Fe. Barceló was born in Sonora in 1800 and was educated there. She was a literate woman who had received some formal education. Her family, which included a brother, two sisters, and a mother, appeared to have migrated northward to an area near Albuquerque, and in 1823, she married into an old New Mexico family. She was four years older than the groom, and she was four or five months pregnant at the time she married.[47]

These circumstances of her marriage were not uncommon: Santa Feans sanctioned common-law marriages because priests were scarce and church weddings expensive.[48] Brides often were pregnant, and some even had children when they finally did marry, officially. Why so much attention has been focused on Barceló, the individual, and then has been generalized for all women, is intriguing. To understand why this occurred involves shifting the analysis momentarily away from women and focusing it on their society, as well as on the newcomers inspecting Santa Fe.

Some explanations for the lack of differentiation of women in the memoirs or travelogues of the period reside in the personal background of each of the writers; mostly middle class and primarily Protestant, these men could hardly distinguish one class from another. It is not surprising that in other ways they homogenized the local population, forsaking divisions based on status and fixating instead on their own misperceptions of poverty, race, or sex and gender. Soldiers, merchants, and travelers shared this tendency. James Josiah Webb, a merchant with nearly twenty years' experience in a partnership with William Messervy of Santa Fe, lamented that "the Pinos and Ortizes were considered the 'ricos' and those most respectable leaders in society and political influence, but idleness, gambling, and the Indians had made such inroads upon their influence that there was little left except the reputation of honorable descent."[49]

Again, Brewerton's work proved to be central to the developing castigations against Mexicans, some of them being based on sex, others on culture; and when those failed, religion could be counted on to emphasize the point (see Figure 2.6).

Cultural attributes, murderous conduct, thievery, and drunkenness were never far behind as subjects for criticism. Lieutenant Kendall argued that Mexicans were an "anti-go-a-head race," and immortalized a Captain Salezar (Salazar?), a brutal leader who rounded up Kendall and the Texan troops (who were en route to conquer Santa Fe in 1841), shot the stragglers, and cut off the ears of those who disobeyed him.[50]

FIGURE 2.6 Father Ignatio Moved by the Spirit

Consistently, such writers elevated one or two figures to hold the audience's attention—Barceló, the Ortizes or Pinos, or Salezar—with little regard for differences of any kind. In the literature, Barceló shared her individuation with the other women and men mentioned; she was lifted out of the crowd of women, and her activities were scrutinized; thus, she was labeled "shrewd" and "harsh."[51] In this way, the individual was held responsible for the sins, mistakes, and behavior of everyone; Euro-Americans saw no need to avoid gross generalizations, and as the literary critic Raymund Paredes explains about anti-Mexican fervor, "[Euro-]American writers came to observe the Mexican at a time when they were [most] prepared to hate him [her]."[52]

How locals responded to these pernicious attitudes and lies, if they did so at all, is less obvious but not impossible to decipher. Few Spanish-Mexicans could read or write Spanish, and even fewer read English. Reactions were therefore often restricted to the courtroom. Miguel Sena, for example, criticized Euro-American behavior, particularly in court: "As soon as they enter, they stretch themselves or recline on the seats, and if they are not ordered to stand, they give their answers in that position, and with their hats on their heads."[53] Mainly, Spanish-Mexicans did not denounce Euro-American observations with the same candor Sena displayed, but neither did they understand the customs of the newcomers.

Some reasons for the lack of a more vociferous outcry and resistance against Euro-Americans can be found in life's vicissitudes. Barceló's activities were indisputably anchored in a community shaped by a changing economy, as well as by other political, social, and cultural demands, including the persistent concern for virtue, reputation, and comportment. Orthodox interpretations of La Tules and the other individuals isolated in the travelers' accounts have overlooked the primacy of the surrounding turmoil and of Spanish-Mexican values. But individual men were not as harshly described by visitors and merchants as were women like La Tules. By the time of the U.S.-Mexican War, she had become the female object of the easiest, most exaggerated misunderstandings that such complicated frontier colonial situations breed. The exaggerations have been examined from several perspectives, but standard works fail to assess the role sexuality and gender, honor and respectability, played in discussions of Barceló's business and personality.[54] The outcome has been the creation of a legend shaped directly by the disruptions affecting her generation in general, and specifically involving her sex, sexuality, and business.

Gertrudis Barceló was said to have controlled men and to have dabbled in local politics. However, these were insinuations about her sexual prowess and they partially inform her legend. Reporters of her time, professional historians today, and novelists have debated her morals, arguing about her influence over political leaders and speculating about whether she was operating a brothel and whether she was a madam. Early accounts of Barceló, alone with the recollection of contemporary writers and soldiers of their experiences in the "hinterlands" of what until recently had been northern Mexico, consistently reveal these concerns. The impact of the negative images and the anti-Mexican stereotypes in their work helped legitimize the Euro-Americans' conquest of the region. Absorbed and reiterated by succeeding generations of historians and novelists, the legend of Barceló has obscured the complex duality of cultural accommodation and ongoing resistance to the Euro-American takeover. It has instead etched exaggerations of sex and female sexuality in the historical memory of the period.

Moreover, the legend evolving around Barceló affected the lives of other Spanish-Mexican women. Her supposed moral laxity and outrageous costumes became the basis for generalizations that included all the women of Santa Fe. Susan Shelby Magoffin, the first Euro-American woman to travel down the Santa Fe Trail, observed in 1846:

> They were dressed in the Mexican style; large sleeves, short waists, ruffled skirts, and no bustles—which latter looks exceedingly odd in this day of grass skirts and pillows. All danced and smoked cigarittos, from the old woman with false hair and teeth (Doña Tula), to the little child.[55]

This was not the first account of La Tules.[56] Josiah Gregg, the famous merchant, said during the 1830s that La Tules was a woman of "loose habits," who "roamed" Taos before she came to Santa Fe.[57] In his widely read *Commerce of the Prairies*, Gregg likened local customs—smoking, gambling, and dancing—to social and moral disintegration. La Tules embodied, for him and others, the depths of Spanish-Mexican decadence, and it was not, by extension, difficult for the writers to label her a prostitute, a whore. Even Gregg, who had praised her accomplishments, succumbed to this tendency.[58]

What Gregg and the others could not communicate to their audience was that La Tules was adaptable and, before their eyes, disproved their notion that Spanish-Mexicans were "lazy and indolent."[59] She contradicted such stereotypes and magnifications. Her busy saloon hosted nightly fandangos, and she easily became the target for the charge of licentious behavior. No evidence exists to support the contention that the saloon was also a brothel; what we know of the site—one large room—seems not to support this conclusion, although the census documents of the period twice listed "prostitute" as an occupation, suggesting that prostitutes did work in Santa Fe. We are simply uncertain that Barceló was herself a prostitute or was involved in the business of prostitution.[60]

Still, on other western frontiers, historians have linked drunkenness and saloons with the formation of prostitution rings; in colonial situations, scholars have also investigated the link between prostitution and merchant and industrial capitalism.[61] Both sociological and economic phenomena need to be kept in mind when examining the presumed sexual conduct of customers at the saloon, but in this case, the evidence is too scanty to accurately draw any portrait that is not based on conjecture. In the Brewerton sketch of the gambling saloon, one woman is visible, leaning against the wall and surrounded by solicitous men. What they were soliciting—and what women were offering by being present in the saloon—is open to interpretation (Figure 2.7).

The scene in the sketch showed eighteen men, four of them sitting in chairs; gambling is visible only in the left-hand corner, where a hunched-over man eagerly examines a line of cards, over the raised table edge, and a dealer sits pointing to one card rather than the others. A pistol appears to be visible in the corner of the gaming table. Directly behind, and leaning on the left-hand side, a woman's head and parts of her dress and hair are obscured by a man peering eagerly at the line of cards. Although the woman is part of the sketch, her invisibility or partial visibility was intended to make the point that women were present in the saloon where men relaxed, smoked, and conversed. It is difficult to discern among the happy participants the person who is a resident and the one who is an outsider, and the implication emerges that, in gambling, none of that is important; rather, conviviality, conversation, and reception, but not remorse, conflict, or drunkenness, are resurrected by the depiction.

In speculations about women's presence, or even their presumed sexual role within the saloon, other factors need to be considered. The bulk of published "evidence" of women's sexual behavior in the war years comes from memorialists who moralized that excessive dancing, drinking, and gambling signified unbridled sexuality for all women. "Lady" Tules, as she was sketched, investigated, and popularized, brought to the fore in the U.S. popular imagination all that was thought exotic and intriguing about "others"—in her case, Mexican women.

FIGURE 2.7 Gambling Saloon in Santa Fé

The sexual idiom of any society, composed of the values assigned to people, the morals attributed, and the behavior ascribed, to them—in this instance, ascribed to women, by the conquerors from the United States—has many historical counterparts. The scholar Elizabeth Perry has found, in the medical literature of counter-Reformation Spain, that women were categorized and labeled virgins, martyrs, witches, and whores. Nuns were martyrs and virgins, promiscuous women were whores, and eccentric women were witches; it is possible within this taxonomy to conclude that women were split into categories of good and bad. Some of the same expectations associated with "proper" female behavior were transported to, and refined in, the New World.[62]

For colonial Mexico, scholars have begun debating the extent to which upper-class women were cast in similar roles.[63] Some have suggested that gender prescriptions for women of mestiza background can be traced either to the sacrifice of Malintzín Tenepal or to her betrayal, depending on whether one sees her as Hernán Cortés's slave or mistress. To Mexican nationalists, Malintzín—twice sold into slavery and eventually sold to Cortés as a translator—symbolizes the betrayal for Indians; La Malinche, as she is identified in this lexicon, is the ultimate traitor, a treacherous and sneaky woman who helped Cortés conquer the magnificent Aztec Empire. For some scholars she serves other purposes; because of her victimization by Cortés, she is shown in a more positive light. By virtue of her captivity, she is one in a long line of women appropriated by conquerors to achieve their goals.[64]

Malinche was not just a victim. Certainly, she epitomized how the European conquest was achieved. She played a central role as Cortés's translator.

Linguistically, she was supremely capable, initially speaking Mayan as well as the diplomatic language of Mesoamerica, Nahuátl, and, later, Spanish. Her fluency aided Cortés more than the disgruntlements of the many cultures that made up the enormous Aztec Empire. Without her translations, Cortés's meetings with the Aztec leader Moctezuma would undoubtedly have been different.

Who Malinche was, or what she was not, is crucial to how we understand the position of Spanish-Mexican women in their communities because they bore the burden of this and other legends. Theirs was and is an engendered inheritance. The "La" placed before nicknames or diminutives at once isolates their popularity as it elevates it; it refers to more than "the." It sets women apart. Men are not identified, objectified in this way. Emerging even in the folktales and popular culture of seventeenth-century New Mexico is a heroine who battled—in a male disguise—the "infidel" Moors; because of her consistency and sexual fidelity, that figure is known as "La Constancia." Even more recently, Chicano Studies programs throughout the country continued offering courses on "La Chicana." From "La" Malinche to "La" Constancia, from "La" Tules to "La" Chicana, lie traceable patterns socially and linguistically constructed, a continuum that places individual women on a pedestal by particularizing them on the basis of their sex or gender.[65]

Moreover, the accusation of betrayal—and holding one woman responsible for "selling out" an entire nation—is cast in a language that silences all but the strongest girl or woman accused of Malinchismo. "Don't be a Malinche," children warn girls during play to silence the tattlers. Families also warn female children or adolescents, as well as adult women, to avoid being labeled a "Malinche"—in other words, to maintain privacy or to keep the family secrets. In this way, the supposed treachery of an Indian slave/mistress becomes a historical tale laden with multiple and duplicitous meanings, and a primary tale designed to keep women under control; its continued creation and re-creation across the ages facilitates any number of patriarchal agendas, but these must be understood in multiple contexts.[66]

The fear and threat of lust and sensuality lie just below the surface in the admonitions, both contemporary and historical, because the division polarizes the figure, first by her sex, then by her gender and actions. Boys and men are not accused of Malinchismo. Associating the breach and actions with her sex means that only women can be castigated, that only women can play the role of Malinche. The binary division hoisted on the figure of Malinche and the dialectical, unequivocating categorization of women into good or bad—like the categories used to describe New Mexico's women—revolved around particularly caustic attitudes about femaleness. Although some of these originated in Europe, these developed differently in the New World during the initial European conquest of Native peoples.[67]

Nineteenth-century New Mexicans observed similar codes for women, which were marked by a regard for virtue, honor, and reputation, but they frequently ignored or railed against them as well, as court cases and individual case studies have demonstrated. As in the economic structure, where merchant capitalism shifted, but nevertheless constrained, people's activities, the social structure on this frontier community tolerated many contradictory forms of sexual expression, while it outrightly denounced others. Another way to put this is to call it an operation of a Spanish-Mexican and a constructed female-ness or womanhood, a categorically debased version of it, according to the Euro-American social commentators—in other words, the creation of different female roles, unappealing in their differences.

Within Spanish-Mexican frontier cultures, other aspects of femaleness and related renditions of women's role were at work. Although the ghost of Malinche implanted itself in the Mexican national consciousness, and was resurrected from time to time on the New Mexican frontier, it was not the only salient role into which women were shoved. For example, in the soured relationship between the Euro-American John Scolly and the unrepentant Santa Fean Juana Lopes, the judge did not condemn Lopes's conduct, on paper, nor did he charge her with prostitution; he did not admonish her harshly or question her loyalty to her husband. He only asked her to stop philandering and to assume a more wifely role.[68] In cases where men were charged with adultery, the alcaldes usually stopped short of banishing the guilty and instead urged marital reconciliation. In an economy burdened by scarcity, that advice was sensible because the community or poor relatives could hardly shoulder the burden of caring for the abandoned. Therefore, practical considerations as well as loftier ideals about appropriate conduct for women and men guided the dispensation of justice in the courts and are as important as assessing the extent of the societal impact of any rigid sexual or role definitions laid out explicitly and across all periods for women.[69]

Outside the courts, and during the decade of the 1840s, another compelling ethic surfaced and marked social relations as much as ancient role definitions and gender ascriptions did. In their memoirs and travel literature, Euro-Americans pretended to describe—as well as to inscribe—Spanish-Mexican women's sexuality in the consciousness of the United States. Again, Davis provided examples of wayward women he observed at the gambling hall and concluded that "the standard of female chastity is deplorably low."[70] His remarks were based on ignorance *and* a dismissive understanding of differences, an utter intolerance of non-Euro-American forms of dancing, gambling, or dressing.

Many similar descriptions developed around the figure of La Tules. Matt Field suggested that Barceló was promiscuous, recording that he had first seen her "dashing" by in a "gaudy," mule-drawn carriage, and that she had smiled invitingly at the alcalde with whom he was walking.[71] In the works of such Euro-Americans, and because of her high visibility around town, La Tules's reputation was unrivaled. But, in Spanish-Mexican folklore, where the saloon girl and the female bar owner are not altogether unfamiliar, her persona did not necessarily convey the notoriety it did in the accounts of the writers Matt Field, W. W. H. Davis, Josiah Gregg, George Brewerton, or William Kennerly. Few Spanish-Mexicans would have agreed with the artist Alfred Waugh, who generalized that women in Santa Fe "deem chastity no virtue."[72] As one historian of colonial New Mexico has shown, on the contrary, the society put a great deal of stock in preserving virtue and honor, qualities associated with purity and virginity.[73] Repeatedly, court cases reported women's failures to uphold those elements of the sexual idiom, but this does not mean that this Catholic community did not value chastity or modesty—for women. The society might not have punished transgressors as severely as Euro-Americans would have liked, but it certainly promoted chaste conduct in its folklore and codes of behavior.[74]

The sexuality assigned Barceló thus requires, like Manuela Baca's retreat in the courtroom, that historians refocus temporarily on men to understand not necessarily their motives but how their misunderstandings of local culture and society, juxtaposed here against women's responses, actually encouraged women's resistance, while uncoincidentally impugning their characters. The contradictory pattern posed by the gulf between what was said and what actually existed is one of the more intriguing features of colonization's impact on women: The chasm between the image portrayed and reality is narrowed by the fact that Spanish-Mexicans accommodating newcomers to Santa Fe—allowing them in, to begin with—had the unintended effect of preserving in the historical record a clear pattern of women's responses and resistance to men's encroachments. In other words, around questions of sex and gender, and in the ways colonizers assigned particular roles to women like Barceló, cultural accommodation and a form of gender resistance coexisted. Moreover, because 99 percent of the newcomers were men, that interaction was shaped from the outset by a sex and gender imbalance; the men's memories that were committed to paper and subsequently published meant that the activities of Spanish-Mexican women became nationally known, albeit inaccurately, and therefore, as contemporary literary critics might say, "gave these women a voice" (see Table 2.1).

Thus the origins and meanings of the sexual aspects of Barceló's legend can be attributed to social and cultural discord, misunderstandings, and racism, or to the methods of conquest and colonization. They also sprang from continuous, pronounced political turmoil. During the war years, Spanish-Mexicans had allowed merchants and investors, through an elaborate system of bribery and kickbacks, to gain better footholds in Santa Fe than those encouraged even by the Mexican government. Customs officers conveniently looked the other way when Euro-American merchants forgot to pay duties on alcohol or animal pelts. Taxes were collected and never reported. This system was temporary, however, because after 1848 the power of the wealthier New Mexicans was also jeopardized by a new political order so complicated that New Mexico began resembling other besieged frontiers: new certificates of sale, another taxation system, and long lists of rules and regulations imposed by newly appointed federal officers contributed to the confusion. New Mexicans could barely keep abreast of changes in the legal codes. Their land and properties, particularly those once held in common and outside the town, were threatened with seizure if they did not pay taxes. Only individuals who maintained lobbyists in Washington, D.C., were capable of retaining their titles. Within ten years of the signing of the treaty ending the war, 90 percent of the New Mexicans had lost their lands.[75] What the bankrupt and disorganized independent Mexican government had not accomplished in twenty years, the Euro-Americans appeared ready to complete in half the time.

The full, direct impact of these economic and political fluctuations on literary production and on the recorded impressions of women remains inconclusive. But several other issues related to the military occupation of New Mexico are important to the story of how Spanish-Mexican women were remembered. Santa Fe did not initially embrace the soldiers, who, along with the U.S. traders, merchants, and others, made up an alarming 10 percent of the town's population during the occupation years of the war (1846–1848).[76] Spanish-Mexicans reacted in several ways to the military presence. A brief armed resistance movement died when its supporters, avid anti-Euro-Americans, dispersed.[77] The struggle to repel the army quieted and local resistance shrank because Santa Fe's vecinos (town residents and householders) faced deteriorating relations with the surrounding Native communities. The mobile Apaches, Navajos, and Comanches stepped up their raids on the surrounding towns, especially when newer, more efficient weapons were introduced and when Spanish-Mexicans invaded their territories.[78] Once, Barceló even lent the army money to wage a campaign against marauding Indians. Both U.S. reporters and local Spanish-Mexican writers editorialized about the sedentary communities that lived in terror due to the "roving savages."[79]

The problem of worsening relations between Spanish-Mexicans and Native residents had always been more complicated. The population of Santa Fe was quite mixed, racially and ethnically. Perhaps 10 percent of those who considered themselves residents were Native people or of recently mixed Native ancestry. Moreover, Santa Fe's residents were not passive victims of ambulatory Natives who raided gardens and plundered animal flocks. Spanish-Mexicans also initiated raids, not necessarily to retrieve stolen goods, but to capture Native women and children, whom they treated like commodities and subsequently enslaved in the wealthier households.[80] Adding to the developing tensions were the new merchant capitalists who sold guns indiscriminately to Natives.[81]

And, like the Spanish-Mexicans, Native communities contended with their own problems. A substantial number of Native women began working as domestics in the Euro-American households of Santa Fe. Some were Christianized Natives, others were genízaros, also Christianized and of Apache or Navajo origin. How many migrated to the town voluntarily, how many were captured and forced to work there, and how many were children of migrants or captives, remains a mystery; the survival strategies of the Native groups, however, also played into Euro-American hands because they, like the presence of merchant capitalists, disturbed older patterns of settlement and migration. When the market value of captives rose correspondingly, Natives and Spanish-Mexicans suffered because each was susceptible to enslavement by the other.[82]

Santa Fe (Dancing Ground of the Sun) was evidently the economic locus of multiethnic communities comprised of warring factions and competing interests. From its beginnings in 1609, when it was constructed on the ruins of an ancient Native village by Mexican Natives who had accompanied the Spanish colonizer, Juan de Oñate, the town was multiethnic and multicultural. That it had been, or remained, "purely" Spanish is a myth, as much of a myth as Barceló's legendary sexual prowess. No area of Latin America retained its racial purity, just as men were not more inclined to sexual promiscuity than women were. Even the word "Mexican" captured the ancient system of inter-racial mixing. Derived from the name of the indigenous Mesoamericans, whom Hernán Cortés first encountered in 1519, "Mexican" signified the older patterns of racial and cultural interaction farther south. Other regions of the Republic of Mexico sustained a heritage based on this intermingling of the Spanish and the Natives.[83]

Biculturalism evolved throughout Mexico's frontiers into a complex system of communication based on more than the blending of races. Santa Fe built on the legacy of racial mixing and cultural borrowing while conforming as well to another older pattern, that of inter-Mexican migration. Many residents, including Barceló, had been born in other parts of Mexico and had migrated northward. A native of Sonora, a province two hundred and fifty miles southwest of Santa Fe, Barceló traveled at least once to her birthplace. She also visited the area called Chihuahua, four hundred miles south of Santa Fe, and moved there in 1842. Although she returned to Santa Fe two years later, she sustained an interest and some contacts in the south. Once, she hired a harpist from Chihuahua to play at her saloon.[84]

Barceló's trips renewed business and family ties. Mexican migration like hers advanced regional contact and ensured a degree of interregional cultural mixing that contributed in turn to a pattern of mingling. In such ways, the northern frontier remained linked to other areas. And yet the historiography of northern New Mexico, as in the writings about Barceló, erroneously maintained that the region was "more" Spanish and more insular than others and that its residents should and could be termed "Spanish-Americans" because they were "true" descendants of Spanish conquerors. Some were, but many were not; just as Barceló's activities have been exaggerated and misinterpreted, so has the reality of fused ethnicities and consistent inter- and intra-regional migration been obscured. Just as Barceló was an "outsider" in Santa Fe and from another northern Mexican state, many migrants to Santa Fe, "westering pioneers" included, could trace their origins outside the northern Rio Grande's valleys.

It is equally erroneous to characterize the area, given the interplay and variety of ethnicities and interactions, as a "placid, isolated frontier," as some scholars suggest, or as "an arrested frontier society," as some historians argue.[85] The Santa Fe many have depicted—a peaceful, settled pueblo with generations of venerated families—is simply a fantasy that must be reassessed.

Barceló's family epitomized the movements of Spanish-Mexicans in and out of town; La Tules encouraged her niece, Rafaela, to migrate from Chihuahua to the north.[86] And Rafaela affords one additional example of how Euro-Americans were taken in by the complex, multiethnic community: Rafaela gave birth to a daughter and named her Rallitas Washington, the child evidently having been fathered by a Euro-American. This pattern was repeated by other Spanish-Mexican women, according to the first official U.S. Census, which was taken for Santa Fe in 1850. Ten percent of the population, at that point, had Euro-American surnames, and of that group, about 5 percent had Spanish first names, suggesting a pattern of intercultural marrying or mixing, with Spanish-Mexicanness prevailing. The commingling of previous centuries assumed this added dimension in the occupation period, when Spanish-Mexicans, genízaros, mestizos, and Euro-Americans began intermixing.[87]

Despite interaction, economic problems prevailed. Despite Barceló's efforts, social tensions remained. At the gaming tables, soldiers initially drank liquor distilled by local men and women, but the purchase of local alcohol soon yielded to the practice of importing liquor. Merchants, in particular those with strong outside connections, recognized the potential for earning greater profits from the sale of manufactured alcohol than from local liquor sold in a saloon that drew the majority of the town's residents and thirsty soldiers as well. Soon the wagons winding their way between Missouri and Santa Fe listed bottles of liquor among their varied cargo.[88] Economic life—buttressed by the growing military forces—was passing from the stage in which a local product could satisfy demand to an enlarged one in which items from the outside prevailed, a phase characteristic of the stages of merchant capitalism. The important issue concerning Barceló's business, and the town's business culture in general, is that no economic equilibrium reigned before or after merchants began their vigorous efforts to control and Americanize local markets. And the adaptive phase, in the economy, as in politics, was drawing to an end.

Imported liquor and other manufactured products, as well as cultural mixing, were indications of the aggressive changes Euro-Americans were beginning to make, with the assistance of Barceló and others. Cultural strife also deepened as men and women who operated businesses competed for sales. The altered relationships of the marketplace contributed, in turn, to the legend of La Tules. Brewerton recalled that his Missouri guide gambled away his last dollar at the monte bank, and left for Chihuahua, "thanks to that cussed Monte woman, flat broke."[89] Others were less kind about their losses or their dissatisfaction with Spanish-Mexican business culture. James Ohio Pattie rationalized the merchant takeover in this way: "This province would be among the richest of the Mexican country, if it were inhabited by an enlightened, enterprising, and industrious people. Nothing can exceed the indolence of the actual inhabitants."[90] Surely, Barceló was proving him wrong, but neither he nor any of his countrymen seemed capable of accepting that.

The deeply rooted sociopolitical dissension these prejudices and portraits demonstrate has forged legends in other parts of the country. Bleeding Kansas, in the 1850s, for example, saw the development of the James phenomenon when Jesse and Frank James's escapades came to symbolize both political chaos and a people trying to escape the travail of civil war. Many had seen Jesse, some had ridden with him, others were related to him. At their famous trial, the Jameses' mother testified that it was the Pinkerton detectives who had set her sons on the path to rebelliousness when the authorities firebombed her house and left her an invalid. Good sons who sought justice for a grievous wrong against their mother—this sums up one of the James legend's attractions.[91]

Righting a wrong is, however, just one in a long list of activities that folklorists say produce a legend. Different cultures stress different themes. The great Chief Joseph of the Nez Percé tribe has been idolized and canonized as a resister and fighter because he would not surrender to the U.S. Army.[92] The indomitable Apache leader Geronimo remains for many Native people a similar symbol of defiance and activism, despite his lengthy incarceration at Fort Sill, Oklahoma, which lasted into his old age and death.[93] Analogously, Mexicans imbued nineteenth-century heroes with superhuman perseverance, frequently during periods of intense social unrest. Tibúrcio Vásquez, the California daredevil of the 1850s, and Juanita, of the mining town of Downieville, who was the first woman ever hanged in California, illustrate the same tendency among some Spanish-speaking residents of the former Mexican north.[94]

Scholars attribute the creation of these legends to cultural traits as well as to social or cultural strife.[95] It is difficult to ascribe specific rationales or single origins to legends. Not only do legends derive from several sources, but at times they are the vehicle for special purposes. In storytelling, for example, the tale is often secondary; the message, primary.[96] In some Native groups and in many Spanish-speaking communities, the teller of the tale is more important: Her or his intonations, characterizations, and embellishments set a mood or underscore subtle subplots that concern conveyer and audience, linking them by reinforcing cultural bonds and misrepresenting others. Folklorists have quantified these features of legends to suggest that even as simple a fact as a legend's life span cannot be explained. The James and Vásquez legends survived through the years of the Civil War and the conquest of New Mexico and are very much alive today, in the mass media and in countries around the world.[97]

Obviously, legends are neither restricted by time, nor lodged in one place. Folklorists agree that legends can surpass the stories from which they originated, as well as the material or social conditions from which they were born.[98] Legends can distend circumstances—sometimes consciously, at other times not. Some move outside the ordinary confines of daily life to occupy realms and positions beyond realistic comprehension. This can be termed a legend's nonordinary reality and, in the case of Barceló and others, is as important as the true and known details of their daily existence.[99]

Few historians have ventured into the folklorist's terrain to search out a historical figure's significance or to develop a historical context from that angle. But stories form the heart of a historical sensibility, and the evidence in Barceló's case is promising. For her, the exaggerations or distortions only intensified with time; they did not subside when the chief creators of her legend, Euro-American men, settled in Santa Fe. In other words, they were not entirely a by-product of the men's displacement, or of hers. And into the twentieth century, La Tules was upheld in certain circles as an example of a society in disrepair.[100]

Writing later, in the 1930s and 1940s—when some scholars claim that Euro-Americans began revising their attitudes toward Mexicans—the novelists Blanche Grant, Ruth Laughlin, and Anna Burr helped repopularize La Tules. Their books, produced in a period when similar misimpressions of the local population flowed out through the work of the Taos writers' and artists' colony after World War I, further helped solidify the skewed images of La Tules, and women in general, in the minds of many. In some novels she was portrayed as a lady of the highest fashion and as the epitome of refinement; in others, she was considered the downtrodden victim of her own society who raised herself, by sheer willpower and shrewdness, to respectability.

Grant's "historical note," her introduction, repeated the myths but sought to revise them:

> Careful analysis of what was written of Madam Barceló by Josiah Gregg, George Brewerton and others has made me veer away from what historians are determined that we should believe of her. Not a man ever said that he really *knew* her. . . . My own research through many years convinces me that they have maligned her. It has been my intention to draw a fair portrait of Madam Barceló.[101]

Grant did not accomplish her task. Her novel's protagonist, Lona Barcelona, was a woman of Spanish and French aristocratic breeding who left Spain for Mexico—a land inhabited by unsavory, sombrero-wearing men and humble, mantilla-clad women. Her character's favorite people were the Euro-American traders and merchants she encountered en route to Santa Fe. Laughlin also embellished these earlier misrepresentations by describing La Tules, in her old age, as a religious, devout woman who, through charitable works, relieved much suffering among the poor. Burr's representation of La Tules was as a less respectable person, but one that eventually also established, through Christianity and good works, her place among law-abiding citizens. Thus, the fictional portrayals in this century mimicked the earlier memoirs and reiterated the familiar themes of individual accomplishment, a harsh and hardened female existence, especially during the Mexican period, and steady improvement after the Euro-American occupation.[102]

Simultaneously, and often in the same accounts, she denoted the individual who rose from humble origins to defy Euro-American expectations and often those of her own kind as well. Thus she conformed to the hope of upward mobility, yet another ingredient that nourishes legends. Her success in raising herself from obscurity to affluence was a point Gregg originally expressed, and many writers have followed his lead. In the 1940s, Laughlin portrayed Barceló in her later years as a retired madam, orphaned into poverty and a life of slow, uphill struggles that she eventually surmounted. Laughlin's Tules begins as a young stowaway living a childhood in debt peonage, but one from which she blossoms into an expert card dealer and a mischievous political manipulator. "The love of gambling was in her Latin blood," Laughlin writes as she completes the story of the enterprising and precocious Tules.[103]

Her image of La Tules was an improvement over the others produced in the 1930s. In Burr's *The Golden Quicksand*, for example, Barceló reaches affluence but only by manipulating innocents like Peter, Burr's protagonist. A wanderer, Peter has been abandoned by his father and brother and heads west to locate the lost brother and to make something of himself. He arrives in Santa Fe, tired and disappointed by the look of the place—its "squat, brown buildings." His initial fears, however, give way to the bustle and activity of the plaza. En route to Santa Fe, he has heard of the famous gambling halls and numerous fandangos, and so he is prepared for this aspect of the social scene. Quickly, he finds his way to La Tules's saloon and from the moment he lays eyes on her, he cannot stop fantasizing about her powers or attractions. Smitten, he notes that "the turn of her cheek, the curving of lips and brow, [were] made beautiful because she was she." Realizing his longings are evident, La Tules makes her way to him and welcomes him to her saloon with a kiss on the cheek. Peter cannot forget this woman whom his companion has named "Our Goddess of Chance," despite the warning of a gallant Spanish-Mexican, who tells him to "watch your course, Señor, . . . to mount too quickly into Paradise is dangerous. I speak as one who knows." Peter then departs, struggling with his obsession, breathless, and asking himself: Has he stepped into a land "full of enchantment, like the desert cities in *The Arabian Nights?*" That night, Burr writes, he acknowledges his contradictory feelings: "A woman at the head of such a place by rights should make him sick." Burr concludes the scene by depicting a restless young man who, despite his misgivings, has fallen in love with the misbegotten Barceló.[104]

Nearly a century had lapsed between the story of Peter's dilemmas and the first-hand sketches of Barceló, but both shaped her legend and lend evidence to one other, inescapable conclusion. If her legend transmits any single, historical theme, it lies in the portrait the merchants and travelers of the nineteenth century, and the novelists in the twentieth, sketched of themselves: Colonizing Euro-Americans found it difficult to contend with the likes of La Tules and her success, with her culture and its women, who differed from their own.[105] Even those, like Grant and Burr, who set out to correct the imbalances of the historical record became victims of it.

So, while Barceló's mythological incarnations developed in an analogous context of social and political upheaval, and resemble other legends in their origins and development, they nevertheless display special features related to sex, gender, and accommodation and resistance. Resistance to complete colonization can be read into Barceló's activities because she adopted a businesslike, accommodationist stance in her saloon. She brought gambling men to her tables for stakes ranging as high as forty thousand dollars.[106] The woman was, in those instances, the epitome of the business-minded individual. Despite that accomplishment, however, she could not beat the Euro-Americans at their game. Adept at calling their bluffs, having crossed the gender boundaries through business and profit, she still could not entirely throw off the men's misperceptions of her or the strictures of a changing society; nor would historical memory deal her a better hand.

Some reasons for this lie in how her sexual image was sealed in the popular imagination throughout her lifetime and beyond it and then distended to embrace all Spanish-Mexican women. Writing about his visit to Santa Fe at the end of La Tules's career, Brewerton told *Harper's* magazine readers that he had discovered in Santa Fe a woman "whose face . . . bore unmistakably the impress of her fearful calling, being scarred and seamed, and rendered unwomanly by those painful lines which unbridled passions and midnight watching never fail to stamp upon the countenance of their votary."[107] An exaggerated pencil sketch (Figure 2.4) helped shape the article around his message that she was a "woman of deep policy and shrewdness."[108] Whereas Gregg had already called her a whore, others were more prudent or less willing to make outright charges. Susan Shelby Magoffin slyly suggested prostitution and immoral conduct by describing La Tules's "shrewd and fascinating manner necessary to allure the wayward, inexperienced youth to the hall of final ruin."[109] Her style and dress code served only to highlight her sensuality because, as Brewerton remembered, "she was richly but tastelessly dressed—her fingers being literally covered with rings, while her neck was adorned with three heavy chains of gold."[110] Matt Field devoted several articles in the *New Orleans Picayune* to "Señora Toulous [Tules], the supreme queen of refinement and fashion"; these articles dripped with sarcasm, and he concluded that "she was not handsome." He haughtily ended one article: "Such is the fine lady of Santa Fe."[111]

This intriguing feature of conquest and colonization—the tendency to observe, judge, and dispense with locals in this way—has been shown in other situations to have locked women into particular images from which they could not escape. The speculative fiction on this is interesting to literary analysts, folklorists, and others. Edward Said and Gayatri Spivak have argued in their work on Orientalism that fantasy and speculation become the intention of the observer-colonizer.[112] Others concur. In his study of the French postcard photographers who took shots of Algerian women and of the fictional harems in Algeria during the first three decades of the twentieth century, Malek Alloula explores the meaning of the French gaze upon Algerian women. In their need to portray unrealistically Algerian women's fashions and jewelry, their poses, dances, quarters, and bare breasts, the French soldiers and photographers degraded women, making the harem a brothel and claiming that the women within it were prostitutes. They practiced obsessive voyeurism, he proves, while peppering Europe with fantastic images of the "Orient." Postcard photographers imagined, through their art form, that they were freeing Algerian women from their prison, the harem, but not until they were "captured," in an "authentic" style. Alloula concludes that in displaying the harem as a brothel, the postcard procured Algerian women and sent them on a tour of Europe.[113]

The Euro-American observers of the Spanish-Mexican women of Santa Fe shared such tendencies because they similarly fictionalized and eroticized aspects of women's lives and hoped, in doing so, to "liberate" them. The fiction cut both ways—that is, while Euro-American observer-colonizers speculated and treated themselves to a fantasy they had created around women, they also embodied and carried outward to the society, through the spectacle of the gambling house, a zone of liberation for themselves. That La Tules was, or was not, a prostitute is hardly the point in such literature because she was central mainly to its inception and primarily useful to the images that men controlled continuously—in other words, to their elevation.

The images reproduced in the literature of the western American frontier signified more than mere inaccuracy and were far from harmless. The distortions functioned on two interlocking levels—one local and national, another economic and racial. As we have seen, the colonizers came armed with large reserves of capital, which the local economy could not digest; as capitalists, they began remaking the economy and took over the local government. They accomplished this by employing women *and* men, by changing the political structures and the legal codes. Women performed the most basic daily services necessary to their accomplishments in the conquest—initially, washing, cleaning, and cooking, and later, being the men's dancing and sexual partners. Women thus served the newcomers in several capacities, as did the Algerian women who posed for money for the French photographers who accompanied the French militia to Algeria.[114]

Beginning with Zebulon Pike's illegal reconnaissances, traders and merchants had disparaged Mexicans on the basis of their race, ethnicity, and sex. Pike argued that "in national energy, or patriotism, enterprise of character, and independence of soul, they [Mexicans] are perhaps the most deficient."[115] The man credited with initiating the Santa Fe Trade, William Becknell, said, "The people are generally swarthy, and live in a state of extreme indolence and ignorance."[116] James Pattie insisted later that "nothing can exceed the indolence of the actual inhabitants."[117] Other travelers to California and Texas forsook discussions of enterprise to focus instead on appearances and especially skin color. They termed light-skinned Mexican women "nearly the equals of their southern sisters" and editorialized about their beauty in articles bearing objectifying titles such as "Superb Specimens of Womanhood."[118] The judgments they rendered—even the attempts at compliments—were ultimately self-possessing and wrong.

Many motives guided the writing of travelers, visitors, and explorers. In some cases, their aim was to outline poverty and ignorance and then to promote the hope of improvement through enterprise. Such manipulation of scenes and images, the re-creating, as on a movie set, of the sleepy town awakened by the arrival of caravans or merchants, was meant to convince congressmen and the public about the necessity for a takeover.[119] It paralleled the seeming praise that was, in fact, pejorative commentary in the context of what was being said about Spanish-Mexican men. Much of the commentary, whether backhanded or direct, ended in the same place: Despite the shortcomings of Mexicans in general—and not unlike the women of Algeria who "enticed" the French to photograph them—New Mexicans, and especially the women, were depicted as anxious to reform their wayward habits.[120]

Alloula ends his essay not by concluding that Algerian women were completely victimized or entirely submissive. Rather, he argues that their stylized posing turned the gaze back on the colonizers; women used the photographers by looking back into the camera's eye and thus returning its glance through their own.[121] In that way, women who had been captured on postcards resisted colonization.

Similarly, the colonizers of New Mexico, soldiers, merchants, and travelers, having availed themselves of women's services, began to "claim" the women, to possess them, by writing about them, by drawing caricatures of them and of their society. Neither they nor any other colonizer were entirely successful, as we shall see in the next chapter, when women's strategies of resistance and survival are more closely examined. Yet the propaganda served several purposes: It made "knowledge" of Santa Fe's women a national preoccupation. It made disgracing those women one method of contextualizing their presence under a different political regime. Just as Alloula found when he described the *algériennes* as the "metaphorical equivalent of trophies, of war booty," New Mexico's conquerors first used women as servants, but then continued in their writings to view them metaphorically as prizes.[122] Although the colonizers dismissed women through a steady stream of negative commentary—a practice they shared with other colonizers—they simultaneously used women to secure their own social and economic position in Santa Fe. Behaving like the French in Algeria who initially misunderstood the harem and required the women to do suggestive poses, these colonizers of New Mexico overlooked women's places in their community and alternately focused on their "quiet" demeanors, or their enslavement; they intentionally misportrayed women's roles, exaggerated their "oppression," and instead underscored Spanish-Mexican excesses. Calling Spanish-Mexicans "priest-ridden," "servile," and "humble," describing women as "toilers" and their husbands as "swarthy thieves and liars," the newcomers to Santa Fe took their place in history with other colonizers; in this way, they used women to assist their takeover.[123]

Santa Fe's women, if they ever truly accepted the Euro-American invasion, had by 1848 begun to reevaluate their positions in such a changing society. Partly, reassessments came with the pandemonium that exploded on the plaza and elsewhere after the Army of the West arrived. The eighteen hundred soldiers proved to be a rambunctious crew.[124] Intoxicated, they roamed the streets, yelling and screaming and victimizing any who attempted to control their activities. The first Euro-American woman who lived in Santa Fe, Susan Shelby Magoffin, commented on the commotion: "What an everlasting noise these soldiers keep—from early dawn till late at night they are blowing their trumpets, whooping like Indians, or making some unheard of sounds."[125] The English traveler George F. Ruxton believed that the soldiers and traders in Santa Fe were the "dirtiest, rowdiest crew" he had "seen collected together."[126] Some frightened citizens took their complaints to court, but it was unclear whether the soldiers could be tried there or not (see Figure 2.8).

The skewed demography, and the new Kearny Code, approved by Congress as an interim plan for military rule until territorial status was achieved, served as ever-present reminders that the community was under siege. The alcaldes attempted to appease angry residents and to scold the troops but they held little control over the situation.[127] Scant evidence exists for surmising that the wearied citizenry might, on this score alone, have applauded La Tules's business, but it is possible to conjecture that they appreciated how her saloon temporarily kept the soldiers off the streets; they were probably less appreciative of her sale of liquor to newcomers who had, ironically, been charged by General Kearny to "maintain order." That goal was never accomplished, and the bur-

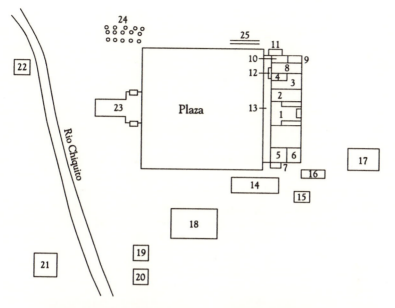

FIGURE 2.8 Santa Fe in 1857. Information for this rendition was drawn from W. W. H. Davis, *El Gringo*, 1857.

Palace of the Governors
1. Legislative Council Chamber
2. Executive Chamber
3. Cámara de Representantes
4. People's Gallery
5. Secretary of the Treasury's office
6. Storeroom
7. Post Office
8. Library
9. Office of Supt. of Indian Affairs
10. Greeting room for Indians
11. Calabozo
12. Indian Market
13. Portal

Other buildings
14. Courthouse
15. Penitentiary
16. Military Garrison
17. New Statehouse
18. Lomy's New Cathedral
19. Boys Boarding School
20. Girls Boarding School
21. San Miguel Church
22. Our Lady of Guadalupe
23. Military Chapel
24. Hay and Grass Market
25. Burro Alley

den of restoring the peace fell on Spanish-Mexicans, even if it meant entertaining the disorderly soldiers Kearny had left behind at the gambling hall and countless fandangos.[128]

Women did more than tolerate the invaders. Doña María Gertrudis Valdez de Beremende, for example, had married James Wiley Magoffin, the most important businessman in the Mexican north. Magoffin learned Spanish quickly and served as U.S. consul in Chihuahua. He was known as "Don Santiago" among Spanish-Mexicans, and Doña Gertrudis helped him adjust to his new life on the Mexican frontier, but the marriage symbolized more than that. Along with his brother, Samuel, and their friends, his solid position and the *marriage = womanhood.*

lucrative profits of the local trade lured others to Santa Fe.[129] Although the majority of traders, like James Josiah Webb, who conducted business in partnership with William Messervy for over twenty years, recalled that "there was nothing to induce me to entertain a desire to become a resident," a few others settled in Santa Fe, married local women, and became prominent merchants or politicians.[130]

Several factors predisposed Spanish-Mexican women to cast friendly eyes toward the new men. Historians have indeed advanced many explanations for the women's attraction to the newcomers. One historian argues that mutual physical attraction and romantic feelings accounted for cross-cultural marriages. Another considers the positive economic gains a woman derived from marriage to an outsider. Still another suggests that the relatively higher sex ratio of Euro-American men to single women might be responsible for the percentage of intermarriages. Still others theorize from another angle—the men's search for intimacy in the newly conquered territories. Inevitably, this argument maintains, the lonely male married the indigenous female.[131]

But none of these explanations closely examines the acrimonious cultural and economic context within which Spanish-Mexican women forged relationships with Euro-American men. During the tumultuous decade of the 1840s, the suits and official complaints between newcomers and locals, as well as between men and women, multiplied. Fines were imposed on Euro-American men for misdemeanors such as "making a fandango without a license," selling liquor without a permit, and disturbing the peace and thieving.[132] In their haste to accept intermarriages as examples of cultural unity, some scholars have overlooked the examples of social disharmony and raging turmoil. The harsh underlying tensions on this multicultural frontier also molded men's and women's interactions, but some historians have shied away from focusing on these intensifying relations. Bringing their own mythologies to bear on the evidence, and leaning toward promoting cultural understanding, these scholars have hastily depicted the positive aspects of racial and cultural intermarriage.[133]

Why intermarriage ask, given what is involved in wit.?

The evidence for New Mexico requires other explanations. The hostilities between rival factions, like those between Baca-Sena and Le Grand, or Scolly and Lopes, suggest that the move to rob these relationships of their contentiousness might be erroneous. Moreover, dissension, as the intellectual historian Warren Susman has written, molds societies, shapes communities, and is as central to our understanding of social and cultural history as the unraveling of complex economic and political phenomenon.[134] Previously, and in this discussion, I have depicted the lack of consensus for both reasons—many studies of Spanish-Mexican and Euro-American interaction do not demonstrate the underside of social relations, which are laden with tensions and misunderstandings, while other works rely on relatively small quantitative samples to assess relationships that court testimonies indicate were far from harmonious.[135]

Moreover, the historical legacy of intercultural mixing throughout Latin America, as well as the specific role that Barceló's saloon played in forging the ties that bound westering men to resident women, suggest that the intercultural contact of the pre- and post-war periods occurred consistently within or against a backdrop of strained *and* changing relations. This was as true for the Euro-American conquest as it was during the colonial period throughout Latin America. Mestizaje, the mixing of Spanish and Indians, was often a violent act, especially on the frontiers of northern New Spain.[136] The historian Antonia Castañeda has demonstrated that the policies of the church and state in northern California were designed to encourage soldiers and others, in the absence of Spanish women, to settle down with Indian women, even if it meant capturing and raping the Natives.[137] In New Mexico, the earliest contact between Europeans and Indians was equally violent, but by the nineteenth century, and in Barceló's saloon, the systemic violence and horrors of previous centuries had abated.[138] In the rowdy, friendly atmosphere of the gambling hall, newcomers bartered misapprehension for companionship. In winning and losing at monte, all card players looked alike; this leveling was not lost on the Spanish-Mexican women who frequented the saloon.

Over cards and drinks, the soldiers and merchants might not have entirely shed their mistrust of the life and people of Santa Fe, or entirely suspended their judgments, but they did participate in the commmunity's fun. They drank with men and danced with women. On many evenings, the gambling table yielded to the dance floor. Field insisted that "traders often lose the profits of a whole season in an hour's play, and when the last dollar is gone they walk off to a fandango, choose a partner, and dance away care, never dreaming of curing misfortune by suicide."[139] This socializing eventually extended beyond the saloon and into the home and church.[140] Many men arrived at Barceló's establishment as strangers, but left as friends.

How many local women married the westering men is unknown because the crucial census taken in 1845 is missing several barrios (neighborhoods) and the next one was taken in 1850.[141] Other documents that would help determine numbers, such as wills or marriage certificates, are similarly incomplete or exceedingly varied in quantity and quality. Percentages after the Treaty of Guadalupe-Hidalgo of 1848 remain tentative on several additional counts. Until 1880, the federal census did not cite relationships between household members. To assume that a man and a woman of similar age were married might be erroneous, especially in a community where households included extended families. Moreover, work on marriage and the family indicates that couples often lived together without being officially married.[142] Still, by using the 1850 census as a guide, which reveals that nearly 50 percent of all Euro-American men in Santa Fe resided with Spanish-Mexican women who appear to have been their wives, conclusions about the numbers of intermarriages are possible.

The work of quantifiers and social historians in calculating and determining the extent of intermarriage in Santa Fe is as interesting in its assumptions as in its conclusions and signifies the difficulties of drawing definitive lessons about the extent of intercultural understanding from the mixed marriages of Euro-American men and Spanish-Mexican women. In one article, a historian has argued that nearly 63 percent of all Euro-American men in Santa Fe in

1870 were married to Spanish-Mexican women.[143] On the surface, that percentage seems extremely high. However, the total sample of Euro-American men was only five hundred. The number of Euro-Americans married to Spanish-Mexicans neared three hundred. In 1850, when 50 percent of the Euro-Americans are listed with Spanish-Mexican women, the group of men totals 239, and the number of intermarrying men is about one hundred. The percentage rose each decade, but never comprised more than a few hundred individuals in a community of around four thousand Spanish-Mexicans.

In the context of Spanish-Mexican demography, then, the numbers are not nearly as impressive as the percentages imply. Inverting the figures by placing the emphasis on women reveals that not quite two percent of all Spanish-Mexican women were married to Euro-Americans in 1870, and fewer than that in 1850. The question thus remains as to why scholars recently have become so interested in showing intermarriages statistically, and yet have not paid attention to the actual numbers of Spanish-Mexican women marrying non-Spanish-Mexicans. Many have been concerned primarily with showing extensive intercultural and interracial contact, while fewer studies have attempted to link the statistics to other circumstances of daily living, including cultural misunderstandings. In any case, the conclusions are open to debate because the numbers actually place the intermarrying group in the category of a minority, although they made up an important cluster in Santa Fe. In other words, whatever number of new men marry local women, it is important because it shows people establishing interracial and intercultural relationships, but not because Euro-American males made up a great proportion of the population, or because it necessarily signifies their acceptance by Spanish-Mexicans. Santa Fe remained a Spanish-Mexican town, and most Spanish-Mexicans continued to marry each other.

Highlighting the intercultural or the interracial marriage may fulfill a contemporary desire to focus on "cultural interaction," a phrase nearly synonymous, among some western American historians, with cultural unity or blending. But the evidence in the case of New Mexico suggests a need for other explanations. So many arenas were not as hospitable to the newcomers as the gambling hall was. In the courts and in church, Euro-Americans were despised, reminded that they were strangers in a foreign land. Practiced in Anglo law, they found themselves misunderstanding Spanish legalities, many of which originated in Roman Catholic doctrine and in medieval ideas concerning property and inheritance.[144]

Primarily of Protestant origins, the outsiders found themselves in a Catholic community where the line between civil, religious, and military authority was often blurred, and where, even under the Kearny Code—which promised to respect religious and legal traditions—women sustained their right to retain property in their family names, even in marriage; to sue in a court of law; and to initiate divorce in certain circumstances. Santa Feans regularly filed complaints in court and at the church, a practice that, Euro-Americans argued, further deepened an already hopeless dependence on priests.[145]

It was not just Catholicism that frustrated the newcomers. Mainly English-speaking people, the migrants discovered that they were expected to master

Spanish. And such expectations, they decried, thwarted them at every turn. In civil and ecclesiastical courts, they were sometimes fined for the same offense, a practice they also disliked.[146] Santa Fe, they fumed, was nothing but "a parcel of brick yards," its streets "narrow and filthy," the walkways filled with "monte banks" and "beggarly" people, the residents "treacherous" and "proverbial liars," who "have three or four prices for everything" sold.[147]

Not surprisingly, by 1848 many of the disgruntled and disappointed were ready to move on. Some were enticed by better investment opportunities in California during the Gold Rush period, and abandoned Santa Fe in a "restless desire for prosperity."[148] Their brief visits, however, had undoubtedly made life more difficult in the besieged community. Sojourners increasingly began to direct the New Mexico trade after the war, and locals could only hope, with each new wave of merchant capitalists descending on the town, that the disorder they caused and the negative opinions they unleashed would abate.[149] They did not. Lieutenant Dyer reported problems one year after his arrival: "Still it began to be apparent that the people generally were dissatisfied with the change."[150] In January 1847, resisters in Taos, fifty miles northeast of Santa Fe, caught and scalped Governor Charles Bent, leaving him to die.[151] Hints that the same spirit guided others toward revolting against the Euro-Americans persisted. The murder of a lieutenant who had been pursuing horse thieves occurred in the spring. Forty-three Spanish-Mexicans were brought to Santa Fe to stand trial for the crime.[152] In October of the same year, some months after several revolts had been suppressed and their instigators hanged, Dyer reported "a large meeting of citizens at the [Governor's] Palace," where speakers expressed "disaffection at the course of the commissioned officers."[153]

Despite Barceló's work, and despite the incorporation of some Euro-American men into Spanish-Mexican society, local disaffections and political turmoil persisted. In the late 1840s, Navajos and Apaches stepped up their raids, and reports of surrounding mayhem filtered in.[154] Relations had been badly strained after 1844, when a peaceful delegation of Utes in Santa Fe sought justice for a Spanish-Mexican raiding party that had mistaken them for enemy Navajos. They never received an apology or compensation. Fighting erupted on the plaza during their visita (visit), and many were killed, including the esteemed warrior and chief Panasiyave.[155]

The activities of the ricos exacerbated the problems. Governor Manuel Armijo, with whom Barceló was reputed to have had a love affair, was exactly the sort of merchant and politician whose forbearance with distant, bothersome officials had worn thin and he threw his support to the Euro-Americans. He began to sell land, just before the war broke out, imposing arbitrary duties on the traders and lavishing favors on others. During his administration, some Euro-Americans were granted Mexican citizenship, as in the case of Alexander Branch, who resided in Taos. James Kirker, a native of Ireland, did not become a naturalized citizen like Branch had, but he was in such good standing that he was empowered to lead a campaign against the Apaches.[156] Branch's and Kirker's confidants, the merchant group that Armijo led, eventually supported the U.S. military takeover because it promised to improve trade relations and "pacify" the Apaches, Comanches, and Navajos.[157]

The consistent arguments for accepting the army were advanced in speeches by the conquering officers and contrasted sharply with the multiple edicts of the irascible Mexican officials to the south, who appeared unable to settle on a single course of action to resolve frontier problems. Hence, in 1846, Euro-American soldiers, merchants, and other migrants of various occupational groups, like traders and trappers a generation earlier, captured a community's interest, and the immediate possibilities for making money with them outweighed any deeper concern about the ramifications of a descending militia.[158] When Kearny and the soldiers arrived, it proved too late to repel the Euro-Americans. Hence, the sporadic outbursts against the unjust actions of the military probably indicated the degree of frustration among locals who had noticed no improvement in the economy, nor received much relief from interethnic tensions.

Conquering soldiers, like traders and merchants, came to Santa Fe armed with purpose and commitment. They brought plans and realized them: The building of a fort above the town was begun the day after Kearny marched into Santa Fe. Soldiers built a two-story flagstaff, and this imposing structure on the plaza attracted visitors from the surrounding areas who supposedly came to admire it, but probably also to assess the military's strength.[159] What better symbol of the power of the military than a new garrison and an obtrusive monument rising high for all the people to notice? Soldiers hailed these "crowning" achievements as signs of blessings from God to a nation destined to control the hemisphere.[160] Locals were not pleased. Tensions multiplied as soldiers continued to move in and out of town. The garrisoned soldiers grew impatient and acted rashly. Dyer reported, "A Mexican was unfortunately shot last night by the sentinel at my store house. Tonight we have a rumor that the Mexicans are to rise and attack us."[161]

Recriminations and sensationalism focused national attention on the region, and Santa Fe's rowdiness was disdainfully portrayed in the presses and periodicals of the eastern and southern United States.[162] The bad publicity in reports to the outside world made matters worse. And resistance broke out periodically, fueling new stories and highlighting the disaffection of locals toward the soldiers. Despite their unhappiness, however, poorly armed and disunited Spanish-Mexicans could do little to repel the eighteen hundred soldiers moving in and out of Santa Fe. Problems with them as well as with warring Natives began to signal the end of one era and the beginning of another. Some Euro-Americans were beginning to settle in Santa Fe, with the assistance of Spanish-Mexican merchants and politicos, like Armijo, and entrepreneurs, like Barceló. The two decades following the war, as the next chapter notes, witnessed the arrival of lawyers and investors who made the work of the previous generations of Euro-American trappers, traders, merchants, and soldiers appear almost innocuous. The wealth of the new class of migrants was exceeded only by their ambitions to secure the land and property of New Mexico for the United States.[163]

Even in her departure, Barceló offered the worsening situation some meaning: After 1852, when she died, her skills were discussed and her legend continued, indicating that her role extended beyond the immediate helping hand she had lent Euro-Americans. No documents written by her, except a will and a deed dictated before a local magistrate, have survived to indicate whether she even recognized her accomplishments or if she read much into the assistance she had given the Euro-American cause.

It is at once strange and yet somehow fitting that we know so little about her through her own words. Instead, the material conditions of her life and her political achievements have spoken for her. Her wealth suggests that she might have harbored an understanding of her influential status in the process of colonization. She willed three houses to different relatives, including two nieces and adopted children. Her sister and brother were given mules and the cash remaining in her estate, but she also willed money to the church and to the local alcaldes for charitable causes. Ultimately, in her will and in her final wishes, the well-off Barceló exerted control over her finances in a way that most women, who were poorer, could not.[164]

The next chapter assesses the poverty and survival strategies of the bulk of the poorer women and of a few wealthy ones, suggesting how much the business style of women like Barceló and Manuela Baca yielded in the face of everchanging political and economic structures. In that context, her legacy conveys the painful lesson of a loss; despite the gamble she had taken as a businesswoman, her solution to the changing military and economic situation ceased to be effective. Interestingly, the loss of privileges gained or of status acquired, folklorists also say, enhances a legend's appeal. This is certainly the case with La Tules.

Irrespective of its folkloric meanings, however, another aspect of Barceló's legacy remains, whether she or her detractors realized it or not: Beginning with her, the accommodation of Euro-Americans by Spanish-Mexican women proceeded on other levels. Barceló had inaugurated one level, at the gambling hall, and set the stage for the second, whereby a few women began marrying the newcomers. In that, she had become the unsuspecting architect of a plan that reconciled the Euro-Americans to Santa Fe and Spanish-Mexicans to the Euro-Americans. She had sustained Santa Fe's multicultural heritage because she encouraged the acceptance of another group of newcomers, even as the power balances shifted around her.[165]

Barceló could be blamed here, as Malinche and other women have been blamed, for the problems that intensified between the two cultures after the war. She should not be, however, because she symbolized the transformations and opportunities plaguing Santa Fe and much of the former Mexican north. She symbolized as well how an older community had handled the arrival of men from a new, young nation still seeking to tap markets and find a route to the Pacific. If we imagine the Euro-Americans as being, first, illegal immigrants, then migrants, and, finally, colonizer-settlers, it seems appropriate to label La Tules a member of a "greeting" generation—and this explains my focus on the word (or concept of) "accommodation." Moreover, she exemplified contact between independent, female Catholics and westering, male Protestants. If she continues to be made a legend, or if her activities are now made legendary, it should be done while we also keep these multiple and shifting contexts in mind.

Traveling to California during the 1830s, Richard Henry Dana, the sailor-reporter, mourned the seemingly wasted opportunity presented by land still in the possession of Spanish-Mexicans. "In the hands of an enterprising people, what a country this might be!" he declared.[166] His fellow sojourners to New Mexico concurred. What Dana and the other Euro-Americans failed to see was that the land and its communities were already in the hands of enterprising persons such as Barceló. Rather than acknowledging the truth, they disparaged her. Their conquering minds could not comprehend her intellect, her enterprise, and her success. Barceló, they believed, had erred. Her life's story suggests that she had not.

In giving herself to the conquest, but not the conquerors, La Tules survived and succeeded. She drew betting clients to her saloon. They played, and won or lost that round. She gambled and won in her own way because, in the end, the saloon that had attracted conquerors released men who had been conquered, if only temporarily. Ultimately, Barceló's losses were the losses of the people of her community, but her accomplishments were theirs as well; she had acculturated many Euro-Americans to Santa Fe. She was a woman with a keen, practical business sense and a creative spirit who had dealt the Euro-Americans a hand and won because in the saloon, momentarily, they accepted her rules, if not her, and suspended their wariness and prejudices over card games and social interactions. Among the *ricos* and in her family, she was accepted as the businesswoman that she was. Regardless of the positive and negative opinions and regardless of whether the commentary came from travelers, soldiers, reporters, or, later, novelists, she attests to the central role women played in the conquest of New Mexico. In that sense, her life mimicked that of many others and indicates why historically she has become the most well-known woman of Santa Fe.

Still, in reevaluating her image and life, it is important to bear in mind that her fame and glory were produced in a situation of conquest, were central to the achievement of that conquest, and have been reproduced in this century to sustain certain images of the ongoing colonization of New Mexico. La Tules remains on paper as much a symbol as always; her importance and contributions will continue to be masked until a wider range of explanations and portrayals are exposed to round out the known facts and established details. Moreover, precisely because she is a figure who shows us a link between the historical with the symbolic, she has been examined in this chapter from several angles and against traditional perspectives. The historiographic value of presenting her in several dimensions is that it is not—as the cliché states—history that judges, but the people who write and read it who do. La Tules and the other women of Santa Fe thus deserve our reassessments.

Women's Survival Strategies

Gifts and Giving as Methods
of Resistance, 1846–1880

The widow Chaves was blessed, luckier than many women of the postwar generation. She was born into a prominent Santa Fe family, had inherited land and livestock, and had managed to preserve and improve her estate. Wealthy, but in poor health in 1871, unable to read or write English, the widow turned to the law clerk Edwin Dunn, whom she asked to draw up her will. Having found her attorney absent, she hired Dunn because he seemed capable and was interested in helping her. Luckily, though to her horror, as she later told a friend, her son returned from a trip and examined the will, only to discover that the law clerk and an unscrupulous priest were colluding to dupe her. Apparently, the will Dunn recorded contained unapproved donations to the church and the poor, as well as a substantial sum of money for the clerk's law office.[1]

The situation of the widow and the details surrounding her sad tale of conniving lawyers and unreliable priests suggest the extent of colonization and its potential impact, even on upper-class women. Indeed, by no means poor, the widow Chaves was played upon because she owned property and because the new men with whom she dealt carried prejudices to Santa Fe regarding women's intelligence or wherewithal. Evidently, they did not think that she would show the will to anyone. That was their first mistake. Will-making among the women, and perhaps the men, of Santa Fe did not entail secrecy or necessarily require privacy—expectations that some eastern Euro-Americans apparently harbored. The documents were a public matter—relatively public, that is—because several people witnessed and signed the documents, and the

79

alcaldes and priests themselves often transcribed the wishes of the filing parties.[2] Several people in the community thus knew of a will's contents and the
growing number of wills written after the war suggest that the practice of writing them was becoming more prevalent as Santa Fe grew. After the war, more
foreigners flocked to the old capital city; in the 1870s alone, over one thousand new Euro-Americans migrated to Santa Fe. And, they were as ignorant
of Spanish-Mexican customs and laws as their predecessors.[3]

If the colluders in the widow Chaves's case misunderstood aspects of
Spanish-Mexican culture, such as the relationships that encouraged mothers
to show sons or daughters their wills, they seemed even less inclined to admit
their ignorance. By attempting to take advantage of a widow illiterate in
English, the law clerk's actions—which were to be repeated many times in this
colonial situation—had unintended but positive results, for Chaves. Perhaps
sensing that something was amiss, she turned to her son for assistance because
he read English but also because the matter concerned his inheritance. Further,
Chaves asked her neighbor, "the widow of Juan Delgado and mother of Juan,"
to witness the burning of the disputed will. Her son and neighbor thus recti-
fied the impropriety and helped ease Chaves's situation. Chaves's strategy for
coping with the problem of an unauthorized document was therefore family-
and community-based, a stategy that ultimately saved her children's inheritances.

The law clerk and the priest who conspired against Chaves demonstrated
more than ignorance of Spanish-Mexican values and practices; their miscom-
prehension was just one of the intriguing aspects of this case. Evidently, these
newcomers and others like them were incapable of understanding that this
widow and other women like her were not helpless, although that is also an
important part of the story and was another of the law clerk's mistakes. Like
previous colonizers who labeled Gertrudis Barceló a whore or a madam, the
person who told the widow's tale was equally misinformed: He was the newly
appointed Territorial Secretary William G. Ritch, and he injected in his memoirs—from which the widow Chaves's story is drawn—his own notions and
exaggerations of women by fashioning the widow into a respectable figure.
And, his notion of respectability, cast as it was over other women involved in
this case, had not changed much since the days when Josiah Gregg and others
disparaged women like Barceló and any who resembled her. Chaves, Ritch reported, was one lady who no longer "had the supreme confidence in the priest-
hood that she once had. Nor would she yield to them in matters which apper-
tained to her business and were entirely foreign to the Church."[4] Ritch, and
the promoters of takeover, still individualized women, or set them apart. Any
heroic qualities women supposedly exhibited elevated them, but only temporarily, in the eyes of the conquerors. Moreover, the individuation was in-
tentional because it signified more than an effort to separate the wealthy or
unsuspecting from the crowd. Some women, Ritch suggested, were ready to
embrace Euro-American reforms. Even Catholic women, he seemed to say,
were willing to accept a change, one separating church from state. In that way,
his recollections resembled, ideologically, those that had been written in pre-

vious decades, but promoted a new form of colonization in the postwar era, one that accepted those women who lent themselves to "American" ideals and values.

Colonization, which I previously used to describe a process involving the imposition and impact of Euro-American values, ideologies, economies, and political practices, as well as the systematic importation of sexual and racial attitudes, operated differently in the postwar period because some members of the wealthy class were now potential citizens. Some aspects of this function of colonization will be discussed later in this chapter but other aspects are equally important to the analysis.

Theorists of colonization—across many disciplines and over periods—have explained that the impact on the colonized carries both immediate and long-term implications, many of which are recognized by colonized communities as conquest is under way. Women like Chaves assuredly understood the changes Euro-Americans had institutionalized in places like the courts or in the church. Colonization, some scholars have also shown, has a profound impact on women, on societies and communities, and on relations between men and women. As such, its impact can be said to be universal, because it reaches across arenas to shape all other relations.[5] The practices of colonization, connected in this way to the tendencies of an earlier generation of colonizers, suggest that what postwar colonizers like Ritch did with their information about the women of Santa Fe, and what they did to them, was typical. They manipulated their stories about women, popularizing one type over another, to achieve a similar end: to contain the local population, to quell resistance toward Euro-Americans and discussions of resistance, and to secure the lands and properties of the colonized for themselves. Dunn and Ritch shared this with others.[6]

But colonization had indirect consequences as well. The extensive writings about women ensured that those who might have been hidden from written history were not. Skewed though the images were, they nevertheless preserved documentation about women that can be reorganized to create different portraits of their lives. Moreover, the actions and responses of these women— even when purposefully depicted by men to suit their needs, as in the case of the widow Chaves, who demonstrated certain qualities Ritch prized—were acceptable to the newcomers only to a point. That is the juncture Ritch did not reach but that historians have begun to approach using evidence like his: The widow Chaves may have had the last laugh by finding a way to gain lessons about the new territorial laws and accompanying practices, by testing men like Dunn and the new court system now controlled by Euro-Americans. Knowing that her son would examine the will, her strategy contained a safety mechanism.

On one level, even Ritch could not ignore what motivated her. He stated several times that she was wealthy, a descendant of the affluent Armijo family. On a strictly financial level, he was suggesting, she reflected the concerns of the upper class. She had married well; her husband, a merchant, Ritch believed, had left each of their daughters a large inheritance of $17,000. One daughter was an invalid and incapacitated to the point of being confined to an

institution in Colorado. She intended to leave her brother her share of the estate, but a New Mexico law of that period prevented invalids from bequeath-
ing to any one sibling more than one-third of their inheritance. Buried in
Ritch's lengthy account of the widow's predicament, this last detail further clar-
ifies Chaves's actions. Presumably, the complicated legal situation, coupled
with the gravity of her daughter's and her own illness, motivated the widow to
seek assistance from the conniving law clerk.[7]

What Ritch and others after him overlook, however, are the understated
facts of such women's lives. Upper-class women like Chaves made it into the
historical record after the war because they appeared to be acting appropriately—that is, in ways Euro-Americans understood. The separation of church
and state, of religion from business, which, presumably, wealthy women now
sought, were important to men like Ritch. As a federal appointee, he came to
Santa Fe to promote such practices and to legally and politically change institutions to reflect this thinking. The opinions and actions of Ritch's group have
been documented by other historians to make that point.[8] But, given that situation, few historians have asked what motivated women like Chaves to turn
to men like Dunn in the first place. If Spanish-Mexican women were growing
increasingly suspicious—and with cause—of Euro-American men, was the
widow Chaves testing the newcomers to see if they would support her because
of her upper-class status? Was she relying on the new territorial structures to
help resolve her dilemmas?

Probably, all these issues motivated her. But the presence of others can be
proven by examining the broader context of church affairs, which her case also
involved. The church, like the economy and government, was changing, and
Spanish-Mexicans were frustrated by the equally domineering Euro-American
Catholic leaders who came to town shortly after the treaty ending the war had
been signed. Essentially, the Vatican removed the diocese from Mexican and
U.S. hands and placed it in the hands of a European, a native of France, Jean
Baptiste (John Baptist) Lamy, whom it appointed vicar apostolic.

A cold wind blew into Santa Fe in the fall of 1851 with his arrival. Just before his appointment, the ecclesiastical jurisdiction of the conquered territory
had been transferred from Durango to Santa Fe. Lamy initiated a series of blus-
tery changes in the predominantly Catholic community. First, he surveyed
church properties. Second, content that the church was in solid standing, but
convinced that its priests and parishioners "lacked drive and ambition," he sys-
tematized maintenance of the eleven churches in Santa Fe, including the
chapels around town.[9] He rode the countryside inspecting other parishes and
eventually got around to visiting churches as far south as El Paso. In that first
month, he also sustained a steady correspondence with friends around the
world. In letters sent to France and to Cincinnati, he pleaded, cajoled, and argued for desperately needed supplies, including robes, incense, and religious
medallions. These items were either scarce, he claimed, or not made locally to
his liking.[10]

Lamy was a man driven to action. In style and ideas, he bore a remarkable
resemblance to the ambitious politicians and lawyers pouring into Santa Fe—

men like Ritch and Dunn. And he proved to be as astute as they were, in his energetic quest to change the situation. Some of the older Euro-American merchant class had grown disheartened or had settled into a life of easy old age. The more ambitious had struck out for California, while others had taken to drinking and gambling.[11] In the decades after the war, another type of Euro-American man appeared among these others: the civic humanitarian. Vigorously Protestant, such men, particularly those planning to settle in Santa Fe, cared deeply about such issues as public education. In the 1870s, they established a commission to study the lack of public schools there and they argued for a separation of church and state in educational reform.[12] Popularizing the need for the separation was in the interests of the new leaders. The widow Chaves and her complaints were perfectly suited to their campaign, and for that reason, Ritch championed her responses.

[margin note: Protestants trying to undermine Catholics]

Although Lamy resembled these newcomers, his own issues and the fact that he was the designated Catholic leader of the region, distinguished him from the others. The Protestant agenda, however, concerned him less. Lamy devised plans for several Catholic schools, and he began pinpointing problems extending beyond the lack of a formal educational system. He was dismayed by the absence of orphanages or asylums and was distressed as well by the number of poor persons roaming around without work or places to live. His concern was somewhat misplaced—and not because the poor and vagabonds were not acknowledged. Many indeed observed their presence on the streets and in the countryside, but generally, Santa Feans remarked that the impoverished were taken in and that orphans were adopted. But the problems of beggars, of unemployment, and of abandoned children became more severe after the war, when the economy experienced a turn for the worse, when the prices of eggs, vegetables, and flour rose because of the strain created by so many newcomers.[13] Lamy did not, however, comment on the causes of the problems but instead focused on their solution. As early as 1851, he requested that the Sisters of Charity send a delegation of teachers to Santa Fe. Additionally, four Sisters of Loretto from Kentucky arrived and established a school and an orphanage. Lamy continued lobbying on other fronts.[14]

[margin note: after 1846 impoverisht beggars, + aband. children food ↑ ↑]

His thorniest problems remained with the priests, who were used to receiving orders only from the distant Catholic seat of Durango. They had disobeyed some edicts or improvised to get around others, especially because their requests for supplies and money often went unheeded. The type of Catholicism that emerged under this situation of scarcity was, of necessity, rather autonomous; despite any efforts to strictly regulate or completely control the parishes of the north, the bishops in Durango and those presiding further to the south had no way of knowing whether their instructions were being followed. Occasionally, they visited the frontier areas, but even then, the church could not supply priests to most towns or villages. Catholicism in Santa Fe, then, had developed in a distinctive manner, and this Lamy did not appreciate.

He approached the reform of priests earnestly but also naively. In dismay, he wrote Archbishop John Baptist Purcell of Cincinnati about "a priest who does not preach to his congregation but only once a year, and then on the con-

Am priest trying to reform others that will reform priest

dition that he will receive $182."[15] Few records exist that might assess the extent to which Lamy's concerns were accurate, but his frustration with recalcitrant priests—who were poorly paid through tithing and fees raised for administering the sacraments at birth, marriage, and death—evidently deepened. In May 1852, he attended meetings in New Orleans where other bishops listened sympathetically to his complaints about New Mexico and to his hope for modernizing the church in New Mexico. There was little, however, they could do to help; throughout the 1850s, Lamy pursued a policy of complaining to the outside world, receiving mostly sympathetic replies, while he attempted to locally resolve economic and social problems within the church.[16]

Over a decade later, the designated leader of New Mexican Catholics could report some progress as well as resistance: "The school of the Sisters and that for the boys are doing well but now that I have commenced to reform some abuses, and to lay down a few rules for the clergymen, I have met with a great deal of opposition . . . , having been obligated to suspend a few Mexican priests for the most notorious faults. . . ."[17] Although Lamy rarely explained, in his correspondence, the origins of many of these problems, he recognized the gravity of the situation. Several priests, including a resister and famous anti-Euro-American, Padre José Martínez of Taos, refused to acknowledge the bishop's authority.[18] Lamy faced ever-stronger opposition in Santa Fe: "The old vicar of Santa Fe is very much put out because I have divided his parish, leaving him one good half, and offering [it] to him in the immediate neighborhood. . . . He gets more than I keep, but he would not accept, and refuses to give his services."[19]

Lamy had replaced, and was now displacing, the aging vicar, so his edicts were bound to be aggravating. His actions did not catch Spanish-Mexicans unawares. By the 1850s, locals had watched several waves of newcomers enter Santa Fe and implement ambitious plans. Lamy was no exception. When he began fund-raising to build a new cathedral, everyone—including the Euro-Americans—contributed.[20] When he recovered a chapel that the military had appropriated on the plaza to shelter soldiers, people lauded his effort. But Lamy promptly turned around and sold the property, an action that needled devout Spanish-Mexicans who were already put out by disorderly soldiers and litigious merchants.[21]

Other issues irked Spanish-Mexicans even more and detracted from Lamy's program of reform. His harangues from the pulpit did not help. He justified them by saying that "some scandals are so public, and so notorious, that it is necessary to denounce them often and often in the pulpit."[22] He reported to Bishop Zubíria of Durango, in April 1853, that several priests "tuvieron una junta en esta ciudad, burlándose de mi autoridad y escribiendome una carta que firmaron cuatro de ellos" (they had a meeting in this city, mocked my authority and wrote a letter to me signed by four of them).[23] In the decade since his arrival, Lamy had faced a worsening situation, despite his mastery of Spanish and his building program.

Lamy might have learned Spanish, but he was abysmally untutored—or willful and uninterested—in the art of defusing challenges to his authority. In the midst of the worst difficulties with priests, he revealed aspects of his deepest feelings when he said that "I feel badly and until this day I have treated them more as equals than as inferiors, but I can no longer tolerate their craziness."[24] Presumably, Lamy intended next to begin meting out the punishments these subordinates deserved. As the problems multiplied, he became obstinate: "For my part, I am determined that they obey or resign."[25] When he tired of their refusals "to administer properly the sacraments . . . ," as he put it, he excommunicated some.[26] Such impatience, however, came at a time when he also lamented the lack of priests and mourned the deaths of others.[27] His requests, requirements, and ambitions only added to the general disgruntlements of Catholics, who had rarely been treated well by the church hierarchy in Durango, and who, perhaps expecting that a central figure living among them might change that, instead witnessed disruptions in daily religious worship.

The excommunications and the acrimony between the priests and their new leader affected many women from a distance, but some of Lamy's denunciations bothered them for other reasons. From the pulpit, Lamy also began denouncing "immoral" women and he refused to hear their confessions. Seeing this as evidence of a campaign against concubinage, as well as prostitution, some Euro-Americans added to it. W. W. H. Davis, an acting governor for a period, argued that, indeed, "the vice of prostitution has become so prevalent that the whole moral frame-work of society is rotten and undermined."[28] Such comments, coupled with reflections about social mores, ignored the economic hardships of most women. Many Catholics postponed weddings until they could afford them, and lived together in the meantime. To such observers as Lamy and Davis, these women were immoral. In fact, they were simply poor.[29] Few seemed capable of understanding this. Even those who should have been more sympathetic, because of their charge to "alleviate suffering and minister to the poor and ignorant," were critical of local conditions and customs: Sister Catherine Mallon remembered her "first impression[s] as we approached the city of Holy Faith; they were not at all favorable either to place or people."[30]

Against this background marked by Lamy's and other visitors' proclamations as well as those of Euro-American politicians, it is understandable that Spanish-Mexican women began searching for methods to resolve their precarious positions as Catholics and as working women. Some resolutions, such as laboring for wages, as laundresses, domestics, and seamstresses, were probably arrived at without calculation. Need and poverty determined where and how women sought work in their changing community. Lamy's and others' actions intensified their search and contributed to their impoverishment. After he reclaimed the chapel the army had been using, Lamy himself began noting the lack of currency and the problems caused by scarcity: On the same lot as the chapel, "stood four stores and one house. The stores yield a rent of [a] hundred dollars a month as everything is extremely dear in this place."[31] Rents were rising because of people, like Lamy, who sought to establish themselves in the marketplace. The new church leader might have noticed that the price of mutton, butter, and eggs had risen.[32] Surely, Lamy recognized the dollar's power. Through firm, friendly gestures, he recovered the chapel and lot, collected the rents for the church, and allied with the merchants on the plaza. In also befriending the local politicians, the acting governors, and the territorial legislators, he persevered in a larger plan to link Santa Fe to the outside world, even if his mission offended Spanish-Mexicans or caused inflation.[33] He even charged his own guests, the Sisters of Charity (whom he had invited to Santa Fe), rent on a building, part of his former residence, that was to become their hospital.[34]

If the church was growing but in turmoil, and if Spanish-Mexicans felt ostracized by Lamy's actions, the economic changes of the 1850s and 1860s played an even greater role in displacing them. The symbols of "progress," as Euro-Americans defined it, were everywhere. Food carts gave way to stores and shops stocked with the supplies newcomers needed. New commercial establishments and a well-equipped fort—built to accommodate over a thousand soldiers—gave the place a different flavor. The old building used for politics and business, the Palace of the Governors, yielded to a new capitol built of brick.[35] Lamy's cathedral rose on the dusty ground beyond the plaza—an enormous church made of the stone common in his native France.[36] During the next two decades as construction proceeded, the local newspapers lauded his efforts, saying in an editorial that the cathedral would "prove the antidote for the mud epidemic which, transmitted from generation to generation, has become hereditary."[37] Although he had to import the building's materials, and the masons who could work on it, Lamy remained undeterred in a quest for better Catholics and more-European-looking places to worship. Promoted to bishop in 1853, and despite all of his troubles, Lamy pursued his plans. Like the merchants and politicians in Santa Fe, the Catholic leader sought to transform the place and to prosper.

But for all of its appearance of growth and of thriving, the group which comprised the majority in Santa Fe, Spanish-Mexican women, lived under harsh conditions and remained mired in poverty, despite wage work. The miniscule 5 percent of that group who might conceivably be accorded upper-class status also suffered. Seventy-five percent of the female adult population (over the age of fifteen) labored as domestics, laundresses, or seamstresses in 1860; by 1870, the percentage rose to 80 percent and in 1880, it had increased by another 8 percent. Domestics in this period earned from $1.50 to $2.00 daily in 1880, if they were "American," as the census termed them, or between $.50 and $.85, if "Mexican." Similar wage inequities existed in laundering and sewing (see Table 2.3).[38]

Not just difficult jobs and low wages detailed the grim contrast between Spanish-Mexican women and prosperous immigrant men. Net worths portrayed another disparity. The censuses of 1850, 1860, and 1870 inquired into people's personal income and property. The enumerations showed few non-Spanish-surnamed males with real and personal estates worth below $100. One-fourth of four hundred newcomers in 1860 claimed personal yearly incomes of between one and four thousand dollars. Another twenty-seven individuals listed estates exceeding $5,000. Within a decade, those amounts had quadrupled (see Table 2.2).[39]

At the other end of the financial spectrum stood Santa Fe's impoverished women. Until 1870, not 1 percent of their number claimed net worths surpassing $100. The overwhelming majority claimed less than $50 estates. Their lack of financial security deepened while the prices of food and goods continued rising. When Kearny's soldiers first entered Santa Fe, corn cost $3.50 a bushel. Five years later, the soldiers and others had strained supplies and the price had risen another dollar per bushel. The cost of eggs doubled, and in less than a decade, the value of mules quadrupled.[40]

The low and barely rising wages for domestic, laundering, and sewing jobs meant that working women had no protection against such spiraling costs. Beyond that, shortages became common. The same amount of crops and the number of livestock continued to support the expanding population, with the only difference being that the land and animals now belonged primarily to the newcomers. The scarcities led such observers as Sister Blandina Segale of the Sisters of Charity to report in the late 1870s that many poor women poured into the plaza on Sundays, begging for food while trying to exchange precious possessions like Indian blankets. The shortages affected not just Santa Feans but also people in the surrounding areas who came to town hoping to find relief, but instead induced shortages themselves.[41]

Spanish-Mexican women could do little against rising inflation. They had previously supplemented their incomes by raising hens for the eggs, but never in a sufficient quantity to compete with farmers from the outlying areas in the marketing of chickens. Now women began raising animals. Local men bought sheep and pastured them on plots outside the urban area. The flocks proved to be a nuisance, in both instances. Sheep devoured good grasses and left the hillsides bare; chickens were noisy and difficult to keep penned. Regardless, the locals could not compete with the newcomers who latched onto cattle and hogs as better investments. Such changes, however, had a rippling effect that extended all the way to people's diet: Beef and pork replaced chicken and mutton as delicacies. Cattle and hogs, which the immigrant class purchased as rapidly as possible and leased out to pasture, or pastured on lands they were also buying, became unofficial currency worth more than some luxury items. The value of chickens and sheep fell correspondingly. No matter how much they tried, Spanish-Mexican women could not fight against inflation.[42]

Economically, Santa Fe was a town turned upside down. But its demography had also changed. Between 1850 and 1860 the non-Spanish-surnamed population increased from 6 percent of the population to 9 percent; it rose again to 13 percent in 1870. The 1870s became the decade of greatest migration because over thirteen hundred new Euro-American men and eighty Euro-American women entered Santa Fe. (See Table 2.1.)

Investors and newcomers in that decade used their money to construct new mercantile houses, a hotel, homes, a hospital, and an industrial school for orphans, mostly Native-Americans. By these outward appearances, the economy was growing, the demography changing, but growth did not imply prosperity or improvement for Spanish-Mexican women, who constantly labored for the newcomers.

In the matter of jobs and in working for wages, women's circumstances became governed by Euro-American needs and this ensured growing dependency, for both. Powerful religious leaders, lawmakers, military officers, and merchants determined the course of women's lives in new ways because they were directly responsible for employing them, and because they were building structures and passing laws that indirectly affected women.[43]

In this altered social and economic landscape, it is intriguing to speculate about whether Euro-American men's opinions about women had changed since the decades before the war. Ritch's comments on the widow Chaves and Lamy's on concubinage suggest not. But, an interesting difference distinguishes the treatment of Chaves from the treatment of Doña Gertrudis Barceló, and points out how attitudes toward women on the part of the newcomers might have begun to change. Barceló was never either fully accorded the potential for reform or granted status as a businesswoman by the colonizers. Women like Chaves, by contrast, were beginning to be viewed as possible converts to Euro-American business ethics and as influential people in their own right—a matter of some significance.

What had changed? For one thing, the 1870s in the United States were years of rapid industrialization and it was a decade when work culture began taking on different meanings in the lives of managers; although women were still largely invisible, others, including immigrants and working-class men, were regarded as potential converts to American-style business values. The qualities necessary for the conversion included industry, frugality, independence, and perseverance. In that sense, Chaves also fit the requirements because by breaking away from the church and the overbearing priests, she was abandoning tradition and adapting to the newcomers' ways. Ritch, as a federal appointee in the newly created territory, could not have been happier to have found an example of such a person, and a wealthy one at that. She was a perfect fit for his need, and for that of other officials as well, to propagandize—indeed, to justify—their actions on the frontier. The wealthy Spanish-Mexicans were contributing to the modernization of Santa Fe, these men thought, by appearing to make its residents willing practitioners of a different way of conducting business, of conveying property and worldly possessions. Ritch could thus take pride in the widow's outrage at a priest who expected to be taken care of, at a church greedily violating its ascetic principles.

Even deeper concerns emerge from Ritch's report of the episode. Being anti-Catholic, and suspicious of Catholicism in general, his story suggested, like the memoirs of Josiah Gregg and of others, that the takeover of New Mexico had indeed been destined, inevitable. This, he believed: Protestants had been chosen to wrest control of education from the domineering Catholics, Euro-American or not. Ritch called the strongest opponent of public education, Father Donato M. Gasparri, an Italian Jesuit, "that carpetbagger from Naples." Gasparri had the means to debate Ritch because he owned and operated a press that supplied the schools with their textbooks; he also printed a widely read newsletter in Spanish. Ritch was indeed battling the power of the church on many levels and displayed the disdainful (in New Mexico in this period) affectation of a southern Confederate. His account of the widow Chaves assisted the campaign against Catholic influence over the schools and it offers insightful commentary on the lives of women in decades of rising Euro-American migration and of continued, significant national economic, religious, and political upheaval. It also racialized the situation, perhaps inadvertently, but importantly, by calling forward the racism of the Civil War era and its aftermath: Italian, Catholic "foreigners," even if they were just immigrant citizens, were to be lumped together with a local and oppressed populace.

Next, this chapter examines the changing face of colonization, of women's responses to it, in the tumultuous decades following the war. It places upper-class women like Chaves and many poorer ones at the center of a transformation aimed at understanding women's difficulties and at probing their often contradictory methods of survival, given their difficulties with altered institutions like the church, the governor's office, and the courtrooms. Expressing their final wishes in wills and in other documents, many mothers like Chaves sought to control their losses of land and property by giving their eldest sons the bulk of their estates. They thus departed from previous practices, when they tended to leave their estates to daughters (and when fathers left their lands and manufactured articles to sons).[44]

Unsurprisingly, as we have seen in the preceding chapter, men like Ritch preserved their basic stereotypes about women and advanced them in tracts designed to garner sympathy for the ongoing Euro-American invasion. Their attitudes and concerns were deeply embedded in the mythologies of conquest and takeover. A Protestant, Ritch resembled the other anti-Catholics of the prewar years. Even the subtitle of the document (an official report) in which he recalled the widow's dilemma is indicative of the depth of his misunderstandings: "How a lawyer and a priest undertook to fix the will of a widow lady in the interest of Truchard [the priest]." Ritch twisted the last part of the story to end on the same note: The widow publicly accused the priest of malicious conduct and in response the priest began excommunication procedures. He would rescind them only if she sought his forgiveness. Of course, the widow Chaves did not ask for it. Smugly, Ritch wound the narrative to its suggestive finale, claiming that the widow Chaves was now a disheartened, if unrepentant, Catholic. And even such a grave consequence as excommunication would not get her to yield to men who had no business meddling in her affairs.[45]

An interesting development, however, guided this and other postwar reflections and distinguishes them from the accounts of the pre–U.S.-Mexican War period. While the memoirs, letters, and diaries of the earlier generation had been written in a period when an institutional and structural takeover had not yet been accomplished, officials like Ritch wrote in an era when Euro-American merchants, lawyers, and priests firmly controlled the economy and government of Santa Fe. In the decades before the war, their hold on institutions was weaker and it is possible that, given their economic advances after the war, they became more likely to describe women less pejoratively because the local residents and the political situation in general were less threatening to their programs of advancement, of Americanization. If in the earlier, prewar era, any hint of women's independence or autonomy, vis-à-vis men, was viewed as a challenge to the success of conquest, in the postwar era, those challenges could now be diffused by institutions firmly in the hands of Euro-Americans.

In the courts, as in the schools and churches, the evidence of Euro-American control abounds. Justice of the Peace Facundo Pino complained in 1853 that his two-year appointment had not expired before John E. Mink took his seat. On the same day that Pino submitted a signed complaint, Mink entered the court and rendered judgment on another case. Subsequent cases were signed by both judges, indicating that Pino did not readily vacate the seat. Finally, after six months, Pino's name disappears altogether from the record.[46] Displacements took place in the higher offices as well, especially after 1860 and under the guidance of two men whose names became synonymous with land-grant swindles, Stephen Benton Elkins and Thomas Benton Catron. Both had come to New Mexico with the army, one having joined the Union forces and the other the Confederate forces. Elkins left for southern New Mexico after 1864 and became U.S. district attorney for New Mexico; meanwhile, Catron settled comfortably in Santa Fe in 1866. He mastered Spanish and became district attorney for the judicial district in 1867. Once in federal office, both men joined hands to form the law firm of Elkins and Catron, a partnership which dominated the great land-grant takeovers of this era. According to historian Howard Roberts Lamar, both appointees had higher political aspirations and each "dreamed of reaching the United States Senate one day."[47]

Catron and Elkins led the legal battles that predominated in the scramble to prove claims to land, or to lay claim to untitled lands. Onerous instructions were given to the first surveyor general, William Pelham, and he was ordered to unmask other confusions which marked the saga of Spanish-Mexican land losses. Under the Treaty of Guadalupe-Hidalgo (1848), Spanish and Mexican land titles and claims were to be recognized by the new government. That much was clear, but everything else was ambiguous. Some laws passed under the Mexican government, like the Colonization Law of 1824, placed limits on the size of individual grants while others contradicted this regulation and others. The Congress of the United States, final arbiter in these matters, ignored the law limiting size and, by its action, cleared the way for a multitude of contradictory claims and wholesale land-grabbing. The task of the surveyor general was to assess the validity of all claims, and the burden of proof resided with Spanish-Mexicans, who—because they had held titles in some cases for several generations and, in others, held communal titles through the *ejido* (public land)—could not always produce the evidence of ownership Euro-American courts demanded. The surveyor general's job and his orders were based on the presumption that land was not "legally" owned until proven, while Spanish-Mexican laws, especially on the frontiers, held that land collectively claimed and granted retained that status unless it was dissolved by an action of the local government or the state. In effect, the surveyor general and Congress were arbitrarily designating the ejidos, as well as private Spanish-Mexican claims, as null or void unless titles and documents to the contrary were produced. With the disruptions caused by the break from Spain, plus the hundreds of years which had lapsed from the time of original settlement, Spanish-Mexican claimants were in a bind. Meanwhile, as Gov. E. G. Ross claimed, the situation was primed for "sharp, shrewd Americans." Elkins and Catron led a bevy of attorneys representing themselves and other buyers who had laid claim to thousands of acres of land. The builder of the new capitol, Joab Houghton, was also an attorney for twelve land-grant claimants. Judges who were attorneys, like John S. Watts, reported handling up to forty-three land-grant clients at once, most of them Euro-Americans.[48]

Lawyers and politicians like Elkins and Catron, as well as federal appointees like Pelham, also wielded power in other arenas. A new system for collecting fines from gamblers and for assessing taxes on property helped them steal from individuals as well as communities. Small-farm owners were troubled by taxes of one hundred dollars while such merchants as Solomon and Abraham Spiegelberg, they claimed, were hardly taxed at all.[49] The New Mexico Mining Company, owned by Euro-American lawyers and merchants, excavated outside Santa Fe and realized over forty thousand dollars in profits one year, but paid only three hundred dollars in taxes to the federal treasury.[50]

Changes in the church and courts were not the only indicators of how Santa Fe was changing. Newcomers caught on to how Spanish-Mexicans registered deeds, titles, and testaments at the church. In 1852, three pages of suits and property transfers appeared in the files of the diocese, among another set of pages from the marshal's office. E. L. Spencer and Henry Grandjeans sued Tomás Valencia over unpaid bills; Juan Bernadett sued Valencia as well. The documents, presented to the priest, declared that "having given public notice, . . . the said premises were struck off to Richard Owens for the sum of one dollar and twenty-five cents, he being the highest bidder."[51] Valencia thus lost his estate, and a Euro-American purchased it for a pittance. By depositing the documents at the church, the newcomers displayed their ability and desire to manipulate a local practice for the practical goal of acquiring property.

Trickery and duplicate filing at the church, as much as the institutional changes Euro-Americans had instigated, signified the extent to which newcomers had integrated themselves in Santa Fe. Now, Euro-Americans mastered, and used, the church and courts to achieve their own goals of Americanization. They allied themselves in a dizzying pattern of partnerships, sometimes with Lamy, other times with the handful of wealthy Spanish-Mexicans who managed to hold on to their property. The goal of lawyers and investors, of men like Catron and Owens, was to snap up property when it became available or to contrive methods for taking property even when it was not for sale. In this stage of besiegement, local women devised some interesting responses, but even those were constrained by the changing character of the institutions within which they framed their responses.

The stories of women who had married Euro-Americans provide some insights into the dilemmas Spanish-Mexican women confronted and offer, at the same time, an example of a worsening scenario in which women could do so little to alter the situation in their favor. The wealthy widow Tomasa Fitzmaurice—married to a man born in Ireland, who had come to Santa Fe and became wealthy in merchandising—presumably had done well for herself. But, upon her husband's death, Fitzmaurice encountered the tremendous power Euro-Americans wielded in the courts. Before a Euro-American judge, the widow argued that her husband's will, which named her an executor, was indeed authentic. When asked about the length of her marriage and repeatedly questioned about why she had the only copy of the will, Fitzmaurice sounded worried: "I have always lived in Santa Fe," she argued. Unable to read or write, she marked her "X" on the document, departed, and then filed at the church, with a Spanish-Mexican priest, her testimonial about the authenticity of the document and its wishes. She could not understand why "these foreigners are so preoccupied with affairs that are, [she said], my own, with our business and customs."[52] Fitzmaurice managed to hold on to her estate and inheritance but she had good reason to worry. Called again before the Euro-American judge, she had to sign additional documents proving that she had legally married her husband.

Fitzmaurice's ire was raised by the insinuations of an impropriety, but she was luckier than many others. Ana Marta Carson was called before a Euro-American judge to tell him why he should not grant custody of her four-year-old daughter to Henry Carson, a Euro-American. The mother lived outside the town with her own mother, and she pleaded poverty when questioned about why she had "abandoned the child, leaving it with its father and his new wife." Other cases of legitimacy and adoption convey similar problems. Florence Donaghue petitioned to adopt his infant daughter because the mother, Antonia Gallegos, was "quite poor and unable to support and properly care for said child." Gallegos appears in the census as a seamstress and was born in Mexico, so poverty might also help explain her or her child's predicament. She argued before the magistrate that she did not support the petition and that "she took care of her child as [she] best could."[53] Donaghue won his case but Gallegos's loss might have been alleviated because she later appears in an inventory of his estate as Antonia Gallegos de Donaghue.

In both of these cases, however, a crucial issue is exposed, irrespective of final outcomes: Euro-American men held power over women, rich and poor alike, but Euro-American men also used that power to accomplish many things. In some instances, they won custody of their children against the wishes of the Spanish-Mexican mothers. In others, they won fights over property. In almost all cases litigated in the courts in the years following the war, whether concerning children, inheritance, or property, Euro-American men solidified their authority and exerted control over Spanish-Mexicans. The point, however, is to focus not on the concerns of fathers for their offspring but on the grim contrast these cases suggest between the power of emigrating men and that of local women.[54] Even in instances where power differentials could presumably be lessened, such as in intermarriage, inequalities cannot be ignored. In fact, there they also dominated social relations. Fitzmaurice had to prove her relationship to her husband; it had been questioned. Similarly, Ana Marta Carson and Antonia Gallegos fought against Euro-Americans for custody of their children and had to prove that the children were "properly cared for." While some aspects of these struggles might shed light on the problems plaguing intermarriages—and can be examined with that in mind—more important issues ultimately reside in the unequal weight judges gave men's testimonies. Because of the power differentials, coupled with the rapid turnover in the court system and the changing ethnic composition of judgeships, Spanish-Mexican women were indeed vulnerable, and losing their cases.

As some Spanish-Mexican women discovered, Euro-American men in this era were specifically concerned about inheritance and legitimacy. Newcomers were rapidly acquiring property and they had no intention of letting it slip back into Spanish-Mexican hands or, in some cases, of leaving it to the children of mixed marriages. Problems between parents like Florence Donaghue and Antonia Gallegos point out the trauma of the undocumented, intercultural relationship in a period characterized by many programs of change and of Americanization. Even when surrounded by an aura of legitimacy and propriety, as in Fitzmaurice's case, a cloud of dust was raised by the suspicious judges charged with overseeing the proper execution of her deceased Euro-American husband's final wishes.

Yet Spanish-Mexican women had been filing their own wills long before Euro-Americans arrived in Santa Fe. Their witnesses in the courtroom and those they invited to appear with them before the priest (with whom they also deposited the documents), were almost always other women, relatives, or friends. Never much of a secret, the written document conveyed strong, decisively public messages about a woman's final wishes and expressed as well her devotion to family and to her religion. Women usually opened these documents with lengthy proclamations to God and to favorite saints; typically, they penned prayers at the beginning of the will. Will-making was in this way an act of faith, but it had its practical side as well. The document gave dying or ailing women a sense of order and perhaps strengthened them; many said as much.

This final act also served as a bridge between life in the present and the hereafter; and in dispersing worldly possessions in this way, pious Catholics connected temporal and spiritual worlds. Even in death, relating to succeeding generations positioned the woman in her Catholic community and centered her among kin, neighbors, and friends. This singular act—her distribution of material possessions but also the declaration and its inventory of devotions—symbolized so much more than the passing of life or the giving of effects. It conveyed meaning on many levels—psychological, religious, and financial.

Perhaps Spanish-Mexican women's wills are emblazoned with these meanings because women's property was protected under Spanish law, under "Las Siete Partidas" (The Seven Sacraments) of 1265 and under the Laws of Toro of 1369. Dowries—either the property women brought to a marriage or that given by a man to the woman he married—were strictly governed by the same laws, although the codes were somewhat modified in Mexico after independence. Husbands were entrusted with women's estates, to preserve and protect them, though they did not always do so. In widowhood, women were allowed to retain the dowry and were also granted the right to half of the property accumulated in marriage and to whatever property they owned separately and had not surrendered in marriage. Altogether, the laws governing inheritance, property ownership, and men's or women's rights were strictly enforced; widows could act as executors and coexecutors of an estate, women could oversee children's inheritances, and estates passed on through the maternal side were valued by heirs as much as those from the paternal side.[55]

There is some evidence, for other parts of the Mexican Republic, that the importance of dowry among the upper classes, and especially among the nobility, had declined rapidly in the first half of the nineteenth century. In New Mexico, the incomplete notarial records and the scattered extant wills make discerning such a pattern nearly impossible, but a few women did note in the margins of their wills or in testimonials what they had brought to a marriage, what they wished to pass on as a dowry to unmarried daughters, or what they had acquired separately and wished to pass on through the maternal line. The importance of the dowry in tracing changing patterns of marriage is uncharted terrain in the case of Spanish-Mexican women living in the frontier towns, but its connection to the selection of marital partners and, by extension, to the preservation of estates is indeed important. The dowry, but also all of the possessions women owned, guided a woman's final wishes and determined, in particular, the course of her children's lives.[56]

The wills of the Baca family portray some of these patterns across several generations. On April 22, 1830, María Miquela Baca appeared before the alcalde to give her last testament and to declare herself "free from debt." Finding herself "ill and in bed the past days," Baca began the document with long prayers and then listed the articles and property she wanted to bequeath, including blankets, pots and pans, silver ladles, crocheted tablecloths, some rooms in a house, an orchard, and some animals. Twenty-six years earlier, almost to the day, her mother, María Rafaela Baca, had done the same. Her prayers were shorter, her properties fewer. But like her daughter, she gave her worldly possessions to her children, willing the bulk of her estate to her daughters. Nearly thirty years after María Miquela Baca's will had been tendered, her own daughter, María de la Sur Ortiz, also went before the court, offering prayers and submitting her final decree, in a manner reminiscent of her mother's and her grandmother's dispensations. All three wills favored daughters over sons; all passed on, through the maternal line, dowries and properties acquired during marriage.[57]

Three generations of Baca women had performed maternal duties. All had borne several children; all had been widowed; all had passed their properties onto their children. María Miquela remarried and had eight children altogether from the two marriages. Her mother was also widowed, she remarried, and she gave birth seven times. María de la Sur had twelve children with her husband of twenty-two years; she did not remarry and was still a widow when she wrote her will. Marriage, widowhood, and motherhood thus united these women; all outlived each of their husbands and many of their children. In that sense, they were truly matriarchs who lived to oversee lands and small pastures scattered around Santa Fe. The arrangements of their wills and the properties conveyed demonstrate marital patterns and more. The Bacas were upholding family tradition, preserving inheritances, and passing on to a succeeding generation more than simple obligations.

Turning back to the widow Chaves (cited earlier in this chapter), we find that an inventory filed in probate court in December 1870 for Maria Nieves Chávez—if they were in fact one and the same—suggests her wealth as well as her predicament. She had five large portions of lands in the environs of Santa Fe, each estimated in value at over $200, household articles that were worth over $250, and herds of sheep, lambs, and goats, worth over $223; these items placed her net worth in the thousands of dollars. Debts against the estate alone totaled over $1,447. Her heirs, including her sons Alejandro, Francisco, Andres, and Martin received houses or rooms in some of the properties owned as well as livestock and supplies. Her daughters, Teofila and Manuela, received housing, land, and livestock, as well as firewood, santos, and mattresses.

Thirteen pages of inventory detail that the Chávez estate was of considerable size, and indicate inheritance patterns different from those for wills filed in the earlier part of the century. For one thing, sons are consistently included in the wills of the 1870s, and the portions of estates they receive are usually more substantial than those of daughters. The hijuela (conveyance) of Maria Nieves Chávez suggests the older concern for settling all debts (page four of the will detailed the sum owed the carpenter for the coffin itself, and a sum of $40 to the priest with whom she filed her will, Truchard). No paid masses were specified in this document, as was the case in the other sixty-five wills I have surveyed (covering the period between 1770 and 1870), nor were novenas stipulated for other, departed souls or relatives.[58]

An inventory is not the same as a testimonial, so drawing the conclusion that the listing of debts and items conveyed all the final wishes of Maria Nieves Chávez would be erroneous. Still, in other inventories, paying for masses that were to be recited and the general tendency to pass on most household items and land or livestock to daughters held true until this period of time.

Perhaps only the poor could sustain this custom, but in some cases, even they appear to have given in to the notion of willing most of their few articles to men. Desideria Otero, filing her testimonial in the same month and year that Chávez filed hers, had far less to bequeath than Chávez had. She had been married to the late Pablo Quintana, and they had had three children, all deceased at the time she filed. To her comadre (best friend or godmother of her children), Ventura, she willed a saint; to another female friend she left some petticoats plus three plates made of china, two cups, and two spoons. But to two male executors, Ygnacio and Antonio, she left the bulk of her worldly possessions, including a candleholder, a crystal saltshaker, a metal trunk, and some bedspreads.[59]

These aspects of inheritance and will-making ripened with time, and the act of writing a will, which might be evaluated primarily as ritual, in fact assumed far greater importance in the decades after the war, as the demography of Santa Fe changed and as both the socioecclesiastic and political structures were reordered. In that period, will-making became, among women, the primary means of preserving inheritances and of keeping property out of the prying hands of Euro-Americans. Many women like the widow Chaves and the

Bacas played an important role in preserving inheritances but, by extension, they also occupied a central place in the struggles to control the market, the economy, and the town in general. The battles of such upper-class women, and the resistance they waged against Euro-American takeover, occurred not just in the public square, in courtroom confrontations, or in other public arenas; rather, many women systematically fought colonization through will-making—through the artful composition of final wishes carefully considered.

Not just wealthy women composed wills. Bárbara Baca, not known to have been related to the other Bacas, filed her will in a year during which she had suffered serious injuries. She complained before a magistrate that she awoke in the middle of one February night to find two men in her house. The burglars forced her to give them the keys to a closet, from which they took money and other valuables. When she called to her son, who was sleeping in the kitchen, she was beaten on the ribs, the knees, and was "bruised in other places." A physician gave a detailed description of her injuries and spoke in the same testimony about the woman's religious devotion, hinting that her Catholicism had saved her from worse distress. The doctor ended his report with a sorrowful plea, asking for general assistance for this widow and her son.[60]

Baca filed her will in December of that year. Although she pleaded poverty and at the same time solicited assistance from the court, her final decree does not portray a woman severely destitute. She gave her small house and the surrounding land to her son, because "she had no daughters." She also willed him all of her other worldly possessions, which she enumerated as: two cows, a mule, four burros, ten bottles, six jars, six bowls, two forks, five mattresses, five sheets, ten coverlets, three sarapes, two storage boxes, three chairs, one bedstead, nine saints, two bultos, two cast-iron skillets, two spoons, two cooking pans (one made of copper), and a tablecloth. She included foodstuffs as well: sixty sacks of maize, five bushels of beans, and another bushel of peas.[61]

Baca's hardships can be surmised. She worried about her son's welfare, alluding to an ongoing illness or to his injury since childbirth. Remarried, and widowed for a second time, Baca evidently had inherited some property from both husbands, and this she passed on to the ineffectual son. Her will revealed that the concern over careful, systematic listings of all household articles—no matter how small the item—was important. It also showed how important children were in the matter of inheritance. Baca said in her will that she would pass on "all the possessions of my dead husband, Manuel Pino, to our son, José Pino." While she might have fretted over her son's capabilities or worried about his health, the inheritance, she hoped, "would keep him from becoming a burden on others." The owner of few material possessions, she nevertheless seemed like the other widows writing wills who communicated, above everything else, a sense of obligation and resignation, an acceptance of death, and also, a rather compromised but implicit faith in the future that they gained through their children.[62]

Not all women writing wills were widowed. Not all were affected by the economic downturns of the postwar years. One example comes from María Josefa Martínez. Of all the wills recorded in the *Probate Court Journal* between 1856 and 1862, none was longer than hers, which included five pages of items and a prayer of over three hundred words. "Finding myself ill and in bed, with a disease God has inflicted, but of sound mind and memory, I do freely and voluntarily give my worldly possessions as follows . . . ," Martínez stated. She continued with perfunctory reference to her husband and to a marriage which was in its twenty-fourth year, during which they "neither had, nor procreated, a single child." Further, the childless woman stipulated, "Neither my husband nor I brought to our marriage any inheritance from our parents. Our goods are ours and ours alone."[63]

Understandably, the wealthiest woman among those who deposited a will in court during this period would sound the most individualistic, and contributing to this tendency was the fact that she had no blood relatives who might have been heirs. She was evidently acquisitive because she listed numerous holdings, including, she noted, "the house in which I live," another next door, and a ranch outside the town with a small house on the property; at another location, she stated that she owned another half acre. She had just purchased that land and ordered that her husband "keep the document signed from the [recent] sale." Martínez listed many livestock, including oxen, cows, sheep, and goats. She had over five hundred sheep, but some of the livestock, she also said, did not belong to her. Evidently, she had been pasturing the animals for José de Jesús Luján of Santo Domingo Pueblo, a Native community ten miles southwest of Santa Fe. Her own animals, plus those she took on consignment, grazed on other properties scattered around the region; she used these to rotate the animals and assure that the animals remained fattened.[64]

Few documents so richly detail enduring aspects of a colonial economy as Martínez's does, or so sharply delineate a role in that economy as hers does. Her will depicts a rural system of pasturing that harkens back to an earlier time, before the advent of the large ranch. It was nearly extinct or extinguished in her lifetime by the new men who purchased acreage, fenced the land, and undercut the rotational patterns of livestock owners like Martínez. Despite her diversified landholdings and her large flock, even Martínez looked poor in comparison to such renowned ranchers as John Chisum or the lawyer Catron, who also owned sheep and cattle ranches.[65]

Martínez's operations, based on a feudal pattern termed transhumance, whereby shepherds moved, under contract, animals around to different pastures, evoked patterns of ranching common in Latin America but not in the western United States, common in preindustrial eras but not in the nineteenth century. Her style of ranching was conducted from a town or a city; livestock was divided into smaller herds and fanned out to shepherds contracted for a period of years. Martínez stipulated in her will that she "had rented pasture to José María del Real of San Francisco beginning on the 5th of January 1859, and for a term running until the 5th of January 1864." Martínez pastured some goats with Don Miguel Montoya and his wife, María Filomena, and, as part of that agreement, she paid them "with five goats and five sheep each year." These arrangements, she urged, should continue and be renewed.[66]

Martínez's decree offers so many clues as to how women maintained their properties in marriage and increased their holdings independently of their husbands. Martínez managed a large number of sheep and goats, herds that required an elaborate system of rotation and much attention. Did that alone encourage a degree of autonomy and of financial security unavailable to most women who were poor? The question cannot be answered on the basis of the type of evidence available, but other issues are in fact raised by Martínez's will. The older economic system upon which her estate relied, a colonial and even precolonial one at that, implies that some aspects of women's inheritances and of the economy remained unpreempted by the new practices of powerful church officials, like Bishop Lamy, or federal appointees, like William Ritch. And, her large estate, her endurance, and her role in retaining it are as important as the deeding of property by other will-makers to daughters or to sons, and suggest the way a select group of upper-class women remained uninvolved in a merchant-capitalist economy, if only momentarily. The few who managed to retain property and to pasture large herds of livestock evidently weathered the crisis of the postwar era.

Every example of an exception to a pattern, however, can be countered by contrary evidence. There were in Santa Fe other, equally wealthy women, like the widow Chaves, whose enumerations were as lengthy as Martínez's and whose wealth rivaled hers. But there were several differences among them. Martínez claimed that she had not inherited anything; she had built up her large estate. Chaves had inherited some of her property. Chaves had willed all of her land and livestock to her husband and children, but Martínez seemed disinclined to unconditionally do so. Rather, she asked that her husband be required to continue the contracts she had undertaken. Compared against each other, the contents of the two wills imply that fewer restrictions, fewer inhibitions among the wealthy provided greater diversity in their methods of dispensation, of will-making.[67] For a small minority, which I estimate to be only 5 percent of the testators, the implication is that rich women could rise above their daily conflicts, the problems of land losses, inflation, and deepening poverty that afflicted the majority of the population.[68]

Many other wills, numbering over thirty, more conspicuously reflect the straitened circumstances of women's lives. Athough these documents do not fully portray the external conditions that changed life for women, rarely state occupations, and tell little of daily troubles—such as Bárbara Baca's assault-and-robbery situation, which only other court records revealed—they do suggest lives marked by hardship and poverty, and imply that will-making was an act important beyond ritual because they were often the only thing these women actually controlled. For destitute women such as these, the act was cleansing and a method of instituting order in an otherwise chaotic world.

On August 31, 1868, Juana Terrasas proclaimed that she was "close to death." After a short introductory prayer, she stated that she had four young children, "Selsa, Antonio, Carolina, and Emiliano," and that all were "hijos naturales mios" (my out-of-wedlock children). To these heirs, she would leave her worldly goods, which included two houses in El Paso, Texas, one near the Franklin Plaza, composed of "four rooms and a corral," and another of two rooms near Fort Bliss. Her property, however, was insufficient to cover all of her debts. She owed money, primarily to doctors. She ordered that her fifty-dollar debt to Dr. McGee be paid, and that another, to Dr. Francisco Diffendofer of El Paso, also be settled. She owed the merchant Sigmund Seligman fifty dollars, and she owed Santiago Lopes another ten dollars. Her household items were minimal: two trunks, four mattresses, some blankets, dishes, and saints. She rented the house in which she lived in Santa Fe and owed money to her landlord, Felipe Delgado; she ordered it paid out of the rent her tenant in El Paso owed her.[69]

Terrasas had few possessions, save for her two houses, and insufficient cash to pay her rent. She ordered that an ox be sold and the money used to cover her funeral costs. She left one daughter the saints she had and a mattress. The others received only their bedding. In addition, she stipulated that, in the event of her death, all the children be given over to the hospital and orphanage of the Sisters of Charity. Finally, she declared in her will that her daughter Carolina was "the daughter of Guillermo Mills and I order that she be turned over to him, if he will take her, and if he does, her share of the house shall be divided among the other three."

Although not exactly in desperate straits, Juana Terrasas was quite poor, so poor that she indeed had to turn her children over to the nuns' care. She left her children nothing more than a roof over their heads and their bedding and was evidently counting on Guillermo Mills to assume responsibility for one of them. Terrasas's name does not appear in the census of 1850 or 1860, indicating that she was, in all likelihood, a resident of El Paso and without family in Santa Fe. Her sojourning demonstrates the continuing pattern of interregional migration among the poorest women, however difficult or insecure their employment might have been. Her move to northern New Mexico further suggests that women who might have sought refuge in a town known for its changing marketplace might, instead, just as well have stayed put because good jobs, steady employment, and reasonable rents were hard to come by in Santa Fe.

Even the poorest women of the besieged community, however, had some recourses. They relied on relatives for support. Living arrangements reflect this practice. The 1880 census listed Miguel García, age forty-one, and his wife, María García, age thirty-seven; they were living next door to Leonore García, age twenty-nine, and head of her household. She had four children, and their ages ranged from one to ten. Miguel was a laborer, María worked at home, and Leonore was a laundress. In the same neighborhood, the widower José Dúran, forty-one years of age, lived with his niece, María Dúran, twenty-two years old, and her infant sons, Juan and Eugenio. Agapito Lucero was also widowed, and he lived with his stepmother, Trinidad Gonzalez, her nephew, Pantaleon Lucero, and her niece, Teresa.[70]

In this cross section of the census enumerations, several important aspects of people's living arrangements suggest answers to the question about how poorer women survived the Euro-American onslaught. All of the men of the households investigated were or had been laborers, and each of the women worked as a laundress, taking work into the home or going outside it to wash others' clothes. The widowed tended to live with their children, and unmarried adults often lived with their siblings. The widow Cruz Ortiz Pino was fifty-six years old and lived with her adopted son, Petrolino, who was twelve. One widowed grandmother, Gregória Chávez, lived with her daughter, also widowed, and three grandsons, plus an unmarried daughter.[71]

These family arrangements mirror still other aspects of life that wills—no matter how precise they are about identifying relatives—cannot disclose. There was no such thing as a typical family in Spanish-Mexican Santa Fe; therefore, there could not be a standard pattern of inheritance. Through the tumultuous decades following the war, households also became exceedingly complex, that is to say, varied, in composition: The widowed, the elderly, adoptees, nieces and nephews, and some who had no other place to turn to, comprised the postwar generation. The average household size rose by two members between 1850 and 1880; also, the average income fell, and the number of persons in semiskilled or unskilled work nearly doubled. More new people moved into Santa Fe, but reliance on relatives grew stronger.[72]

The Ortega family demonstrates how these arrangements jelled. Albino and Antonio, brothers in their mid-thirties, lived next door to each other with their wives and children. Josefa Ortega, their mother, and Juan Ortega, their father, lived next door to them. An unmarried brother and a niece lived with the parents. Ten years earlier neither of the two brothers was married, all lived at home, and the household included two other Garcías, probably the couple's nephews. Meanwhile, next door, Dolores and Catalina García worked at home. Their ages suggest that they may have been Josefa Ortega's sisters.[73]

The children of such extended households imply another characteristic feature: Younger children were the responsibility of the extended family and incurred certain familial obligations, as Juana Terrasas's will also illustrated, the equivalent of inherited property. Testators attempted to secure care for children by specifying the relatives with whom they should live. The majority of will-makers, however, tended to be mothers of grown children. For that reason, the wills present a somewhat skewed picture of family relations. Other sources, like the census, are needed to sketch women's patterns of giving because evidently the group of testators does not represent all women of the postwar period.

One relationship not tested or undermined in these documents is that between bequeather and the Catholic Church or its saints. Women's faith in both church and saints was upheld in the practice of crafting a will. The statement "I have lived under it [the church] faithfully" appeared regularly. Supplications to the Virgin Mary extended the long, introductory prayer that became the basis of the will-making ritual: a Virgin Mary whose "pure, divine, and mysterious web and divine word" rarely supplanted devotion to "one, holy, almighty God," but to whom all these women offered their devotion and from whom, in return, they sought benediction. María was also the most common name among the testators, usually paired with another first name—María Gertrudes Casados, María de Jesus García, María Dolores Lucero, María Josefa Martínez, María Francisca Quiron, and María de la Sur Ortiz, to cite all of those listed in only one book of the four comprising the *Probate Court Journals*.[74]

Will-makers displayed yet one more consistent habit, however, that attested to the importance of female kin and friends. Women without children or husbands most often gave their possessions to their sisters, and even women with husbands and children first willed clothes and land to sisters, then to adopted daughters or to other women. Desideria Otero, the widow who wrote her will in December 1870 (as discussed earlier), calls to mind "female gift-giving." She had left her "comadre, Ventura" a saint, and she said, "To Juanita, I give two smaller saints. I own nine altogether." What she did with the rest is not noted; her children were all deceased, and Otero seemed preoccupied primarily with leaving two of the saints to her friends. She evidently valued the icons more than her other meager possessions, which included a mirror, two barrels, seven pillows, one shirt, one sheet, one burro, and six mattresses. A closer textual analysis of the style and tone of such bequests made by women might conclude that despite the tendency to dispense property to sons or husbands, another, more hidden purpose existed within these documents—to sustain female friendship or to pass on family heirlooms like saints or dowry items to women.[75]

Otero appointed two men who lived nearby as executors of her estate; she had invited them to be her witnesses and she asked that they be entrusted to "comply with [her] wishes."[76] Otero's witnesses and her friends demonstrated that a woman without relatives sought friends and neighbors as her heirs. In most instances, the items that were to be given carried no appreciable market value and seemed intended as gifts of remembrance. In that way, willing became an act of giving. But it conveyed more than one message about the value of kin and friends and about the importance of gifts. It sustained a system of social relations that made relatives and others important to Spanish-Mexican women, while reinforcing the ritualistic tradition of making a will. Otero's executors were present because, she implied, they were to be trusted; as a result, they also became privy to her final thoughts and last wishes.

Although the practice of writing wills, their inventories, and requests displayed timeless concerns, by 1870, so many other transformations, including new establishments on the Santa Fe plaza, more Euro-Americans in town, and the railroad tracks lying thirty miles outside the town, signaled some dramatic shifts in the ways people would begin organizing their lives. A shift in the tone and the organization of wills indicated that the chaos of the past decade and of the current one had finally caught up with the women of Santa Fe. Between 1877 and 1883, 37 Spanish-Mexican women filed their final testaments, 50 percent more than in any previous set of recordings. The number of women who filed, but also their distinctly complex, heightened preoccupation with their sons' (and not the daughters') status, marked a divergence in will-making.

The Gonzales sisters—María Jesus, María Refujio, and Petrona Borrego—filed their wills on the same day, as if urgency were of the essence, and gave their plots of land and livestock to husbands or brothers. Dolores Montoya, a mother, gave her property to her husband, and María Josefa Montoya, a widow, gave hers to her son.[77] María Josefa Prada named her husband as her heir, and her widowed sister, filing a will on the same day that she filed, named her sister the "receiver of all her goods." When the widow and her sister died, both their documents say, María Josefa's husband would inherit their estates.[78]

After 1870, the new structure of the wills was as important as the trend of giving property to men. Sisters opened their wills with one short declarative prayer, barely longer than two sentences, and they rarely listed their parents' names. They even now began giving their saints to men and rarely to daughters. They described fewer articles inherited from mothers, and their worldly possessions excluded clothes or dishes. The lists focused nearly exclusively on livestock, houses, and plots of land, indicating that secular and economic matters occupied women as never before. María Juana Prada lamented that she had "not a single, solitary heir."[79] Therefore, she gave her property to her sister, whom she apparently did not consider her heir. Two generations earlier, women had in fact considered their sisters their heirs, but evidently that practice was now ending.[80]

Women were consenting to different decrees; their concerns lay elsewhere. The female world of gifts and giving was yielding under the pressures of Americanization, and to a (Euro-American) male world of getting or taking. In this scenario, "female" signifies the distribution to female heirs and "male" signifies the skewed demography of Santa Fe, as well as the financial power of the emigrating men. The evidence for an increasing lack of choices among women is glaring. Antonio Mora, María Chávez's husband, said he "got five cows" and "took eight sheep" from Chávez's estate.[81] Women rarely used the same language. María Miquela Baca, earlier in the century, said she had "received a trunk from [her] mother," and she ordered that it be sold to pay for the recitation of masses for her mother's soul; she left her maids and their children livestock as well as furnishings.[82] Later, fewer women bequeathed much to their servants. Desideria Otero "gave saints" to her friends. Women's and men's worlds had changed, and the language of key phrases in these documents alone denoted the extent of the radical transformations sweeping their community.

Generalizations about the uniform impact of these changes must, of course, be avoided because there is some evidence that poor women writing wills in the 1870s retained the longer prayers and appeared preoccupied with equitable dispensations, with listing even the smallest of articles. For example, María Teresa García, twice widowed, gave a long introductory prayer and willed her "rooms" to her children. She gave her hoe, an ax, a shovel, and a quilt to her son; she asked another to sell the burro and to have four masses recited for her soul; and she willed a third son, she said, "a skillet, a metal spoon, and a piece of land that my mother gave me." Her will resembled the earlier ones in its conveyances of articles, but in its conveyances of property to sons, it differed from them as well.[83]

Sorting through specific trends in the period after the war, and using documents like wills, requires care because, while there can be no doubt that these women's lives were affected by the changes Euro-American men induced— and such changes would indisputably be mirrored in daily life, even in rituals and ceremonies—linking cause and effect can be risky. Even beyond the fact that men also shifted their positions and strategies (Lamy was outwardly friendly at first, increasingly impatient and less friendly later on), saying that women's practices in writing wills are "timeless" gives the documents a coherence markedly absent elsewhere in the society. Will-makers committed wishes and ideas to paper; theirs was inherently an act of structure and organization, or of orderly activity. Simply appearing before a judge in the probate court to detail such a document, or gathering witnesses to attest to its completion, provided consistency amid turbulence. The activity itself was symbolic—an attempt to preserve order and induce a semblance of harmony.

Timelessness is a characteristic attributable to the wills for other reasons, on other grounds. Perhaps what is timeless about the wills of the widows Desideria Otero and María Teresa García is that they had few material possessions; whether most women composed their wills in 1850 or 1870, the most impoverished exhibited similar modes of continuity. Poverty lent the appearance of changelessness to their lives. They were born into it and remained poor throughout their lives. Possibly, their concerns for survival were as enduring as their concerns for giving away prized possessions, and to make the latter more significant might be erroneous. Making a will became, for these women who were poor and Catholic, a matter of appeasement and also signified resignation. They repeatedly said so, listing the frailties, illnesses, or other physical problems that forced them to think through this process. The act prepared them for death and, by declaring their belief in God and the sacraments, they expressed their hope for an easier time in heaven.

The orderliness of will-making displayed by rich and poor alike in the probate courts, and at the church or in neighborhoods, can ultimately be best understood as a symbolic intervention in the disorder predominating in the outside world dominated by Euro-Americans. The subtle and striking changes in tone and patterning of women's testaments continued to occur against the backdrop of Euro-American encroachment. The 1870s, interestingly, were the decade of greatest Euro-American migration to Santa Fe; their numbers tripled and at one point during that decade, they constituted 25 percent of the population (see Table 2.1).[84]

Of the newly arrived group, many were drawn into, or involved themselves in, shady activities. The infamous land and tax scandal of the 1870s, whose leaders were dubbed the "Santa Fe Ring," involved many of the new attorneys and politicians pouring into town. Even the federally appointed governors were linked to land speculation and fraud, but none seemed to care much about their reputations as they hastened to purchase Spanish-Mexican land grants. The best grazing lands fell into the hands of the largest investors and cattle barons, leaving even women like María Nieves Chaves, one of the wealthiest Spanish-Mexicans in Santa Fe, unable to continue her rotational practices, strapped in her efforts to find good pastures for her large herds.[85]

The wealthier women could not compete with foreign-owned land companies, of the sort that began to predominate after 1870, or with the largest of the land-grabbers. The purchase of the Maxwell Land Grant placed two million acres of land in foreign hands and made several Santa Fe attorneys wealthy. The estates of women like Chaves paled in comparison to such landholdings.

Moreover, speculators preyed on women and men who could not read or write English. Few were as lucky as the widow Chaves. Beyond the immediate confusions created by arbitrary taxes and penalties, the conflation of federal land laws, local Spanish laws, and territorial practices proved incomprehensible, even to a Congress charged with deciphering myriad legal codes. To people used to settling issues of water usage, boundary disputes, and pasturing problems before the familiar alcaldes and priests, the newer, larger problems of the 1870s must have indeed appeared bewildering.[86]

We can only hypothesize about the impact of these changes on women's authority and independence, on the different roles they must have necessarily adopted within their families. Other literature on colonization suggests extensive, wide-ranging shifts in male-female relations, in family structure, and in community positions. But mainly we can only surmise the full impact in the case of Santa Fe because few women recorded their thoughts, and few men, Euro-American or Spanish-Mexican, wrote about the detrimental side of their activities.

Several conclusions, based on the evidence revealed by a close examination of wills, can be drawn: Only a minority escaped the hardships suffered by the postwar generation. Most women had to increasingly rely on men to help them sustain their small estates, their precarious positions in a new economy. As we have seen in the previous chapter, labor segregation, in jobs that were the most physically demanding and the lowest-paying ones, solidified women's positions at the bottom of a transposed wage-based economy. Dual jobs marked women's working lives; most slaved either as laundresses and seamstresses or as domestics and laundresses for pennies a day.

How the Spanish-Mexican women of Santa Fe survived these hardships has something to do with their ability to withstand the worst effects of poverty, something to do with the reliance even in the postwar years on friendly neighbors, kin, and the extended family. Almost all family members were similarly constrained; women and children worked harder than ever before and they maintained the gardens and animals that had sustained people in eras when manufactured items, market goods, and foodstuffs were scarce. The talents and skills honed under a subsistence economy, plus the fact that merchant capitalism had been slowly implanted, perhaps as early as the late eighteenth century—then slowly across the prewar years, and, finally, with greater force in the postwar period—gave women some time to adjust to the truly drastic changes wrought in the 1870s by Euro-Americans carrying large reserves of cash, and by the changes in the political, religious, and economic structures. Their economic colonization, if not their social and political one, was slow and methodical.

Women had been tested at every turn in the previous decades and as the railroad approached their town, it became evident that a different way of life for them had just begun. The full implications of laboring for wages and of institutional segregation are, to this day, largely unnoticed by the dominant Euro-American residents of Santa Fe. Women's adaptation to a wage-labor system, to a different method of land ownership, and to a political system based on the election of those who could read and write or had formal education, secured their survival, but it was a survival which to a certain extent was based on poverty and a great deal of expectation or hope that it would be eradicated. Few women outwardly resisted Euro-American encroachment after 1880, at least not publicly. Rather, their resistance probably took a different turn, became less visible, and removed from the ways that Juana Lopes and Gertrudis Barceló had followed or themselves devised. In their church groups and in their families—private spaces where records are scarce or nonexistent—these women evidently regrouped, or else they would not have survived and there would be no Spanish-Mexicans in Santá Fe today.

What we know about what allows such women as Lopes and Barceló, or Chaves and Terrasas, to continue in life and sustain a culture and a community is extensive. Social scientists tell us that a culture of expectation serves many purposes for people undergoing radical transformation as well as for those gradually experiencing change. It creates hope, but also can implant despair. It can prepare people for further changes, or isolate them in patterns reminiscent of the old ways. In the case of Santa Fe's women, both of these processes were under way. Some changes were fast-paced—buildings sprouted, city ordinances were passed, stores and a fort attracted newcomers; other changes were slower.[87] The church's rituals and functions were altered as Bishop Lamy saw fit, but celebrations and holy days continued with minor changes. Children, when they married, evidently continued to live near their parents; men and women began working for wages at the same time. The pace and method of the changes, I am suggesting, is also important to consider when evaluating degrees of cultural change and continuity, when considering or contrasting women's changing positions within their society before and after the war.

This chapter and the preceding ones have assessed both the extent of colonization and the variety of women's responses during and after the war between Mexico and the United States. I have sought to measure cultural change and continuity when that seems possible, but mostly to position women's responses within a range of viable possibilities, to find meaning in their activities in ways that meaning has not been previously assigned. Many of the examples I presented in this chapter, to establish women's centrality in colonization, came from over seventy-five wills or testaments—in the case of La Tules, from over two hundred comments about her and from an equal number of published travelogues, diaries, or memoirs; and in the discussions of women in the courts, from over two hundred court cases that directly involved women. To suggest that the evidence is scanty or impossible to find, as many historians do to justify excluding women or gender, is to ignore the sources or the women in them.

This work has also implied that peeling away the layers obscuring women's lives also exposes the layers that have obscured men's. Both sexes were part of a changing world. At the same time, women's values, aspirations, arguments, and behaviors have not been lost in the rush to thoroughly examine, or exhaustively portray, a besieged community. I have been especially conscious of that tendency in recent works in Chicano history that attempt merely to plug women into male-determined categories, which become as oppressive to women as were the habits and tendencies of Euro-American colonizers more than a century ago. When historians begin to cross cultural, racial, and sexual frontiers, as I have sought to do in this work, we must revise all categories of culture, politics, race, ethnicity, economy, sexuality, and religion, no matter what our orientation or training may be. To do less is to fall into the trap of "contribution history," as the historian Suzanne Lebsock argues, meaning that we merely line up women as just one more category, one more constituency, or one more group.[88]

Whether they were insiders or outsiders, at the bottom or at the top, the Spanish-Mexican women of Santa Fe defy easy categorizations, resist linear graphings. Some, like Barceló, adjusted, and others, like Lópes, did not, but many survived. Their survival was based on no coordinated program of resistance based on their gender, but still they obliged their colonizers (and now, historians) in at least one respect: They left us a legacy, an inclination toward many responses. It seems important therefore to know something about them, to return the favor, and to exorcise their omission from history by suggesting patterns, revealing linkages between their society and culture and that of the encroachers, and insisting on more complex readings of their lives.

The Politics of Disidentification and Recuperation

Notations about the "New" Western American History

This book has suggested a framework for unraveling historically the positions and situations of Chicanas by examining their history in one community across a relatively short expanse of time last century (relative, that is, to their presence in the region studied). Its structure and its arguments have made the point that a different angle of vision is necessary if we are to unpack the implications of colonization. Becauses they were persistent, accommodating survivors, it is not surprising that the Spanish-Mexican women I have written about persevered and that their grandchildren, the Chicanas of Santa Fe, presently endure ongoing colonization. What is surprising, however, is how hidden female ancestors have been in the stories men have told of Santa Fe—how undervalued or invisible they have been in these renderings, even in recent decades. This chapter situates these oversights in the context of newer writings that deal with the racial and sexual politics surrounding the "encounters" between westering Euro-American and Spanish-Mexican frontierspeople. It offers a critique of that literature and proposes different possibilities—as each chapter has in this book—for examining the lives of women on this and other colonized frontiers of the world.

Recent scholarship on the American West, including the surveys and texts by Elizabeth John, Edward Spicer, and Patricia Limerick have improved our understanding of "how the West was won"—how the southwestern United States became dominated by Euro-Americans and how Native Americans and Mexicans were practically erased from the scene in textbooks, but interestingly, not in the popular fiction of the time. Similarly, the works of historical sociologist David Montejano, of colonial historian Ramón Gutiérrez, of Chicana historians Antonia Castañeda and Emma Pérez, to cite just a few, have served to rectify some of the imbalances, as have monographs, articles, and anthologies by Paula Gunn Allen, Bea Medicine, Clara Sue Kidwell and other Native American scholars.[1]

Older works did not always make the effort to account for systematic cultural erasure.[2] The invisibility itself reinforced the prevailing notion that non-heroic action was reason enough for the oversight. The inattention testified to the insignificant treatment given the act of takeover by historians writing about western American history, who stuck closely to the guideposts laid out by caravaners and sojourners to the West, the hardy traders, mountain men, and pioneers who formed the heart of the old cowboys-and-Indians paradigm. But in history, as in other arenas of life, balances and interests have shifted, or are shifting. Suddenly, renewed focus has been given, in varied forms, to the mythologies of conquest; to the topic of cultural diversity; and to the realities of social, racial, economic, and cultural oppression. Now, suddenly, not just Chicano scholars discuss the role of Chicanos; not just women discuss the significance of women in the conquest of the frontier. Indeed, a renaissance, fostered and encouraged by a different type of researcher, by social and quantitative history, by investigations into the production and producers of western American narratives, by historians trained in comparative history, has reorganized an entire subfield of the history profession.[3]

Revision is not new to western American history. From Frederick Jackson Turner to Patricia Limerick, the thread spun weaves a familiar pattern, while it discerns particularities and adds to the previous body of knowledge. The individual battling heroically against the odds—which Turner termed one of the singular achievements of westward expansion—the struggle of human beings against nature, the refrains of regenerative salvation, achievement, and progress, reappear from time to time in the scholarship. One new development, however, is the view that much more was at stake than simple land takeovers when white, westering Americans took to the wagon trail. The Euro-American claims to the land and its resources came at the expense of others, especially Natives and Mexicans, some historians argue, and the outright swindles by land-grabbers—who themselves were often the most respected members of society, politicians, lawyers, federal officers—are now an accepted part of our "telling" of western American history.[4]

What has become equally important, especially among ethnic-minority and feminist western historians, has less to do with explaining who did what to whom and more to do with the assumptions and implications involved in the situation of giving and taking, of the swindled and the swindler. Such scholars argue implicitly (and not always explicitly) that the hierarchical imposition of conquest—that is, the superimpositon of domineering values, ideologies, and practices—remains with us today. Another way of saying this is that in the American West we continue to live with, and within, the pattern of domination. These historians suggest that understanding the history of the American West must first begin with such sensitivity but also with a theoretical grounding in the stories and implications of conquest.[5]

In this way western American historians share one feature with historians understanding colonization anywhere: The mutual focus resides in surveying patterns but also in situating the implications of takeover, or in not losing sight of domination as a prevailing universal paradigm of social relations in almost all situations involving conflicts. Foucault called this power while other scholars concerned with semiotics, rhetoric, and ideology, but basically in agreement with him, have asserted that even studies of the dominated and oppressed assert a hierarchy, by repeatedly focusing on the institutions and patterns that created the imbalances in the first place.[6] The message among deconstructionists, demystifiers, cultural workers, and others is similar in that it states that few of us live immune from, or removed from, hegemony, understood varyingly as a Third-World-versus-First-World phenomenon, as an unholy set of associations between overdeveloped-versus-underdeveloped countries, and in cultural criticism, more recently and optimistically termed "the decline of the Western European Age."[7] Hierarchies of domination are being studied everywhere, and many other subdisciplines besides western American frontier history are increasingly shaped by these discussions, for the better. Still, some cautionary markers are evoked along the way, particularly by ethnic residents of the U.S. western frontiers, when we question one fundamental theme that runs through the newer literature: It is unclear that a postcolonial age (as much of this scholarship assumes) has been truly achieved, especially when, through our personal histories, we link causes and effects, when we recognize that modernization—including electricity, health care, and public education—is available in many rural areas of the southwestern United States, but to a selected group of people and not to all.[8]

Ethnic-minority scholars of the western United States have been at the forefront of these and other debates that, for several reasons, call into question the deeper implications of colonization for the majority of the population in this society. Although labeled argumentative, or scholars with an ax to grind, such debaters often succeed in raising the understanding of the larger society by tackling such contentious subjects as bilingual education, affirmative action, and voter registration. An entire generation of Chicano scholars is oriented in the direction of establishing and assisting social justice through their academic work. Without these linkages between community and institutions, many issues at the congressional level would remain unexamined. An excellent example of the impact of this focus is the way scholars shaped the debates—popular, academic, and bureaucratic—on Japanese internment and on redress. Without such broad-based involvement, a fundamentally critical issue in American racial politics would have taken far longer to address.[9]

Although in the United States we can debate that most citizens are not used to closely examining the relevance of class, race, gender, or sexual oppression in everything they do, the importance of those categories themselves can no longer be ignored by any subfield or group of scholars, even while their existence in the society might somehow be overlooked or minimized. Scholars have begun tackling their interconnections, deciphering them, for many reasons including the fact that the color of the professional academy is changing and that the interpretations of world events are multiplying.

Global affairs, rapid communications systems, and teaching courses in a technocratic society have begun affecting western American frontier history, an area of study once thought to reflect, with positive evokings, all that was good about America. From James Fenimore Cooper's novels to Daniel Boone–like characters, the frontier righteously captured "the spirit of America." But even that understanding has been more critically examined, in compelling works that point out how nationalism, violence, and mythologizing are interconnected and lead to a type of western history that purposely overlooks residents who became "minorities," overlooks the roles and fates of women and children in situations of conquest. This is especially evident in newer scholarship grounded in an understanding of unfolding and continuous economic displacements, which were and are integral to an analysis of westward expansion. For example, in assessing the significance, of water in western American history, Donald Worster argues that reclamation was a singular act of domination over limited natural resources, that it became wholesale robbery and quickly displaced thousands of people.[10] In assessing the importance of gender in the Spanish conquest of California, Antonia Castañeda assails past glorifications of European men capturing indigenous California people, but she also focuses on women in particular, who at that moment in their history were peaceful.[11] Our mythologies about the American west are being continuously deconstructed and reconstructed, a feature that should not surprise historians, even Turnerians. This regenerative, cyclical quality is basic to western historiography and even to the continuity of western American practices.

Today the challenges to historiographic tradition come from many quarters, as I am implying in these remarks. Although some challenges are persuasive, a few take longer to become accepted; some extend historians' fallacies. One grave arena of current concern has to do with the sensitivities surrounding race issues, where the trend among some historians is to overlook, or underrepresent, racial tension. The historical record is informative on this score, to use only the example of the Spanish-Mexican women of Santa Fe; many subverted the colonization processes, many expressed disinterest, even anger, toward the colonizers. Few, the record suggests, appeared happy about the Euro-American presence, and even fewer were appeased by the soldiers entering their town. To suggest that colonization for them was just one more event on a continuum is to underrate the significance of particular processes; it denies the severity of the impact of conquest, and its telling results, but also neglects—as I have suggested—the methods these women used to reverse the conquest.

For the Spanish-Mexican women of Santa Fe, colonization spelled certain disasters, some of which linger in the present. It implanted for some a wage-labor system that was discriminatory and forced many others to adapt to the new conditions, but few had chosen or invited those changes. To view their choices or decisions as self-conscious action, as mere adaptation, or, from a slightly more proactive position, as an adoption of "something new," implies complicity or motive based on knowledge, implies—in ways consistent with liberalism—an egalitarian lineup of choices.[12]

This was certainly not the case. The institutions brought to Santa Fe after the war were hierarchical and prearranged; they required that their guardians be literate in English, be male, and have some formal education. Ignoring the relevance of these details, robbing them of their patriarchical, but also hegemonic, influence, makes for complicitous and inaccurate history. But, as my work has also suggested, ignoring the women's recourses to action is equally pernicious. Actresses and victims often occupied the same stage and a woman could simultaneously be both; similarly, richer and poorer women could be affected by colonizers' mentalities, values, and attitudes, so class or status did not necessarily protect the women of Santa Fe.

To focus on women undergoing colonization removes us somewhat from the legitimate questions regarding aspects of life perhaps less affected or shaped by the larger political or economic issues of the time. Again, documents detailing the conflicts between ordinary citizens are suggestive, but only to the extent that these, too, are drawn from institutional life—that is, the courts or jailhouse records. Next, I outline elements of conflict as depicted in the archival material from the 1880s, with an eye toward presenting a methodology (one that does not abruptly end the story, but continues it) for reassessing women's lives.

In 1888, Rafael Muñiz sued Quirina Montoya for custody of his two children, ages 8 and 5, citing how Montoya had "abandoned the home," "without reason whatsoever." The document goes on to detail Muñiz's wrath or anguish: "Said Quirina Montoya left with the aforementioned children along with all of the personal property of said petitioner." Next, Muñiz contended in his petition that Montoya left the home to live a "dishonorable life, a libertine existence, and a scandalous one," setting for the children a "bad example, perverting their innocence, and ruining their morals." Having been informed that his ex-wife had passed the time in "a scandalous and corrupt manner," Muñiz concluded that if his children were not removed from such "diabolic" companionship, they, too, would meet their ruin. Worse, Quirina Montoya appeared to be unwilling to place them in school so that they could "learn something," and instead, they were left "loose to roam the streets, viewing and doing [undignified] things for youngsters of such tender age." He asked the probate court to intervene, to remove the children and place them under the care and guardianship of someone who was capable of "giving them love and showing respect for virtuous living by good example," until such time as the regular court could convene to determine their fate, and hopefully, return them to him. Moreover, Muñiz requested that his ex-wife be ordered to come before the regular-standing judge and address these charges.[13]

In the period between Juana Lopes's 1832 appearance in court (described in chapter 1) and this one by Muñiz in 1888, much had transpired, the very documents attest: The probate clerk in this instance, Marcelino García, accepted the petitioner's testimony on October 27, 1888, by writing a note on the overleaf, in English.

Language was not the only issue at stake. New Mexicans had begun to move matters away from the courts and toward the legislature (the larger political entity); these matters had once been handled at the local level, by magistrates or justices of the peace.

Although Muñiz's petition was written in Spanish, questions of guardianship were beginning to glut the court system, so much so that the legislative sessions of the territorial government entertained large numbers of petitions concerning adoptions and legitimacy—local concerns as well as territorial ones. Other reasons also explain the move toward the legislative body, including the fact that the federal system was designed to supplant local authority not only in questions of governance but also in petition matters. An April 1884 volume that covers such local and special laws, contains an entire section devoted to "Acts of Legitimation." Seventeen separate acts confirmed the petitioners' requests for legitimacy, adoption, and name changes, driven by—as the petitions stated frankly—concerns over inheritance. Both men and women filed such petitions and the territorial authorities passed legislative acts recognizing their requests, printing the acts first in English, followed by the Spanish translations.

These so-called protections that recognized Spanish as the dominant language of the resident population, although neglectful of the indigenous languages that also reigned in the upper Rio Grande Pueblo world, were designed not exclusively as a right or a recognition, but rather as an immediate solution to the problem of monolingualism—that is, the use of Spanish mostly for social relations and of English for business relations, for practical reasons. Their ongoing, complex blending in official statements and in federal documents suggests that colonization was methodically, if slowly, proceeding.

Other venues depicted similar trends of disenchantment or of developing tensions. The jail and arrest records in the decade of the 1880s reveals deep rifts, as the majority of those arrested were Spanish-Mexicans who were mostly without recourse to probation. About the only resolution for an unjust arrest among the several hundred who were imprisoned for more serious crimes, such as larceny and threat with intent to murder, in the years after 1885—when the local penitentiary was established—was via special petition directed to the territorial governor. The office indeed pardoned the indicted ones, but most served out their sentences for crimes ranging from murder and battery to "singing in the streets," and "steeling"; other bases for arrest apparently included "asult," "personating an officer," "distroying property," "breaking house," and "braking peace." These misspellings in the records might suggest that English was making inroads at a sluggish pace, but the magnitude of arrest statistics based on surname, when correlated to the crimes committed, fundamentally attests to a tense social atmosphere, no matter what meaning we find in the numbers of releases or pardons. Many of those arrested for minor offenses were simply fined and released, if they could pay, or, in the case of women—who until the turn of the century tended to be charged but not incarcerated because the penitentiary could only accommodate men—were usually placed on probation.[14]

One generalization from such evidence is that not all Spanish-Mexican women, whether criminals or noncriminals, divorced or separated, rich or poor, were equally affected by the colonizers, but the majority were indeed affected by their *program* of colonization. Another is that ignoring women creates a burdensome oversight in shaping frontier history because it conveys many messages, such as the one that women were primarily reactive participants and are principally absent in historical documents. For New Mexico's women, and across these pages describing territorial imperatives, local court decisions, or jailhouse records, the evidence abounds to the contrary. Women were present, rarely absent, and Euro-Americanism affected them as it did all others.

The key issues of contact and conquest, of visibility and impact, influence more than ever the history we write of Chicanas in the Southwest. When Chicano historians began putting together what were essentially community studies, few consciously included women in their narratives. Up through 1990, Chicano history texts treated women as appendices by mentioning them in chapters on social relations, under such titles as "Chicana Occupational Structure," "The Chicana Worker," and "Female Employment and Matriarchal Families."[15] Spanish-Mexican women either fit under the headings depicting male activities or they were entirely ignored. This trend may shift not only as Chicano historians grapple with the implications of omitting a group constituting the adult majority of nearly every Spanish-Mexican community, but also as we grapple with the notion that more fitting subtitles might focus on questions of adoption, inheritance, children, and on crime and divorce—that is, subjects governed by internal social relations as opposed to the external concerns stemming from an imposing structure of governance.[16]

It is interesting to contrast general historiographic and methodological trends across subfields and within the field. Comparing the decisions of Chicano historians to exclude women with the work of other historians of the "new" western history, who seek to rectify imbalances by tracing just intercultural relations—meaning, at their most basic level, relations between westering men and local Spanish-Mexican women—is a fruitful exercise. The works focus on both men and women, but usually from the perspective of the outsiders, the arriving Euro-American men, their concerns, and their values and interests. Many of these pay less attention to the dynamic and creative tensions intrinsic to cross-cultural and interracial meetings, instead emphasizing cross-cultural contact. Difficult to assess, because many of the same scholars concentrating on intercultural relations are also proponents of multicultural approaches to frontier history, this work is also in need of some revisions.[17]

Historians tracing the intercultural and cross-racial relations between Euro-Americans and Spanish-Mexicans consistently have contended that marriages between these two groups allowed Spanish-Mexican women to assimilate or acculturate.[18] The conclusions are based on the erroneous notion that mixed marriages generally led to upward mobility or that Americanization was an aspect of cross-racial marriage. But, in fact, the evidence for New Mexico does not support these conclusions. First, Euro-Americans until 1870 were a minority of the population and intermarriages occurred infrequently. If acculturation was at issue, it operated in the opposite direction: Like the soldiers La Tules accommodated at her saloon, the larger community of Spanish-Mexicans was "Hispanicizing" the smaller numbers of strangers. Up through the 1880s, Santa Feans referred to these newcomers as "norteamericanos," while continuing to Hispanicize their first names. James became Santiago, John was translated into Juan, Susan was Susana. The question can then be asked about who was acculturated in this process, and to *what* in this context.[19]

Second, in the decades of greatest Euro-American migration to Santa Fe, only 10 percent of the marrying population paired up across ethnic and racial boundaries. Looking closely at the partnerships, we find that a symmetry in class and in property worths emerges. Of the women listed, in the 1860 census, as partnered or living with Euro-Americans, the majority reported estates worth less than $100; they reported their occupations as seamstresses, laundresses, and domestics, and they lived with men whose occupation tended to be that of a day laborer. None of the intermarrying women were paired up with proprietors, property owners, merchants, other businessmen, politicians, or federal appointees. None of the intermarrying women lived with men whose estates totaled over $250. Upward social mobility was surely not operating in these marriages, neither as cause nor as result.[20]

It is interesting that western frontier historians have chosen to write about these relationships in terms that imply that women, worth nothing, married men, worth something, and that Spanish-Mexican women gained mobility as their Euro-American men in turn gained entrance into Spanish-Mexican society.[21] The data reveal a basic flaw in these arguments and suggest caution. A more appropriate line to pursue has to do with class parallelism and with religious compatibility. The most common interracial, cross-cultural relationship in Santa Fe was formed between working-class Spanish-Mexican women and Irish immigrant men, and both tended to be Catholics.

That poor women married Catholic immigrants speaks directly to a host of other factors that make intermarriages interesting; if generalizations can be drawn from these relationships, they must first account for class, religion, and ethnic status: Did women marry Irish immigrants because of an affinity based on class and religion? Did Irish immigrants also experience degrees of ostracism in the new country? Is that why they emigrated to Santa Fe? Finally, we know little about the experiences of these new immigrants and about how long they resided in Santa Fe. A random selection drawn from every fifth relationship between an Irish-born immigrant and a Spanish-Mexican woman indicates that the children of these unions resided in Santa Fe and that their first names were Hispanicized. The pattern in the evidence suggests that the intermarrying Irish became permanent residents and that they were being acculturated to Spanish-Mexican customs.[22]

Inverting the categories and refusing to abide Turner's model—because it would keep the focus on the Euro-American (immigrant) men—signifies a subtle but critical shift in the way intermarrying Spanish-Mexican women are portrayed and assigns different motives and understandings to their relationships with others. The goal in this method of unraveling the intimate encounters between Spanish-Mexican women and Euro-American men is to look at them from a southern perspective, through a Mexican, but not a European, focus, and from a gendered perspective, through the eyes of resident women but not sojourning men. It thus becomes a way to "other" those who have traditionally been "othered," whose actions have been explained entirely as if conquest is a foregone conclusion or have been interpreted by historians who willingly accept a hegemonic enforcement of colonization even in their studies on interracial relations. In the case of intermarrying women, this is neither desirable nor necessary.[23]

The neutralizing effect of the studies—their tendency to register all relationships on a hypothetical plane of equality and ignore surrounding and pronounced political and social turmoil caused by outsiders or insiders, and sustained by both types of interactions—is cause for concern because when it assesses differences at all, it reduces them or renders them insignificant. "American men found Mexican women attractive both physically and socially, and Mexican women were likewise attracted to American men," the historian Sandra Myres wrote. "Intercultural marriages were fairly common occurrences in early California and throughout the Southwest," she continued, and "for some Hispanic women, marriage to an American brought improved social and economic status and started the process of assimilation between the two ethnic groups."[24] Another feature of these studies of intermarriage is the focus on Euro-American cultures, an imbalance which presents difficulties because the conclusions are based on scanty supporting documentation.[25] Why, or how, Euro-American men could defy convention and marry outside their race is the question embedded in every intermarriage case investigated, as if the inquiry must necessarily reside on the emigrating man and not on the resident woman.[26] If Euro-American men were suing for custody of their children, the questions continue, does this not suggest their humanity?[27] The issues embedded in the question center on the men and ignore the women, center on the Euro-American at the expense of the Spanish-Mexican, privileging émigré over resident. Inescapably, this evidence and the accompanying assumptions have forced historians to conservatively choose their emphases; in the case of the intermarrying women of Santa Fe, I would argue that we should rearrange the traditional focus as much as the evidence allows for a fuller presentation with all of its contradictions exposed.[28]

Other problems plague the scholarship on interracial relations on the frontier and raise questions of emphasis and goals. Even the titles of such works as *Women and Indians on the Frontier*, and titles in history course materials labeled,"fur traders and Indian women," display remarkable insensitivity to aspects of indigenous pasts, to the hundreds of communities, languages, religious systems, and philosophies that characterized Native America, if such broad titles can ever be appropriately applied.[29] Although justifications for the titles and works can be made—particularly when one considers the need for textbooklike material in the field of western American women's frontier history, which until two decades ago, was lacking printed works, the recognition should not prohibit our placing the material in the conquest paradigm, from which it derives, for further clarification. These are works produced by authors searching for meanings in the past, hoping in some cases to draw linkages and perhaps in others to erase the terrible crimes that were often committed in the name of exploration and settlement—polite words, to be sure, and erroneous for several reasons.

The words historians use signify more than a search for some sense of "accuracy." Words like "intercultural contact" suggest less-tension-ridden relations, suggest, or imply, equalities in the methods and processes, and the thoughts and feelings, of people confronting one another, and ignore the inhibitions and sanctions that work against interracial partnerships.[30] Similarly, if a historian chooses "contact" over "conquest," or uses words like "multiculturalism," that historian is situating herself/himself in a particularly open, but also difficult, terrain in the current discussions because the words suggest accord and ignore racial attitudes, prejudices, color codes, and institutionalized discrimination.[31]

Evidence often has little to do with the concepts and the language used because it is often presented as an afterthought and can be stacked up to support many arguments, for historians and nonhistorians alike. My point, however, suggests that the uses of words like "contact," "intercultural contact," and "middle ground" pervasively reflect liberal doctrines that underwrite much of the new scholarship on the American west, contain a hope that perhaps domination has ceased taking place, or that the dominated do more than react and have some controlling agency in their daily lives.[32] A question rarely asked, however, is how much the position or the situating itself reflects pitfalls in the discursive field in which such discussions take place. Is it easier to pretend that Native peoples were not displaced, incarcerated, concentrated, and nearly annihilated last century? Is it easier to suggest that Chicanos caused their own demise because they encouraged Euro-American contact, Euro-American trade? These assumptions were once useful to the field, in the sense that they resulted in another angle from which to view social relations, to explore the settings and meanings of "interactions." But they also were and are explicitly ideological, while overlooking the complicating results, and ignoring the historical significance of political economy, of hegemony, and of redress—concepts as crucial to our understanding of nineteeth-century frontier history as they are to First World/Third World affairs today. The irony lies in how historians who raise these issues are curiously themselves labeled "ideological."[33]

Early in the 1980s, the semiotician Tzvetan Todorov reminded historians of Latin America of the need to look beyond the superficial, to more closely read the texts produced by the conquerors of Mesoamerica. His own reading provided us a valuable reminder that, when excavating the archives we should consider the linguistic manipulations of conquerors as well as their actions, the explicit and the implicit. His book *The Conquest of America* became, in some circles, practically iconographic, an accomplishment whose meanings we might also want to investigate. Importantly, we must concern ourselves with the implications of his close reading of the conquest literature because his book's organization implies that the results of Euro-American inquiries are not always what they seem. His parting shots suggested that the Western European tradition unleashed in the sixteenth century not only "fed Mayan women to dogs" (as his book's dedication stipulates), but actively "consumed" knowledge about Mayans and Aztecs to better displace them. In other words, knowledge reaffirmed and guided conquest; the master colonial narrative might not have disappeared after the Enlightenment, and liberals, academics, and other researchers might well be as contemporarily suspect. Does Todorov's method facilitate a different kind of conquest, this one intellectual and consumptive, but a conquest nevertheless?[34]

In portraying the Euro-American "thirst for knowledge," Todorov's book conveyed many messages and perhaps this accounts for its popularity. This is certainly the contribution of a postmodern reading of conquest, but historians must investigate the dilemmas of the model when we reach for either symbolic or textual interpretations as solutions to the conundrums of history. Todorov's hope is that Mayan women will no longer be "fed to the dogs"—that is, suffer the humiliation of omission and, simultaneously, the indignities of false reification. She is "known" to us as "a" Mayan woman, nameless. His book thus illuminates a different path, but one with clear limitations, in case we who use it forget that any research path we choose is already laid out, to a certain extent, by the time we "discover" it. Although evidence is waiting to be revealed and information ready to be conveyed, historians do very little that is truly new or innovative, and this lesson in humility drawn from the work of Todorov and of others is valuable as well. Todorov becomes his sources—that is, his judgments and interpretations are a compilation of those of two friars, Sahagún and Las Casas, and of the Aztecs, who also recorded their observations of their impending demise.[35]

If novelty eludes historians, different issues continue to plague them. Some historians resist reading from the present into the past, fearing that contemporary values and ideologies might somehow contaminate the "purity" of past renderings. Fear of presentism is simply part of a larger pathology because each generation of historians reinvents the past, using the tools, skills, and interests of their current era to sometimes expand interpretations and offer different insights along the way. Many historians, even traditionalists, argue that the question of objectivity "bit the dust" a long time ago, but few would go so far as to admit that their task is to give the past a rereading, or that their commitments to other ways of seeing the past make this a necessity. Yet most historians attach themselves to their evidence to varying extents; many craft arguments after long, deliberate reflections in which they were immersed not only in the evidence, but also in other literatures. The dynamic tension between current debates, past reflections, and the evidence is one of the least-discussed features of historiography, but so crucial to a historian's tasks that it deserves consistent attention.[36]

Real problems persist even after we admit that what we write about cannot escape being cast—nor do we want it to be cast—in contemporary racial, sexual, or political idioms. The language of domination and takeover pervades the American west today, but it also marked the attitudes and reflections of Euro-American sojourners a century ago, and ignoring it can become as much of a barrier to thoughtful analyses as the mountains and canyons were to westering pioneers and conquerors. One historian's pioneer is another's conqueror. The field is beginning to recognize this as a point of departure for newer work that will not ignore positions, intentions, and assumptions in the writing of history. The creative tensions between and among the places out of which we write, and between us and our evidence, are as necessary to our understanding of how we organize evidence, tell stories, as is specific revelation of assumptions on paper. But that conclusion, I am arguing, is simply the first level of assessment. On another, deeper one, the fact that I am a descendant of the women I have written about does not mean that I cannot be balanced in writing this book; but it does mean that I have particular insights into their situations, that in the evidence, I looked purposefully for the many documents that would support arguments, ideas, intonations I "knew" to be part of that history. This task I do not view as my "ax to grind," but rather as intrinsic to my historical writing, as visiting the sites of Civil War battles might be to an historian of that war. Yet we are, in the current debates about the new social history and the new historicism, trapped by arguments that would rather not address these contestable issues across an increasingly embattled ground, that would just as readily argue for their omission.[37]

These and other specific criticisms can be made of standard works on the Borderlands. The books by historians and authors alike have sometimes been generated without detailed or balanced examinations of archival material.[38] Usually, historians spend enormous amounts of time with primary documents, but in the case of depicting Spanish-Mexicans (elucidating their hopes, fears, and activities), fewer historians are competently trained in the languages of the documents.[39] Some of us, for example, are undertrained in medieval Spanish, nearly a necessity for uncovering the explicit as well as the hidden meanings of key concepts in the law that surrounded inheritance litigation and that lingered even into the nineteenth century, underwriting gender relations across time.

Other historians simply conduct all of their primary research by examining documents written only in English, which limits their discussions of politics, society, and culture because the documents ignore or misportray Spanish-Mexicans, often caricaturing, as territorial Governor Ritch did in the 1860s, local people. "The minds of the people are as barren as the land," argued W. W. H. Davis, temporary territorial official, whose words certainly ring false, especially to the real estate agents currently selling property in Santa Fe at rates comparable to those found in the San Francisco Bay Area and in New York City. Real property values, now or last century, however, were not at issue. Cultural misunderstanding was. Conquest and colonization were, and are, integral to the lives of the people involved. A differently trained historian would seek out the connections between what current cultural and political observers witness as the ongoing colonization of Santa Fe and its colonial, nineteenth-century antecedents. Another historian might focus on processes and not on results, might discuss cultural adaptations but not economic colonization, might not ask where Spanish-Mexican women are socially or economically located today. The latter task requires both a commitment to unraveling the impact of new economic and political structures, and a thorough scouring of the primary and recorded documents, those in English and in Spanish.

The detailed work required is daunting and explains why books such as this and others take so long to complete. Few of the secondary accounts contain adequate population figures for the community of Santa Fe.[40] No historian has done a breakdown of property values using the census records; no study, until mine, had previously counted women or widows or documented the period of greatest Euro-American immigration. Finally, no one had closely examined the Catholic Church archives for the period after the U.S.-Mexican War, or the probate records and the primary testimonials written by or about women. Because so few are engaged in these tasks, the necessary work is multiplied and arduous—and this secondary literature is only now coming into being.

Without more thorough explorations of the Spanish-language archival records, for Santa Fe and for every other Spanish-Mexican community of the Southwest, without examining the Catholic archdiocese records—material so abundant and also so full of examples of discord, of disharmony, but mostly unindexed—historians can unsurprisingly assert that Santa Fe before the Euro-Americans arrived "was an arrested frontier society." However, close readings of the documents reveal, in fact, the opposite: Santa Fe was a vibrant, busy social center for Native Americans from the surrounding environs, for Spanish-Mexicans, and as the century wore on, for Euro-Americans.

Scrutinizing these once-prevalent assertions requires some long hours and specific work in the archives, but is necessary if a Spanish-Mexican perspective is to make its presence felt in the subfield of western American history, and if gender inequalities and women's lives are to mean more than depiction, are to be investigated seriously. For that reason as well, I have chosen in some sections of this book to assess what has been said about Spanish-Mexicans and how it has been said; for that reason, I have been concerned here about the implications of a discursive colonization, that need of Euro-Americans to consume information about Santa Feans, while dismissing their retaliations against, and resistance to, encroachment, even their feigned disinterest in it.

When Spanish-Mexican women went ahead in 1876 with a scheduled rite in the fall—a procession through the streets honoring the Virgin—"La Conquistadora," Mrs. Henry Wetter, newly arrived in Santa Fe and married to one of the wealthier migrants, depicted the following spring in a letter to her sister, not merely the strange customs of the local inhabitants, but their humble, peasant appearance and demure demeanors. Surprised hours later, when during the same festival, local women inverted their behavior—shouting as they celebrated the completion of the procession, dancing and singing loudly at the dance hall—Mrs. Wetter did not mention the revelry, preferring instead to render the women as pious, mantilla-clad Catholics.[41] Actual responses to Euro-Americans took many forms, but Spanish-Mexicans were never credited with those that did not confirm stereotypes already inscribed in the written record. Instead, their emotions were ignored and their counteractivities were conspicuously misrepresented or underrepresented.

The colonization of women in different regions of the American continents has sustained a paralleling trajectory, portrayed most heartedly in the works of many scholars, Latin American and Euro-American, in one of two ways: Women are either passively victimized ("victim" itself implies passivity, but I use the term here to suggest that the encoding and constant linkage are as interesting as the practices from which it derives), or they are single, solitary resisters. The framework transplanted in the Americas for understanding women's activities continuously abides these binary, artificial dichotomies. These make for tidy categorization but are hopelessly inaccurate. Women took on roles and acted out behaviors that cannot be readily lumped into the traditional categories—virgin, martyr, witch, or whore, to borrow the historian Elizabeth Perry's distinctions based on her examination of fifteenth-century Spain's medical literature.[42] Similarly, a new paradigm developed more recently is inadequate because it is a triangle that inserts, again, women such as Malintzín Tenepal (La Malinche), Sor Juana Inés de la Cruz, and others in the historical record, as mediators, as cultural go-betweens, translators, useful to the accomplishments of their own colonization.

The truly gifted Malintzín—"sold" (as noted previously) to the Spaniard Hernán Cortés (who is rarely identified by his ethnicity, gender, or full name)—was trilingual and evidently blessed with the talents of a conversationalist; she, and the poetic genius of Sor Juana, who relocated herself to the more serene surroundings of the convent, as close to a women's commune as was possible in her age, become, in male and centralist historiography, either reified or centered awkwardly in a minefield peopled by other problematic characters.

Typologized, and in such settings, woman is indeed created—a figment of the male imagination. When the female figures, the women, prove a bit too unadaptable, as in Octavio Paz's effort to reconstruct and resituate the recalcitrant but evidently "beautiful" Sor Juana, the only possibility is to position men and their institutions (like the Catholic Church) at opposite corners of the triangle, with "woman" in the middle—male descriptors at the ready to disprove the nasty aspersions cast upon such women today by equally unruly feminist and lesbian historians.[43]

This is especially Paz's worry about the debate over Sor Juana's sexuality—her "supposed" lesbian inclinations, her letters to, and verses penned for, other women. It is interesting, and neither accidental nor coincidental, that Malintzín, a Mayan, receives no such attention and that her sexual laxity and mores are presumed, by virtue of either her enslavement—that is, her status—or her race, "Indian." However, if I practice what I preach, in "recovering" Malintzín as a multifaceted and complex character in history, I would also have to focus on the processes of what for her and others might be termed "disidentification"—complex and multidimensional interactions of inscription and of creating identities based on what *they* (the previously disidentified and the unknown) were not, that is, non-European; I would also have to acknowledge their replacement of an identity based on a recovered self.[44] Using this method of writing history, we find that Malintzín becomes, first and in the present tense, an identified personality and character living in a particular period—a linguist, a resister, and manipulator essential to the conquest of the Valley of Mexico, one of several indigenous mistresses (sexual partners) of the conquistadores, and also a person from whom such facts and attributions have been repeatedly removed, by the original European colonizers and by many generations of historians. Simultaneously, her recovery, reconstruction, and deconstruction across time keep pace with the trends historians and history follow. Like Doña Gertrudis Barceló, she becomes, in the present era, an exemplar, and she might even be said to have occupied that role in her own time.

Similar problematic but unproblemitized inclinations and assumptions inform the work of women historians in the western U.S. frontier, but are not as flagrant in their disregard for women. Such books and articles regularly portray women acting and responding, and they situate women's activities with more attention to differences and to the nuances of takeover.[45] Historians of the frontier, particularly feminist scholars, have reoriented an entire subfield of history to include women, but they also have insisted on reimagining their characters in history. Outlaws, prostitutes, Asian and Mexican immigrants, matriarchs, diarists, novelists, reformers, and soldaderas populate the communities we portray. Domestic ideology, female moral authority, interracial relations, economic colonization, wage-labor discrimination, and household economic activities are just a few of the new subjects presented in current books and articles on women of the western United States. Cultural theory, literary criticism, and the new ethnography have also begun to shape this work that only twenty years ago trudged along behind cowboys-and-Indians history, or consistently played second fiddle in the western narratives composed out of the old, stale ingredients.[46]

Contemporary feminist frontier scholarship is not immune from other problems, some of which originate in the difficulties of locating and deciphering the sources, and others having to do with not comprehending indigenous languages. Until those conditions are remedied and more historians from Chicano and Native communities are trained—scholars who bring to the field "internal" and organic knowledge, as well as that learned from books and in archives—the primary revisions in western women's history will duplicate the shortsightedness found in history written by men about men. The challenge arises not from a need solely for multicultural histories, but from the lags produced because too few historians are excavating the Spanish archives and, if they are Native American, Latino, Asian, or African American, too few are also trained professionally or formally in graduate research programs.[47]

In the subfield of western American history, Chicano historians are more numerous in the academy than are Native American historians. But an interesting set of paradoxes pervades. Historians of Native America—that is, who are not Native Americans themselves—dominate the academic field of Native American history, whereas Chicano history is still largely in the hands of Chicano and Chicana academics.

These facts are crucial to the writing of history because, as the American Historical Association's reports indicate, despite high percentages of retirements in the profession of history and insufficient numbers of people entering the field, ethnic minorities remain severely underrepresented. Ethnic representation in this case signifies the presence of traditionally nationally underrepresented ethnic minorities—that is, the national minority groups of this society, the Native American, Chicano, Asian American, and African American groups—but it also implies another set of problems within the field that has to do with specialization and training. Like other disciplines, history is also currently pockmarked by discussions about the politics and policies of the nonnative studying others, about who has access to sources as well as to jobs.

The entire cycle of misinformation, not only about the Spanish-Mexican women of any nineteenth-century community but also about many ethnic minority women, is self-perpetuating. Without professionally trained, employed historians, students interested in topics in Chicano, Native American, Asian American, and African American history are seriously handicapped. Lacking linguistic facility in indigenous languages, unable to find adequate support for research, scholars suffer additional pressing demands. The nineteen professionally trained Chicana historians in the United States, the equally few Native American or Asian American women historians, necessarily find their tasks as historians hampered by conditions within the discipline and in university settings, where the bulk of resources continue to support work in the history of the nation-state, that is, political history or cultural and intellectual history, but not ethnohistory. The end result is that the entire discipline suffers from an absence of interpretations, from the limitations of systemic exclusion.[48]

These factual details are rarely appended to any monograph written about people considered to be marginal or uncommon in standard U.S. history texts, but the assessments are as crucial as uncovering the evidence about women's lives and restoring them to history, are central to the methods I have deployed in this book. The Spanish-Mexican women of Santa Fe are thus important because they were once invisible, and because that invisibility sheds light on the ways history has been written, not only on the problems of the past but also on the functions of history. To ignore the contradictory implications, political and academic, of this type of social history, of its methods and inquiries, is to perpetuate an injustice on the characters in my story and to further marginalize them. To do less with them and to simply settle for telling the story through the "facts" also compromises the task I set out to accomplish—to weave a narrative so that these and other Spanish-Mexican women would not be ignored, and to open up other possibilities for interpreting their and our lives, even under colonization.

Epilogue

New Mexican women in the nineteenth century suffered the deformation of their social, political, cultural, and economic worlds, emerging from this legacy having won the battle for cultural survival while losing the one over resources. Even in the period of conquest examined here, the speculative fictions about women, the eroticized imaginary of the Euro-American colonizers, wove their way into U.S. society; and we are still recipients of this legacy. Today, the descendants of the women described face many of the same struggles and erasures—being absent from much historical writing, and contemplated from afar by the newly arrived; what separates this generation from previous ones is often hard to comprehend, much less contemplate. As other New Mexicans, such as myself, take a different road—academic, political, or otherwise, within New Mexico or outside it—the strings that pull us back are in fact history's consistencies and ironies.

We can leave New Mexico, but it never leaves us; we can acculturate Euro-American ways, but Mexico and Native callings are never far behind. In fact, in the identity game, our *negotiated* Mexicanness or Indianness, and, especially, the fear of Indianness, which is where much of our identity struggles have resided, provide a link between the centuries. New Mexicans rarely conceived of themselves as either Spanish or Mexican and certainly less as mestizos/mestizas: They tended last century to describe themselves mostly as non-Indians, "gente de habla español" (people who speak the Spanish language), as Roman and Apostolic Catholics, which, again, was established as non-Indianness. Indian meant "non-Christian." Between the time Spain exited the stage and

Mexico named itself, not enough time had elapsed for a political naming ceremony or for a national identificatory practice to take root. That remains one of the larger, unresolved issues as to why in this century New Mexicans took to calling themselves, first, Spanish-Americans, and then Hispanics or Hispanos, but rarely Mexican. In private circles, in familial settings, the word "Chicano" was common throughout the twentieth century. "Mexicano" was also common, but it specified the language spoken ("We speak *mexicano*"). "American" was never in question, but "Euro-Americanism" was. Returning from World War II, New Mexico's Chicano veterans would argue that they were 100 percent American, so much so that more of them died in that war and in the Vietnam War than those from any other ethnic group in the United States.

This ability to philosophize, posture, and profess is probably also inherited from the nineteenth-century testimonies and trepidations so common to the stories and lives outlined in this volume. Moving toward the next millennium, I close with a lesson for all Chicanitas—this is one chapter in our history. Abide it, but refuse the favors colonization imposes. Our resistance makes for a far richer story.

NOTES

PROLOGUE

1. For traditional interpretations of the takeover of New Mexico, see, for example, Ralph Emerson Twitchell, *The Story of the Conquest of Santa Fe: New Mexico and the Building of Old Fort Marcy*, A.D., *1846* (Santa Fe: Historical Society of New Mexico, 1923), and Calvin Horn, *New Mexico's Troubled Years: The Story of the Early Territorial Governors* (Albuquerque: University of New Mexico Press, 1963). For a more complex rendering, see Howard Roberts Lamar, *The Far Southwest, 1846–1912: A Territorial History* (New York: Norton, 1970). On Kearny's speech, see Twitchell, *Story of the Conquest*, 30. On women's poverty, see Deena J. González, "The Widowed Women of Santa Fe: Assessments on the Lives of an Unmarried Population, 1850–1880," in Arlene Scadron, ed., *On Their Own: Widows and Widowhood in the American Southwest, 1848–1939* (Champaign: University of Illinois Press, 1989), 65–90, reprinted in Ellen DuBois and Vicki Ruiz, eds., *Unequal Sisters: A Multicultural Reader in U.S. Women's History* (New York: Routledge, 1990), 34–50. On women in Spanish law, see José María Ots Capdequí, "Bosquejo histórico de los derechos de la mujer casada en la legislación de Indias," *Revista general de legislación y jurisprudencia* 132 (1918), 162–182. On New Mexican women, see Louis H. Warner, "Conveyance of Property, The Spanish and Mexican Way," *New Mexico Historical Review* 5:4 (October 1931), 334–359, and Rosalind Z. Rock, "'Pido y Suplico': Women and the Law in Spanish New Mexico, 1697–1763," *New Mexico Historical Review* 45 (April 1990), 145–159.

2. See, for example, the important work of Edward Spicer, *Cycles of Conquest: The Impact of Spain, Mexico, and the United States on the Indians of the Southwest, 1533–1960* (Tucson, University of Arizona Press, 1962); Elizabeth John, *Storms Brewed in Other Men's Worlds: The Confrontation of Indians, Spanish, and French in the Southwest, 1540–1795* (College Station: Texas A & M University Press, 1975); and Jack Forbes, *Apache,*

Navaho and Spaniard (Norman: University of Oklahoma Press, 1960). A more linear, top-to-bottom interpretation can be found in the first chapters of Richard White, *"It's Your Misfortune and None of My Own": A New History of the American West* (Norman: University of Oklahoma Press, 1991).

3. For a survey of trends, see Antonio Rios-Bustamante, "New Mexico in the Eighteenth Century: Life, Labor and Trade in La Villa de San Felipe de Albuquerque, 1706–1790," *Aztlan: A Journal of Chicano Studies* 7:3 (Fall 1976), 357–389.

4. See González, "The Widowed Women of Santa Fe," in Scadron, *On Their Own,* 65–90 or in DuBois and Ruiz, *Unequal Sisters,* 34–50. In this book, see chapter 3. For examples of the historian's necessity to reiterate the role of marriage for women, referenced in such phrases as "[given] the shortage of men on the frontier," see Rock, *"'Pido y Suplico,'"* 158.

5. For a criticism of the developments, as they resituate critical theory and duplicate a "master" discourse, see Barbara Christian, "The Race for Theory," *Cultural Critique,* 6 (Spring 1987) special issue, *The Nature and Context of Minority Discourse,* ed. Abdul R. JanMohamed and David Lloyd.

6. AASF, "Diligencias Matrimoniales," 1824, Roll 69, frame 591; on the issue of marriage choice, see the work of Patricia Seed, "The Church and the Patriarchal Family: Marriage Conflicts in Sixteenth and Seventeenth-Century New Spain," *Journal of Family History* (Fall 1985), 284–293, and "Marriage Promises and the Value of a Woman's Testimony in Colonial Mexico," *Signs: Journal of Women in Culture and Society* 13:2 (Winter 1988), 253–276.

7. For an example of more prototypical work, see Roger McGrath, *Gunfighters, Highwaymen, and Vigilantes:—Violence on the Frontier* (Berkeley: University of California Press, 1984); an approach deploying gender as a means for discussing the matter of violence can be found in Anne M. Butler, *Gendered Justice in the American West: Women Prisoners in Men's Penitentiaries* (Urbana: University of Illinois Press, 1997). For a newer and alternative historiography, see the work of three historians: Patricia Nelson Limerick, *The Legacy of Conquest: The Unbroken Past of the American West,* (New York: Norton, 1987); Spicer, *Cycles of Conquest;* and Ramón A. Gutiérrez, *When Jesus Came, the Corn Mothers Went Away: Marriage, Sexuality, and Power in New Mexico, 1500–1846* (Palo Alto, Calif.: Stanford University Press, 1991).

8. See USCB, *Twentieth Census of Population* for current statistics that place Puerto Rican women and Chicanas in the lowest percentile of all wage-earning women; for contrasts to other immigrants in the late nineteenth century, see USCB, Tenth, Eleventh, and Twelfth Censuses. On Weber and the iron-cage metaphor, see Ronald T. Takaki, *Iron Cages: Race and Culture in 19th-Century America* (Seattle: University of Washington Press, 1988, orig. ed., 1979).

9. See Roxanne Dunbar Ortiz, *Roots of Resistance: Land Tenure in New Mexico, 1680–1980* (Los Angeles: Chicano Studies Research Center, UCLA, 1980); and Victor Westphall, *Mercedes Reales: Hispanic Land Grants of the Upper Rio Grande Region* (Albuquerque: University of New Mexico Press, 1983). For a recent work that carries forward the implications of land theft and treaty obligations, see Malcolm Ebright, *Land Grants and Lawsuits in Northern New Mexico* (Albuquerque: University of New Mexico Press, 1994).

10. For textbooks that evoke a similar understanding of nineteenth-century American history and trace key differences, see Benjamin B. Ringer, *`We, the People' and Others: Duality and America's Treatment of Its Racial Minorities* (New York: Tavistock, 1983) and Takaki, *Iron Cages.* Specific work on Asian Americans in the U.S. West suggests as well the need to reread chronology and social relations. See Valerie Matsumoto,

Farming the Home Place: A Japanese American Community in California, 1919–1982 (Ithaca: Cornell University Press, 1993) and Judy Yung, *Unbound Feet: A Social History of Chinese Women in San Francisco* (Berkeley: University of California Press, 1995). On African Americans, see Quintard Taylor, *The Forging of the Black Community: Seattle's Central District from 1870 through the Civil Rights Era* (Seattle: University of Washington Press, 1994) and William Loren Katz, *The Black West: A Documentary and Pictorial History of the African-American Role in the Westward Expansion of the United States* (New York: Oxford University Press, 1996). Examples of studies on Native peoples and the matter of survival versus resistance include Albert Hurtado, *Indian Survival on the California Frontier* (New Haven: Yale University Press, 1988).

11. See Dunbar Ortiz, *Roots of Resistance*, and Ebright, *Land Grants*.

12. On the legal codes binding marriage choices, as well as on the matter of terms deployed, see Rock, "'*Pido y Suplico*'," 148.

13. For an explanation which contextualizes merchant capitalism of an earlier period, and suggests that the trade after 1821 should be examined with that in mind, see Gutiérrez, *When Jesus Came*, chapter 10. For an example of the wills, see the settlement of the estate of María Micaela Baca, Santa Fe, 1832, Roll 1, MANM (microfilm, NM-SRC), frame 996; another document for a Maria Miquela Baca can be found in Inventory of Maria Miquela Baca, April 22, 1830, Twitchell Coll.(Manuscript Division, NMSRC); for contrast, see *Probate Court Journals*, SFCR, NMSRC, Books D and E (1870–1897).

14. From the book by that title—John, *Storms Brewed in Other Men's Worlds*.

15. In the past twenty to thirty years, scholars have shifted increasingly their interpretations to describe and detail the resistance of women to domination. See Asunción Lavrin, ed., *Latin American Women: Historical Perspectives* (Westport, Conn.: Greenwood, 1978); Mona Etienne and Eleanor Leacock, eds., *Women and Colonization: Anthropological Perspectives* (New York: Praeger, 1980); Rosaura Sánchez and Rosa Martínez Cruz, *Essays on La Mujer* (Los Angeles: University of California Press, 1969). For monographs on nineteenth-century American history, see Suzanne Lebsock, *The Free Women of Petersburg: Status and Culture in a Southern Town, 1784–1860* (New York, Norton, 1984). For the West, see Paula Petrik, *No Step Backward: Women and Family on the Rocky Mountain Mining Frontier, Helena, Montana 1865–1900* (Helena: Montana Historical Society Press, 1987); Peggy Pascoe, *Relations of Rescue: The Search for Female Moral Authority in the American West, 1874–1939* (New York: Oxford University Press, 1990). And for the late nineteenth century and early twentieth, see Sarah Deutsch, *No Separate Refuge: Culture, Class, and Gender on an Anglo-Hispanic Frontier in the American Southwest, 1880–1940* (New York: Oxford University Press, 1987). Exciting works are being written on colonization and colonialism by international feminists. See, for example, Lata Mani, "Multiple Mediations," *Feminist Studies*, Summer 1990 and Chandra Mohanty, "Under Western Eyes: Feminist Scholarship and Colonial Discourses," *Boundaries* 2:12–13 (Spring/Fall 1984), 333–358. On twentieth-century Chicana history, one of the most revisionary works is Emma Pérez, *The Decolonial Imaginary: Writing Chicanas into History* (Bloomington: Indiana University Press, 1999). Also, see Vicki L. Ruiz, *From Out of the Shadows: Mexican Women in Twentieth-Century America* (New York: Oxford University Press, 1998).

CHAPTER 1

1. *Alejandro Le Grand v. Manuela Baca*, April 6, 1832, JCP, MANM, Roll 15 (microfilm, NMSRC), frames 3–4. This document outlines the lawsuit and the charges; the documents for the summer trial are referenced in the Ritch Collection, HEH, mis-

cellany docket. All primary documents hereafter are listed by their location at one of the four archival sites I used: the New Mexico State Records Center (NMSRC), the Coronado Collection at the University of New Mexico (UNM), the Bancroft Library at the University of California, Berkeley (BAN), or the Henry E. Huntington Library in San Marino, Calif. (HEH). Differences exist in frame numbers in the microfilm editions at each of these locations and not all microfilm collections are complete at each archive. In addition, miscellany, receipts, ledgers, and census notations, are scattered among the papers of individuals—in this case, Governor Ritch, and in others, at the NMSRC, for example, the Chavez or Twitchell papers. In all notes, I have cited the place and nearest location of the miscellany.

2. *La Grand v. Baca*, frames 3–4; on the peso's values, see Warner, "Conveyance of Property," 337.

3. All of the cases selected for this section were chosen from among the cases indexed in the NMSRC under "Judicial Court Proceedings" between 1820 and 1846. The individual cases and documents are cited according to the numbering system employed in the collected microfilm edition in which they were actually used, and not always as they may appear in the available (original) microfilmed records located at the NMSRC.

4. Alejandro Le Grand v. Miguel Sena, February 13, 1832, JCP, MANM, Roll 15 (microfilm, NMSRC), frames 3–4; Sena Family Papers, private collector, Denver. The second paragraph in the private papers, which number twelve pages altogether, reads: "my wife knows nothing of these affairs, but she agreed to manage my own while I was away. Her brothers assisted us in our time of need. All were ensuring that my wishes were followed" (Mi esposa no sabiendo de mis negocios se [encargo]. Sus hermanos nos ayudaron por necesidad y por que yo lo pedí).

5. Tax rolls, Jurisdiction of Santa Fe, MANM, NMSRC, unindexed folders, box 32. The tax rolls were copied for my use by the office of the state historian; I reordered them by year and jurisdiction, but the majority remain unindexed and gaps exist in the order of the pages. In addition, the tax rolls appeared across several private collections at the NMSRC. The best place to begin is with the Santa Fe jurisdiction and then scroll across the miscellaneous documents for each microfilm roll of a particular year.

6. On trading with the Indians and on the complex relations that had formed since Euro-American merchants came on the scene, see David Weber, *The Mexican Frontier, 1821–1846: The American Southwest under Mexico* (Albuquerque: University of New Mexico Press, 1982), chapter 5, especially 95–98. On attitudes toward the Pueblo Indians, see G. Emlen Hall and David J. Weber, "Mexican Liberals and the Pueblo Indians, 1821–1829," *New Mexico Historical Review* 59:1 (1984), 5–120.

7. Several scholars have written about honor in other societies. See, for example, the essays edited by J. G. Peristiany, *Honour and Shame: The Values of Mediterranean Society* (Chicago: University of Chicago Press, 1966) and by David D. Gilmore, *Honor and Shame and the Unity of the Mediterranean* (Washington, D.C.: American Anthropological Association, 1987); for a critique of a pan-mediterranean code of honor, see Michael Herzfeld, "Honor and Shame: Problems in the Comparative Analysis of Moral Systems," *Man* 15, 339–351; on a Greek community, see J. K. Campbell, *Honour, Family and Patronage: A Study of Institutions and Moral Values in a Greek Mountain Community* (Oxford, Eng.: Clarendon, 1964). On New Mexico, see Ramón A. Gutiérrez, "Honor Ideology, Marriage Negotiation, and Class-Gender Domination in New Mexico, 1690–1846," *Latin American Perspectives*, 12, Winter 1985, 81–104; and on colonial Mexico, see Patricia Seed, *To Love, Honor, and Obey in Colonial Mexico: Conflicts over Marriage Choice, 1574–1821*, (Stanford, Calif.: Stanford University Press, 1988). For contrast, about a Bedouin society, see Lila Abu-Lughod,

Veiled Sentiments: Honor and Poetry in a Bedouin Society (Berkeley: University of California Press, 1986).

8. Weber, *The Mexican Frontier*, 97–100.

9. For a discussion of merchant capitalism and merchandising before the independence period, see Gutiérrez, *When Jesus Came*, 318–327. On the terrain, see Max Moorhead, *New Mexico's Royal Road: Trade and Travel on the Chihuahua Trail* (Norman: University of Oklahoma Press, 1958), chap. 1; for photographs, see Joan Myers and Marc Simmons, *Along the Santa Fe Trail* (Albuquerque: University of New Mexico Press, 1986).

10. *Doña Ana María Rendón v. Doña Juliana González*, June 19, 1845, MANM, Roll 19 (microfilm, NMSRC), frames 156–157. On the admonishment, see June 19, 1845, MANM, Roll 19 (microfilm, HEH), the frame without a number, toward the end of the roll. The Sena Family Papers also carry a testimonial note with undiscernible signatures, but which is dated, "June 19, 1845, Santa Fe, Nuevo Mejico." It reads: "I do not know what decent people propose in such a scandalous situation, but I do know the rooms are disorderly" ("No sabiendo que hacer ni lo que gente decente [propone] a una vida tan escandalosa, se que los cuartos estan en desorden").

11. *Juan Pablo Pacheco v. José Antonio Trujillo*, July 16, 1822, JCP, MANM, Roll 1 (microfilm, NMSRC), frame 1262. The matter of annulment was to be taken up later in the ecclesiastical court, the father stipulated.

12. For sources on various interpretations which trace the political economy of marriage and sex, see Gayle Rubin, "The Traffic in Women: Notes Toward a Political Economy of Sex," in Rayna Reiter, ed., *Toward an Anthropology of Women* (New York: Monthly Review Press, 1975); Adelaida del Castillo, "Malintzín Tenepal: A Preliminary Look into a New Perspective," in Sánchez and Cruz, *Essays on La Mujer*, 124–149; June Nash, "Aztec Women: The Transition from Status to Class in Empire and Colony," in Etienne and Leacock, *Women and Colonization*, 134–148; Herbert Gutman, *The Black Family in Slavery and Freedom, 1750–1925* (New York: Pantheon Books, 1976). On colonial Mexican situations in regard to women's rights in the Catholic Church, see Seed, "Marriage Promises," 259.

13. How much ecclesiastical decisions shaped civil ones, or vice versa, is the topic of debate. To trace the contrasts, see Gutiérrez, "Honor Ideology," *Latin American Perspectives* (Winter 1985), 81–104, and Seed, *To Love, Honor, and Obey*; and on the New Mexico case, see Rock, "'Pido y Suplico,'" 148.

14. See the indexes for either the Spanish Archives of New Mexico (SANM) or the Mexican Archives of New Mexico (MANM), NMSRC. On women's property and inheritances in other regions, see Asunción Lavrin and Edith Couturier, "Dowries and Wills: A View of Women's Socioeconomic Role in Colonial Guadalajara and Puebla, 1640–1790," *Hispanic American Historical Review* 59 (1979), 280–304; for New Mexico cases, see Angelina Veyna, "'It Is My Last Wish That . . . ': A Look at Colonial Nuevo Mexicanas through Their Testaments," in Adela de la Torre and Beatríz Pesquera, eds., *Building with Our Hands: New Directions in Chicana Scholarship* (Berkeley: University of California Press, 1993), 91–108.

15. For a different explanation, based on social inequality, see Jane Collier, *Marriage and Inequality in Classless Societies* (Stanford, Calif.: Stanford University Press, 1988). For an earlier and still useful feminist analysis of capitalism, patriarchy, and marriage, see Juliet Mitchell, *Woman's Estate* (New York: Vintage, 1973). For criticism of the model based only on partriarchy, see Seed, *To Love, Honor, and Obey*.

16. *Santiago Armijo v. María Josefa Anaya*, August 4, 1830, JCP, SANM, Roll 11 (microfilm, NMSRC), frame 531. On the accusation on the plaza and the outcome, see the

granddaughter's later recollection of the incident in a family story in the Ritch Collection, RI 1823 (MS, HEH).

17. Civil courts were not the only places where disputes were resolved; complaints could also be filed in ecclesiastical courts, which, until the late colonial period, were the preferred site for conflict resolution. See France V. Scholes, "Church and State in New Mexico, 1610–1650," *New Mexico Historical Review* 11 (1936), 9–76; Gutiérrez, *When Jesus Came*, chaps. 8–9.

18. For a description, see Twitchell, *The Story of the Conquest*.

19. *Roybal v. Chaves*, May 21, 1833, Roll 16, MANM (microfilm, NMSRC), frame 1020. For the document outlining the tragedy, see the same Roll 16, MANM (microfilm, HEH), the unnumbered frame toward the end of the roll.

20. See, for example, Jennifer Coates and Deborah Cameron, eds., *Women in Their Speech Communities*, (London: Longman, 1989) and Ronald Wardhaugh, *Languages in Competition: Dominance, Diversity, and Decline* (Oxford, Eng.: B. Blackwell, 1987). On contemporary manifestations of the significance of language and of Chicana cultural identity or integrity, see Angie Chabram-Dernersesian, "I Throw Punches for my Race, but I Don't Want to Be a Man: Writing Us—Chica-nos (Girl, Us)/Chicanas—into the Movement Script," in Lawrence Grossberg, Cary Nelson, and Paula A. Treichler, eds., *Cultural Studies* (New York: Routledge, 1992), 81–95.

21. The practice of settling many types of disputes before an arbiter is not unusual even in parts of Latin America today; see, for example, the film detailing conflict resolution, by the anthropologist Laura Nader, "Small Injustices," 1983. On the items introduced by the traders, see Marc Simmons, *The Little Lion of the Southwest: The Life of Manuel Antonio Chaves* (Chicago: Sage, 1973), 159–213.

22. See Weber, *The Mexican Frontier*, 44.

23. Ibid, 50.

24. Ibid, 74. On the Franciscans in New Mexico and on the problems of secularization, see Marta Weigle, *Brothers of Light, Brothers of Blood: The Penitentes of the Southwest* (Albuquerque: University of New Mexico Press, 1976), 20–24.

25. For a discussion of tensions in civil and ecclesiastical courts in the colonial period, see Gutiérrez, *When Jesus Came*, chap. 3.

26. I arrived at one thousand by counting, as cases, documents listing complaints of any sort; some are one paragraph long, and others, several pages. I used the period 1810–1840 to mark off a convenience sample, and, within the sample, I selected randomly, in every fourth roll of microfilm, one case for every fifth year; the total number of ecclesiastical documents examined in this way numbered two hundred.

27. [No author] Note To Cura Madriaga, (no day or month) 1830, AASF, LDD, No. 18 (microfilm, NMSRC).

28. Scholes, "Church and State," 15.

29. *Doña María Ursula Chávez v. Don Pedro Bautista Pino*, August 1815, SANM, Roll 18 (microfilm, NMSRC). On Chávez, also see Janet Lecompte, "The Independent Women of Hispanic New Mexico," *Western Historical Quarterly* (January 1985), 25. On the church suit, see José Antonio Chávez to Alcalde Don Manuel Vigil, July 12, 1835, Roll 19, MANM (microfilm, NMSRC), frame 901.

30. *Juana Lopes v. John Scolly*, April 8, 1844, Otero Collection, Bernardo Vásquez Franco Papers (Manuscript Div., NMSRC). For developments in this account leading to the litigation cited above, I relied on the Sena Family Papers, private collection, Denver, including two legible pages of "Complaint and Response" of Juana Lopes in "a Santa Fe court, April, 1844." The collector wishes to remain anonymous, but I have my own transcribed, hand-written copy of the document. The research necessary to link

the document in the NMSRC microfilm collection and the one discovered in these private papers suggests what role luck plays for historians of frontier history seeking evidence beyond the confines or limitations of the library or archive. Many such papers detailing nineteenth-century women's lives are still in the hands of families and heirs. A former state historian, Stanley Hordes, first brought the 1844 document to my attention.

31. See *Gaspar Ortiz v. Juan Nepomuceno*, August 26, 1822, JCP, Roll 1 (microfilm, NMSRC), frame 1270. Also see Ramón A. Gutiérrez, "Honor, Witchcraft, and Sexual Inversion in Colonial New Mexico" (paper delivered at the Western History Association Meeting, Salt Lake City, Utah, October 12, 1984); and Marc Simmons, *Witchcraft in the Southwest: Spanish and Indian Supernaturalism on the Rio Grande* (Lincoln: University of Nebraska Press, 1980).

32. For comparisons to other Spanish-Mexican northern frontier areas, see Albert Camarillo, *Chicanos in a Changing Society: From Mexican Pueblos to American Barrios in Santa Barbara and Southern California, 1848–1930* (Cambridge: Havard University Press, 1979); Arnoldo de Leon, *The Tejano Community* (Albuquerque: University of New Mexico Press, 1982); Mario Garcia, *Desert Immigrants: The Mexicans of El Paso 1880–1920* (New Haven: Yale Univeristy Press, 1981); Richard Griswold del Castillo, *The Los Angeles Barrio, 1850–1890: A Social History* (Berkeley: University of California Press, 1979); Lisbeth Haas, *Conquests and Historical Identities in California, 1769–1936* (Berkeley: University of California Press, 1995).

33. On laundering, but after the war, see González, "The Widowed Women of Santa Fe," in Scadron, *On Their Own*, 69.

34. Petition of Juan Francisco González, (no day or month), 1829, JCP, Roll 10 (microfilm, NMSRC), frame 177.

35. *Cura Juan Tomás Terrazas v. José Antonio Girón*, September 2, 1823, JCP, Roll 2, MANM (microfilm, NMSRC), frame 1295.

36. Proceedings against Rafael Montoya, for the murder of his wife, December 22, 1843, JCP, Roll 32, MANM (microfilm, NMSRC), frame 1295.

37. For Santa Fe after the war, see González, "The Widowed Women," in Scadron, *On Their Own*; for Denver, in the same anthology, see Joyce D. Goodfriend, "The Struggle for Survival: Widows in Denver, 1880–1912. On Los Angeles, see Barbara Laslett, "Household Structure on an American Frontier: Los Angeles, California, in 1850," *American Journal of Sociology* 81 (1975), 109–128.

38. Complaint of María Loreta García, October 20, 1835, AASF, LDD, No.5 (microfilm, NMSRC); for her testimony, see October 21, 1835, MANM, Roll 16 (microfilm, BAN), unnumbered frame.

39. The best discussion of Mexican ecclesiastical divorce is Silvia M. Arrom, *La mujer mexicana ante el divorcio eclesiástico, 1800–1857* (Mexico City, 1976).

40. For another interpretation that describes New Mexico in this period as feudal, see Lamar, *The Far Southwest*, chap. 1. For an alternative theory of conquest, see Mario Barrera, *Race and Class in the Southwest: A Theory of Racial Inequality* (Notre Dame: University of Notre Dame Press, 1979).

41. *Barbara Roybal v. Joaquín Chaves*, May 21, 1833, JCP, Roll 16, MANM (microfilm, NMSRC), frame 1019; see, for her testimony, May 21, 1833, JCP, Roll 16, MANM (microfilm, BAN), unnumbered frame that precedes frame 1024.

42. For examples of folkloric culture, sayings, and proverbs, see "Relación de las provincias internas," May 23, 1825, Archivo General de la Nación (microcopy, Coronado Collection, University of New Mexico). For a collected variety, see Aurora Lucero-White, comp., *The Folklore of New Mexico* (Santa Fe: Seton Village Press, 1941).

43. *Barbara Roybal v. Joaquín Chaves*, May 21, 1833, JCP, Roll 16, MANM (microfilm, NMSRC), frame 1019; for the quotation about her children, see May 21, 1833, JCP, Roll 16, MANM (microfilm, BAN), unnumbered frame that precedes frame 1023.

44. Ibid., frame 1021. On the neighbor, see the unnumbered frame, Roll 16 (microfilm, BAN).

45. For examples, see settlement of estate of María Micaela Baca, Santa Fe, 1832, Roll 1 (SANM, microfilm, NMSRC), frame 996; María Dolores Sandoval, proceedings against Alcalde Juan Garcia, 1833, Roll 1 (SANM, microfilm, NMSRC), frame 148.

46. See Moorhead, *New Mexico's Royal Road*, chaps. 1–3; Lamar, *The Far Southwest*, chap. 3.

47. Included in "Zubíria Pastoral" (no day or month), 1840, AASF, LDD, No. 2 (microfilm, Coronado Collection, UNM).

48. Ibid., 5.

49. *Gregoria Quintana v. Jesús Martínez*, January 10, 1844, JCP, Roll 33 (microfilm, NMSRC), frames 769–770; and *Francisca Romero v. José Sandoval*, October 9, 1843, JCP, Roll 33 (microfilm, NMSRC), frame 1019.

50. For example, see Inventory of Gertrudis Lucero, March 16, 1818; Will of Maria Michaela Baca, April 22, 1830; Hijuela of Doña Luciana Arce, March 27, 1856; and Will of Maria Guadalupe Martin, n.d.—all are in the Twitchell Collection, Wills and Estates (Manuscript Div., NMSRC). For a reading of the significance of ordinary household articles, see Veyna, "It Is My Last Wish That . . . " in de la Torre and Pesquera, *Building with Our Hands*, table 6.2, 95, and Richard Eighme Ahlborn, "The Will of a New Mexico Woman in 1762," *NMHR*, 65:3 (July 1990), 319–355.

51. For the rising price of mules and burros, see Interview of José Francisco Chávez, Ritch Collection, Roll 6, HEH.

52. On class in the colonial period, see Gutiérrez, "Marriage, Sex, and the Family," chap. 8, *When Jesus Came*, 227–235; for the early nineteenth century, see Weber, *The Mexican Frontier*, especially chap. 11. On California, see Camarillo, *Chicanos in a Changing Society*. On Texas, see David Montejano, *Anglos and Mexicans in the Making of Texas, 1836–1986* (Austin: University of Texas Press, 1989).

53. *Juan de Jesús Archuleta v. Juan José Salaises*, March 19, 1844, JCP, Roll 26, MANM (microfilm, NMSRC), frames 144–147.

54. See Gutiérrez, *When Jesus Came*, chap. 5.

55. Proceedings against Juan Trujillo, August 6, 1842, JCP, Roll 32 (microfilm, NMSRC), frame 103.

56. USCB, Seventh Census of Population for Santa Fe (microfilm, NMSRC), found less than 4 percent of the population living alone; the 1845 Census in the MANM is missing entire barrios in Santa Fe; the 1823 Census lists two barrios—see Roll 3, MANM (microfilm, NMSRC).

57. On the asylums and other corrective institutions, see David J. Rothman, *The Discovery of the Asylum: Social Order and Disorder in the New Republic* (Boston: Little, Brown, 1971). On Indian policy for the same period, see Francis Paul Prucha, *American Indian Policy in the Formative Years: The Indian Trade and Intercourse Acts, 1790–1834* (New Brunswick, N.J.: Rutgers University Press, 1942), and Loring Brown Priest, *Uncle Sam's Stepchildren: The Reformation of United States Indian Policy, 1865–1887* (New Brunswick: Octagon, 1942).

58. For an interesting discussion of family, in public and private spheres, see Stephanie Coontz, *The Social Origins of Private Life: A History of American Families, 1600–1900* (London: Versa, 1988), chap. 5. For colonial North America, see Helena Wall, *Fierce Communion: Family and Community in Early America* (Cambridge: Harvard University Press, 1990).

59. On the changing numbers of merchants, especially after problems developed between Mexico and the United States, see Lamar, *The Far Southwest*, chap. 5; he estimates that in 1846, four hundred merchants were entering Santa Fe with Kearny's invading forces.

60. For the view that Gonzales was not a mestizo, see Jacqueline Dorgan Meketa, ed., *Legacy of Honor: The Life of Rafael Chacón, A Nineteenth-Century New Mexican* (Albuquerque: University of New Mexico Press, 1986).

61. See, for details of the rebellions and counter-rebellions in New Mexico, Weber, *The Mexican Frontier*, chap. 12, 264–272; also see Lamar, *The Far Southwest*, chap. 2, and Janet LeCompte, *Rebellion in Río Arriba, 1837* (Albuquerque: University of New Mexico Press, 1985).

CHAPTER 2

1. On Africa and labor resistance, see Robin Cohen, "Resistance and Hidden Forms of Consciousness amongst African Workers," in A *Review of African Political Economy* (July 1981), 8–22. On women's resistance in societies organized on authoritarian and nonauthoritarian lines, see the essays in Michelle Zimbalist Rosaldo and Louise Lamphere, eds., *Women, Culture, and Society* (Stanford: Stanford University Press, 1974), especially Jane Collier's essay on "Women in Politics," and Margery Wolf's "Chinese Women: Old Skills in a New Context." For a contemporary collection of reflections on women and political economy, the state, liberation struggles, and identity formulations, see Chandra Talpade Mohanty, Ann Russo, and Lourdes Torres, *Third World Women and the Politics of Feminism* (Bloomington: Indiana University Press, 1991).

2. Santa Fe remained a predominantly Spanish-Mexican community until the late 1940s; see USCB, Seventeenth Census of Population. On cultural accommodation and the host of factors influencing it, broken down by ethnic group, see Richard D. Lambert, ed., *America as a Multicultural Society: The Annals of the American Academy of Political and Social Science* (Philadelphia: American Academy of Political and Social Science, 1981). On assimilation, see the "theories" of Milton Gordon in his *Assimilation in American Life: The Role of Race, Religion, and National Origins* (New York: Oxford University Press, 1964), and for a valuable critique of Gordon and of assimilation theory, see Harry H. Bash, *Sociology, Race, and Ethnicity: A Critique of American Ideological Intrusions upon Sociological Theory* (New York: Gordon and Breach, 1979); for contemporary reviews, see Stephen Steinberg, *The Ethnic Myth: Race, Ethnicity, and Class in America* (Boston: Beacon, 1989), and Michael Omi and Howard Winant, *Racial Formation in the United States: From the 1960s to the 1980s* (New York: Routledge and Kegan Paul, 1987).

3. Weber, *The Mexican Frontier*, 271–272.

4. For examples of antiauthoritarian activities for this period, see Weber, *The Mexican Frontier*, 19, 25. For discussions of the problems within the church, see Weigle, *Brothers of Light, Brothers of Blood*, 19–51; and for examples of such problems during the colonial period, see Gutiérrez, *When Jesus Came*, chap. 3.

5. On the nature of military conflict elsewhere in the Mexican north, see, for California and Texas, Weber, *The Mexican Frontier*, chap. 13. For another, compelling argument that takes racial inequalities into account as well as economic factors, see Barrera, *Race and Class in the Southwest*, chaps. 2 and 3. On the forms of resistance to the invasion of troops, see Meketa, *Legacy of Honor*, 63–68; Alvin Sunseri, *Seeds of Discord: New Mexico in the Aftermath of the American Conquest, 1846–1861* (Chicago: Nelson-Hall, 1979), 101–104; John Taylor Hughes, *Doniphan's Expedition: An Account of the Conquest of New Mexico* (Washington, D.C.: Government Printing Office, 1914); Lecompte, *Rebellion in Rio Arriba*.

6. On the role of smugglers and of bribery, see John E. Sunder, ed., *Matt Field on the Santa Fe Trail* (Norman: University of Oklahoma Press, 1960), 222.

7. I arrive at the estimates of the percentage who were upper class by examining the Census of 1845 (taking into account that because two entire barrios are missing, it represents a severe undercount), and by plotting the "indices of personal wealth," as listed in the U.S. Censuses after the war; see González, "The Widowed Women of Santa Fe," in Scadron, *On Their Own*, 70, and, in this book, Table 2.2; also see Gutiérrez, *When Jesus Came*, chap. 10, table 10–1, for a breakdown by occupation for eight hundred and forty-six (male) heads of household. For evidence of the displacements of New Mexicans, see the recollections of Rafael Chacón in Meketa, *Legacy of Honor*, 86; and Lamar, *The Far Southwest*, 65–66. On the impact of new tariffs and duties, see Weber, *The Mexican Frontier*, 152–153.

8. For an intriguing analysis of the shift from merchant to industrial capitalism, see Geoffrey Kay, *Development and Underdevelopment: A Marxist Analysis* (London: Macmillan, 1975). Chicano and Chicana scholars have recently explored such concepts as well—for example, see Tomas Almaguer, *Racial Fault Lines* (Berkeley, 1994) on nineteenth-century California; and on the Bourbon Reforms for late colonial New Mexico, see Gutiérrez, *When Jesus Came*, 318–327. The implications of economic shifts in nineteenth-century California are also examined in Rosaura Sánchez, "Nineteenth-Century Narratives: The Hubert H. Bancroft Collection," in Ramón Gutiérrez and Genaro Padilla, eds., *Recovering the U.S. Hispanic Literary Heritage* (Houston: Arte Público Press, 1993), 279–292. For a more complete exploration, but with a focus on literary themes and through a Marxist lens, see Rosaura Sánchez, *Telling Identities: The Californio Testimonies* (Minneapolis: University of Minnesota Press, 1995).

9. Kay, *Development and Underdevelopment*, 101. For an interesting analysis of worker resistance and of the need of capitalism to undermine the social order, see Jeff Crisp, *The Story of an African Working Class: Ghanaian Miners' Struggles, 1870–1980*, (London: Zed Books, 1984). On the influence of gender in the politics and policies of the state in Africa, see Kathleen Staudt, "Women's Politics, the State, and Capitalist Transformation in Africa," in Irving Leonard Markovitz, ed., *Studies in Power and Class in Africa* (New York: Oxford University Press, 1987), 193–208. For a work focusing on the contemporary Southwest Borderlands, see Kathleen Staudt, *Free Trade? Informal Economies at the U.S.-Mexico Border* (Philadelphia: Temple University Press, 1998).

10. On this important matter of the centrality of gender, and its accompanying violence, the best work resides in the articles by historian Antonia Castañeda. See her "Gender, Race, and Culture: Spanish-Mexican Women in the Historiography of Frontier California," *Frontiers: A Journal of Women's Studies* 11 (1990), 8–20, and, in de la Torre and Pesquera, *Building with Our Hands*, her "Sexual Violence in the Politics and Policies of Conquest: Amerindian Women and the Spanish Conquest of Alta California," 15–33.

11. On peddlers and fruit vendors, see Sunder, *Matt Field*, 214.

12. *Chiquita Manuel de Anda v. Madama María Brown*, July 8, 1836, JCP (microfilm, NMSRC), Roll 20, frames 411–412, MANM. On the vendor, see *Doña Bárbara Baca v. Doña Isabel Urioste*, April 25, 1835, JCP (microfilm, NMSRC), Roll 20, frames 388–389. On the 1823 and 1845 censuses, see Virginia Langham Olmsted, *New Mexico, Spanish, and Mexican Colonial Census, 1790, 1823, 1845* (Albuquerque: New Mexico Genealogical Society, 1975), Coronado Collection, Zimmerman Library. On wages and poverty, see the comments in the case of *Doña Peregrina Domínguez v. Doña Josefa Baca*, December 16, 1837, JCP (microfilm, NMSRC), Roll 20, frames 455–458, Roll 25, frames 319–368.

13. See USCB, Seventh, Eighth, and Ninth Censuses of Population, for Santa Fe (microfilm, NMSRC), Social Statistics.

14. The road scene shown here appeared in *Harper's Monthly Magazine* in 1854 and had been sketched by an artist who accompanied George Brewerton on a visit to Santa Fe; Brewerton's articles also appeared in the *New Orleans Daily Picayune*.

15. On the successes of merchant capitalism, see Lamar, *The Far Southwest*, 56–81; and for an alternative view, see Gutiérrez, *When Jesus Came*, chap. 10. On the impact of manufactured goods on the local population, and on poverty and indigence, see Sister Blandina Segale, *At the End of the Santa Fe Trail* (Milwaukee: Bruce Publishing, 1948), 104. Women consistently comprised the majority of the town's population throughout this period. See the Seventh, Eighth, Ninth, and Tenth Censuses of Population, for Santa Fe (microfilm, NMSRC).

16. *María Francisca Sena v. Don Benito Larragoita*, February 25, 1845, JCP, (microfilm, NMSRC), Roll 40, frames 470–472.

17. See Janet Lecompte, "The Independent Women of Hispanic New Mexico," *The Western Historical Quarterly* (January 1981), 20; her source, was a letter, author unknown, dated July 29, 1841, reprinted in *New Mexico Historical Review* 5 (July 1930), 299–304. On the type of work women and children did, from vending to field labor, see Stella Drumm, ed., *The Diary of Susan Shelby Magoffin, 1846–1847: Down the Santa Fe Trail and into Mexico* (Lincoln: University of Nebraska Press, 1982), 131–132, and Sunder, *Matt Field*, 214; on women's work and morality, see John Francis McDermott, ed., *Travels in Search of the Elephant: The Wanderings of Alfred S. Waugh, Artist, in Louisiana, Missouri, and Santa Fe, in 1845–1846* (St. Louis: Missouri Historical Society, 1951), 120–121.

18. W. W. H. Davis, *El Gringo, or New Mexico and Her People* (New York: Harper and Brothers, 1857), 85.

19. Between August 1846, when the soldiers first arrived, and December 1848, when New Mexico was declared a territory of the United States, perhaps as many as fifteen hundred soldiers occupied Santa Fe; the resident population approximated forty-five hundred. On the soldiers, see Dwight L. Clarke, *Stephen Watts Kearny, Soldier of the West* (Norman: University of Oklahoma Press, 1961), 130–135. On the population, see USCB, Seventeenth Census of Population, for Santa Fe (microfilm, NMSRC).

20. For data on James Wiley Magoffin, see Allen Johnson, ed., *The Dictionary of American Biography* (New York: Scribner, 1936). On the numbers of merchants accompanying the soldiers, see Lamar, *The Far Southwest*, 58–59; for more details about the Magoffins and other merchants, also see Drumm, *The Diary of Susan Shelby Magoffin*; on the Spiegelbergs, see Hester Jones, "The Spiegelbergs and Early Trade in New Mexico," *El Palacio* 38 (1935), 81–89.

21. For a rare example of a traveler who found New Mexican women "joyous, sociable, kind-hearted creatures, easy and graceful in their manners," see Milo Quaife, ed., *George Wilkins Kendall's Narrative of the Texas–Santa Fe Expedition* (Chicago: R. R. Donnelley, 1929), 321, 335, first published in 1844; the Texas–Santa Fe expedition was a quasi-filibuster affair organized by Euro-American Texans to purportedly annex New Mexico, and readers should keep that in mind when assessing the seemingly favorable commentary about New Mexico's women. The goal was to annex New Mexico as they had annexed Texas.

22. On Field, see Saunder, *Matt Field*, 194; for more favorable commentary, see Brantz Mayer, *Mexico as It Was and as It Is* (Philadelphia: G. B. Zieber, 1847). For another observer who vacillated between positive and negative opinions of Mexicans, see Abiel Abbot Livermore, *The War with Mexico Reviewed* (Boston: American Peace Society, 1860), 8, 196, 282.

23. For a discussion of this aspect of nineteenth-century travelogues and memoirs,

see Susan Reyner Kenneson, "Through the Looking-Glass: A History of Anglo-American Attitudes towards the Spanish-Americans and Indians of New Mexico" (Ph.D. diss., Yale University, 1978), 102. On Pike, see Kenneson, "Through the Looking-Glass," 130. On Pattie, see William Goetzmann, ed., *The Personal Narrative of James O. Pattie* (Philadelphia: Lippincott, 1962); and James Ohio Pattie, *The Personal Narrative of James O. Pattie, of Kentucky* (Ann Arbor: University of Michigan Press, 1966). For a study of the impact of narratives on attitudes toward Indians in the West, during the same period, see Richard Drinnon, *Facing West* (Minneapolis: University of Minnesota Press, 1980).

24. Sunder, *Matt Field*, 209.

25. Ibid., 210–213; various soldiers wrote in their memoirs that the government often paid them through vouchers and sometimes had trouble meeting its payroll. But the point missed by some who accept comments about the army's poverty is that the merchant-trader class was well endowed and did circulate American currency in town. For descriptions of the soldiers' supposed poverty, see Kenneson, "Through the Looking-Glass," 155–156; her source was, A. Wislizenus, "Memoir of a Tour to Northern Mexico, Connected with Col. Doniphan's Expedition, in 1846 and 1847," *Sen. Misc. Doc.*, 26, 30th Cong., 1st sess., 20. Also see Cooke's complaints about how "the invaders are . . . debarred the rights of war to seize needful supplies," in his *Conquest of New Mexico*, 4.

26. On the value of blankets, especially those from Mexico, see Sunder, *Matt Field*, 204–205. On the precursors to the Santa Fe Trade, see Gutiérrez, *When Jesus Came*, chap. 10.

27. See Moorhead, *Commerce of the Prairies*, 167–68. On Frances Calderón de la Barca, the most famous nineteenth-century traveler and observer of Mexico, see her *Life in Mexico*, (New York: E. P. Dutton, 1954).

28. Complaint of Marcelo Pacheco, April 11, 1846, JCP, MANM, Roll 32 (microfilm, Coronado Collection), frame 185. Also see the Euro-Americans fined for "making fandangos without licenses," in SFCR, *Probate Court Journal*, Jury Book, 1848–1856, 137–40.

29. Sunder, *Matt Field*, 213.

30. Alexander B. Dyer, "Mexican War Journal, 1846–1848" (manuscript copy, MNMHL), 96–97.

31. See "Gen. Kearny and the Army of the West: Extracts from the Journal of Lieut. Emory," *Niles National Register* 71 (November 7, 1846), 158.

32. Max Moorhead, *New Mexico's Royal Road: Trade and Travel on the Chihuahua Trail* (Norman, 1958), chap. 1; Milo Milton Quaife, ed., *The Commerce of the Prairies by Josiah Gregg* (Chicago: R. R. Donnolley, 1926), 105–106. See also Max Moorhead, ed., *The Commerce of the Prairies* (Norman: University of Oklahoma Press, 1954). (I used two different editions of *The Commerce of the Prairies*, and these are hereafter identified by the editor, Quaife or Moorhead).

33. Quaife, *Commerce of the Prairies*, 213.

34. Zebulon Pike, *Exploratory Travels through the Western Territory of North America* (Denver: W. H. Lawrence, 1889), 338.

35. Kendall was also an editor for the *New Orleans Picayune*, and his narrative, published in 1844, was widely read. See Quaife, *George Wilkins Kendall's Narrative*, 366–367.

36. George Douglass Brewerton, "Incidents of Travel in New Mexico," *Harper's* 47 (April 1854), 1.

37. Storms recommended the conquest of Mexico to liberate it from its own de-

structive politicians. See Tom Reilly, "Jane McManus Storms: Letters from the Mexican War, 1846–1848," *Southwestern Historical Quarterly* 85 (July–April 1981–82), 21–44.

38. Thomas James, *Three Years among the Indians and Mexicans* (Philadelphia, 1962; orig. Lippincott, ed., St. Louis: Missouri Historical Society, 1916), 88–89.

39. Brewerton, "Incidents of Travel," 578.

40. Ibid., 589.

41. Quaife, *George Wilkins Kendall's Narrative*, 427–429.

42. Sunder, *Matt Field*, 209.

43. Ibid.

44. Brewerton, "Incidents of Travel," 589.

45. For an intriguing analysis of the effects of gambling on the American character, see John Findlay, *People of Chance: Gambling in American Society from Jamestown to Las Vegas* (New York: Oxford University Press, 1986).

46. Moorhead, *Commerce of the Prairies*, 168.

47. Lecompte, "La Tules and the Americans," 218–219.

48. Euro-Americans puzzled over the practice of common-law marriage; see Davis, *El Gringo*, 95, 134–135, and Moorhead, *Commerce of the Prairies*, 182. For a richly detailed assessment of its implications in the colonial period, see Gutiérrez, *When Jesus Came*, chaps. 8 and 9.

49. James Josiah Webb, Memoirs, 1844–1889 (MNMHL, Santa Fe), 43.

50. Quaife, *George Wilkins Kendall's Narrative*, 292; also see Raymund A. Paredes, "The Mexican Image in American Travel Literature, 1831–1869," *New Mexico Historical Review* 52:1 (1977), 11.

51. Drumm, *The Diary of Susan Shelby Magoffin*, 120, 145.

52. Paredes, "The Mexican Image in American Travel Literature," 25.

53. Quoted in Ralph Bieber, ed., *James Josiah Webb's Adventures in the Santa Fe Trade, 1844–1847* (Glendale, Calif.: Arthur H. Clark, 1931), 61.

54. See, for example, Sunder, *Matt Field*; and Fray Angélico Chávez, "Doña Tules, Her Fame and Her Funeral," *El Palacio* 57 (August 1950), 227–234. For an article that does account for sexual and cultural differences, see LeCompte, "The Independent Women," 25–26; and, by the same author, "La Tules and the Americans," *Arizona and the West* (Autumn 1978), 215–30. For discussions of similar disparities between image and reality, and of the historical consequences of women in colonization, see, on the French in Algiers, Malek Alloula, *The Colonial Harem* (Minneapolis: University of Minnesota Press, 1986).

55. Drumm, *The Diary of Susan Shelby Magoffin*, 145.

56. Simmons, *The Little Lion*, 55.

57. Moorhead, *Commerce of the Prairies*, 168; also see Lecompte, "La Tules and the Americans," 218–219.

58. Gregg's *Commerce of the Prairies* was reprinted three times between 1844 and 1857 and translated into several languages; on the conspiracy against the Euro-American government, and on the instrumental role of "a woman of shady character by the name of Tules Barcelona," see Ralph E. Twitchell, *The History of the Military Occupation of the Territory of New Mexico from 1846 to 1851 by the Government of the United States* (Denver: Smith-Brooks, 1909; reprint, New York: Arno Press, 1976), 298.

59. Waddy Thompson, *Recollections of Mexico* (New York: Wiley and Putnam, 1846), 23.

60. See the Seventh and Eighth Censuses of Population for Santa Fe (microfilm, NMSRC). Those most likely to take this line of argument around La Tules's own role in procuring sexual services for men or employing other women might first read the two

hundred travelogues central to my analysis, to develop a sense of the racist and racial-ist tone of the material in this situation of conquest, and might then examine closely the embedded sexist logic of the conquest idioms. While some graduate students in sem-inars at the University of Michigan have apparently contended that Barceló was a madam, "doing women a disservice," the several hundred references in commentary about life in Santa Fe at the time suggest otherwise and the scanty primary evidence (three–four documents involving La Tules herself) about other aspects of her life leaves much to be desired. The comments of graduate critics were relayed to me by Tómas Almaguer, in Albuquerque, New Mexico, July 1994.

61. On prostitutes in the West, see George M. Blackburn and Sherman L. Richards, "The Prostitutes and Gamblers of Virginia City, Nevada, 1870," *Pacific Historical Review* 48:2 (May 1979), 239–258; Lawrence B. de Graaf, "Race, Sex, and Region: Black Women in the American West, 1850–1920," *Pacific Historical Review* 49:2 (May 1980), 285–313; Lucie Cheng Hirata, "Free, Indentured, Enslaved: Chinese Prostitutes in Nineteenth Century America," *Signs: Journal of Women in Culture and Society* 5 (Autumn 1979), 3–29. On Helena, Montana, see Paula Petrik, *No Step Backward: Women and Family on the Rocky Mountain Mining Frontier, Helena, Montana, 1865–1900* (Seattle: University of Washington Press, 1987), chap. 3. Two important monographs are Anne Butler, *Daughters of Joy, Sisters of Mercy: Prostitutes in the American West, 1865–90* (Champaign: University of Illinois Press, 1987); and Marion S. Goldman, *Gold Diggers and Silver Miners: Prostitution and Social Life on the Comstock Lode* (Ann Arbor: University of Michigan Press, 1981). For an overview of prostitution in the United States, see Ruth Rosen, *The Lost Sisterhood: Prostitution in America, 1900–1918* (Baltimore: Johns Hopkins University Press, 1982).

62. Elizabeth Perry, Phoebe Estelle Spaulding Lecture, "On Virgins and Martyrs," Pomona College, February 3, 1987.

63. See the essays in Asunción Lavrin, ed., *Latin American Women: Historical Perspectives* (Westport, Conn.: Greenwood Press, 1978). In the area of Chicana Studies, see del Castillo, "Malintzin Tenepal," in Sánchez and Cruz, *Essays on La Mujer*. For counternarratives, see Gloria Anzaldúa, *Borderlands/La Frontera: The New Mestiza* (San Francisco: Spinsters/Aunt Lute, 1987).

64. For an analysis of Malinche as a symbol of violation, see Octavio Paz, *Labyrinth of Solitude* (New York: Grove Press, 1961). For a Chicana feminist perspective, see Del Castillo, "Malintzín Tenepal: A Preliminary Look into a New Perspective," in Sánchez and Cruz, *Essays on La Mujer*, 124–149; and Norma Alarcón, "Chicana's Feminist Literature: A Re-Vision Through Malintzin/or Malintzin: Putting Flesh Back on the Object," in Cherríe Moraga and Gloria Anzaldúa, eds., *This Bridge Called My Back: Writings by Radical Women of Color* (Watertown, Mass.: Persephone, 1981), 182–190. For a review of the historical accounting of Malinche and a revision depicting her diplo-matic skills, see Deena J. González, "Encountering Columbus," in Teresa Cordova, ed., *Chicano Studies: Critical Connection Between Research and Community* (Albuquerque: University of New Mexico Press, 1992), 13–19. On her impact on literature, see Sandra Messinger Cypess, *La Malinche in Mexican Literature: From History to Myth* (Austin: University of Texas Press, 1991). For a hermeneutic argument, see Tzvetan Todorov, *The Conquest of America* (New York: Harper and Row, 1982), chap. 2.

65. On the significance of the legend of La Constancia in colonial New Mexico, see Gutiérrez, *When Jesus Came*, 176–177. On the imprint of La Malinche, see Paz, *Labryinth*, chap. 4; for another example, see the first novel written in the New World, *La Monia Alferez*, based on the life of Doña Catalina de Erazu, who became a sword

fighter and muleteer, as documented in Lesly Byrd Simpson, *Many Mexicos* (Berkeley: University of California Press, 1969), 167–168. For a contemporary example of the prevalence of the concept, also see Alfredo Mirandé and Evangelina Enríquez, *La Chicana: The Mexican-American Woman* (Chicago: University of Chicago Press, 1979). On the uses of, and need for, revising the concept of "La" Chicana in Chicano Studies, see Deena González, "Chicano Studies and La Chicana," background paper, in Alfredo González and David Sandoval, eds., *A Symposium on Chicano Studies* (Los Angeles: Loyola Marymount University, 1988). For a slightly different twist to the essentializing tendency, but still problematic—because "mujer" is now theologically constructed in mujerista theology—see the work of liberation theologian Ada Maria Isasi-Diaz, *Hispanic Women, Prophetic Voice in the Church* (New York: Harper and Row, 1989).

66. For an interesting discussion of the meaning of La Malinche and other figures, including La Llorona (weeping woman), see José E. Limón, "La Llorona, The Third Legend of Greater Mexico: Cultural Symbols, Women, and the Political Unconscious," in Adelaida del Castillo, eds., *Between Borders: Essays on Mexicana/Chicana History* (Encino, Calif.: Floricanto Press, 1990).

67. See the work of the historian Antonia Castañeda on colonial California for a demonstration of this point: "Presidarias y Pobladoras: Spanish-Mexican Women in Frontier Monterey, Alta California, 1770–1821" (Ph.D. diss., Stanford University, 1990), 75–113; see also Castañeda, "Gender, Race, and Culture," *Frontiers* 11 (1990), 8–20. On the comparable differences or similarities, the ancient European world of the Romans might initiate some new discussion and seems profoundly interesting in the equation linking the "depravity" of the Cleopatra or even Flavia varieties with their public sensuality or sexuality, which contributed, it was supposed, to revolutionary activism and, therefore, was to be feared by the Second Triumvirate; whether the transported Spanish interpretations of this sort of linkage between women's expressed sexuality and revolution in fact manifested themselves on Spain's northern frontiers is conjecture, but interesting in comparison. See Ron Cluett, "Roman Women in the Second Triumviral" (Paper presented at Pomona College, January 24, 1997).

68. *Lopes v. Scolly*, April 8, 1844; and Sena Family Papers.

69. The same issue about the incongruence between the national images of women and their regional realities has been studied in other parts of the continent; see, for example, Lebsock's explanation for the South in *The Free Women of Petersburg*, introduction. For a study of Mexican women in an urban area, see Sylvia M. Arrom, *The Women of Mexico City, 1790–1857* (Stanford: Stanford University Press, 1985); on the Southwest, see Deutsch, *No Separate Refuge*.

70. Davis, *El Gringo*, 221.

71. Sunder, *Matt Field*, 206.

72. McDermott, *The Wanderings of Alfred S. Waugh*, 121.

73. Gutiérrez, *When Jesus Came*, chaps. 5–7.

74. For cases in which women were admonished to pursue modesty, see *Roybal v. Chaves*, May 21, 1833, Roll 16, frame 1020 (MANM), as well as the lawsuit between La Tules and Ana María Rendón, March 3, 1835, JCP, Roll 20, frames 131–132 (MANM).

75. For discussions of the land-grant fiascos following the war, see Dunbar Ortiz, *Roots of Resistance*; Sunseri, *Seeds of Discord*; Westphall, *Mercedes Reales*; and Charles L. Briggs and John R. Van Ness, *Land, Water, and Culture: New Perspectives on Hispanic Land Grants* (Albuquerque: University of New Mexico Press, 1987). Also see the dis-

cussion of land takeover as one "legacy of conquest" in Limerick, *The Legacy of Conquest*, chap. 7. For ongoing, contemporary significance, see Ebright, *Land Grants*.

76. The estimate is based on USCB, Seventh Census of Population, for Santa Fe (microfilm, NMSRC); on the statistics in Twitchell, *Story of the Conquest*, 35–36; and on Phillip St. George Cook, *The Conquest of New Mexico and California: An Historical and Personal Narrative* (New York: Putnam's, 1878), introduction.

77. On resistance to the invasion north of Santa Fe, at Santa Cruz, El Embudo, and Taos, see James Madison Cutts, *The Conquest of California and New Mexico by the Forces of the United States in the Years 1846 and 1847* (Philadelphia: Carey and Hart, 1847), 231; and Simmons, *Little Lion*, 91–92.

78. Weber, *The Mexican Frontier*, 92–93.

79. Pattie, *The Personal Narrative*, 45.

80. Frank McNitt, *Navajo Wars* (Albuquerque: University of New Mexico Press, 1972), 67.

81. Weber, *The Mexican Frontier*, 98. For a discussion of problems between Natives and Spanish-Mexicans in an earlier period, see Daniel Tyler, "Mexican Indian Policy in New Mexico," *New Mexico Historical Review* 55 (March 1980), 101–120.

82. On genízaros, see Steven M. Horvath, Jr., "The Genízaros of Eighteenth Century New Mexico: A Reexamination," *Discovery* 12 (Fall 1977), 39; and Gutiérrez, *When Jesus Came*, 149–151.

83. On the establishment of Santa Fe, see Weber, *The Mexican Frontier*, 5. On Oñate's travels, see Herbert Eugene Bolton, ed., *Spanish Exploration in the Southwest, 1542–1706* (New York: Barnes and Noble, 1908), 199–280. On the derivation of the word "Mexico," see the glossary in Ignacio Bernal, *Mexico before Cortez: Art, History, and Legend* (Garden City, N.Y.: Doubleday, 1963), 129; and on pre-Spanish cultural mixing, see the same work, 83–85.

84. Lecompte, "La Tules," 218, 224, 228. On the move to Chihuahua, see "Governor's Letterbook," (MANM, NMSRC, 1843), Roll 33 (frame number illegible). For examples of continued Mexican migration after 1848, see USCB, Eighth Census of Population, for Santa Fe (microfilm, NMSRC), 1–7.

85. See Kenneson, "Through the Looking-Glass," 102; Lamar, *The Far Southwest*, 31. On interregional contact between New Mexico and California, see Eleanor Lawrence, "Mexican Trade between Santa Fe and Los Angeles, 1830–1848," *California Historical Society Quarterly* (March 1931), 27–39.

86. Santa Fe, Census of 1841, Original Schedule of Population for Santa Fe (microfilm, NMSRC), Roll 30, frame 327.

87. See the Seventh Census of Population, for Santa Fe, New Mexico (microfilm, NMSRC).

88. Ralph Emerson Twitchell, ed., *The Spanish Archives of New Mexico* (Cedar Rapids, Mich.: Torch, 1911), 1, 124; *House Executive Document* 2, 29th Cong., 1846, 1st sess., 213.

89. Brewerton, "Incidents of Travel," 589.

90. Pattie, *Narrative*, 98.

91. For a general introduction to bandits and heroes, see Eric Hobsbawm, *Primitive Rebels: Studies in Archaic Forms of Social Movement in the 19th and 20th Centuries* (Manchester, Eng.: Manchester University Press, 1959). On the Jameses, see Homer Croy, *Jesse James Was My Neighbor* (New York: Duell, Sloane and Pearce, 1949), 25. Also see *Journal of the House of Representatives of the State of Missouri* (Jefferson City, March 1875), 1, 339–340.

92. N. C. Titus, "The Last Stand of the Nez Percés," *Washington Historical Quarterly*

6 (July 1915), 145–15?; and Alvin M. Josephy, *The Nez Perces and the Opening of the Northwest* (New Haven, Conn.: Yale University Press, 1965), chap. 2.

93. Alexander Adams, *Geronimo* (New York: Putnam, 1971), 308; and Dee Brown, *Bury My Heart at Wounded Knee* (New York: Pocket Books, 1981), 387.

94. Rodolfo Acuña, *Occupied America: A History of Chicanos* (New York: Harper and Row, 1981), 105, 111, 113; and Robert Greenwood, *The California Outlaw: Tiburcio Vásquez* (Los Gatos, Calif.: Talisman, 1960). Interestingly, Juanita appears primarily by her first name, and another woman, lynched or hung, depending on one's perspective, is known only by her last name, Villa; for data on this interesting feature and the accompanying analysis of its significance, see Sánchez, *Telling Identities*, 221–224. The singularity of first/last name, like that of the label "la," has yet to be fully unraveled in the case of Mexican womanhood across the different regions of the former Mexican north.

95. Greenwood, *The California Outlaw*, introduction.

96. For an overview of folklore's organizing principles, see Richard Bauman, Roger Abrahams, and Susan Kalcik, "American Folklore and American Studies," *American Quarterly* 38 (1976), 360–377. On how the various genres interpret one of folklore's building blocks, see Alan Dundes, "Folk Ideas as Units of Worldview," *Journal of American Folklore* 84 (January–March 1971), 93–103. On Native folklore, see Alan Dundes, "North American Folklore Studies," *Journal de la Société des Américanistes* 56 (1967), 53–79.

97. For examples of the extent of their popularity, see Ed McCurdy, "Songs of the Old West," Elektra Records; *The True Story of Jesse James* (20th Century Fox, 1957); and *The Life and Times of Jesse James* (ABC Television, 1965). Other movies, distributed in Italy and Russia, include *The Return of Jesse James*, *Jesse James at Bay*, and *I Shot Jesse James*.

98. Jan Vansina, *Oral Tradition: A Study in Historical Methodology* (Chicago: Aldine, 1965), chap. 1.

99. For an intriguing analysis, primarily Marxist and incorporative of some feminist theory, see Sánchez, *Telling Identities*, chap. 5, particularly the sections entitled "Constructs of the Feminine in Hegemonic Texts" and "The Maiden and the Merchant."

100. See the novels by Ruth Laughlin, *The Wind Leaves No Shadow* (Caldwell, Idaho: Caxton Printers, 1978), and by Paul Horgan, *Centuries of Santa Fe* (New York: Dutton, 1965), chap. 7.

101. Blanche C. Grant, *Doña Lona: A Story of Old Taos and Santa Fe* (New York: Wilfred Funk, 1941), viii. Grant was a writer and an artist; educated at Vassar College, she arrived in Taos in 1921. Among her other books on the Southwest are *When Old Trails were New; Taos Indians;* and *Kit Carson's Own Story of His Life*, which she edited.

102. See Laughlin, *The Wind Leaves No Shadow*, and Grant, *Doña Lona*. See also Anna Robeson Burr, *The Golden Quicksand: A Novel of Santa Fé* (New York: Appleton-Century, 1936). For an analysis of the Taos colony of artists and writers, see Sylvia Rodríguez, "Land, Water, and Ethnic Identity in Taos," in Briggs and Van Ness, *Land, Water, and Culture*, 313–403.

103. Laughlin, *The Wind Leaves No Shadow*, 142; for another sketch, see Grant, *Doña Lona*.

104. Burr, *The Golden Quicksand*, 94–99. The linkage between the portrayal of a character like Peter, Orientalist discourse, and colonialism is best explored in Edward Said, *Orientalism* (New York: Pantheon, 1978).

105. For examples of more disparaging comments, see Moorhead, *Commerce of the Prairies*, 168; Brewerton, "Incidents of Travel," 580.

106. Lecompte, "La Tules and the Americans," 228.

107. Brewerton, "Incidents of Travel," 588.

108. Ibid.

109. Drumm, *The Diary of Susan Shelby Magoffin*.

110. Brewerton, "Incidents of Travel," 588.

111. Sunder, *Matt Field*, 205–213.

112. Said, *Orientalism*; Gayatri Chakravorty Spivak, *In Other Worlds: Essays in Cultural Politics* (New York: Routledge, 1988). For a discussion of the equally disconcerting tendency in Western (European) feminist scholarship and its reflections on Third World women, see Chandra Talpade Mohanty, "Under Western Eyes: Feminist Scholarship and Colonial Discourses," *Boundary* 2:12–13 (Spring/Fall 1984), 333–358. On a Texas frontier, see the comments by Euro-Americans who stereotyped Mexican women as ardent, promiscuous, and voluptuous in Arnoldo de León, "White Racial Attitudes towards Mexicanos in Texas, 1821–1900" (Ph.D. diss., Texas Christian University, 1974), 125–128.

113. Alloula, *The Colonial Harem*, 122.

114. On employment patterns, beginning with the more complete 1850 census, see Scadron, *On Their Own*; González, "The Widowed Women of Santa Fe," 69; and Table 2.3 in this book.

115. Pike, *Exploratory Travels*, 335.

116. See Archer B. Hulbert, ed., *Southwest on the Turquoise Trail* (Denver: Stewart Commission of Colorado College and Denver Public Library, 1933), 64–65.

117. Pattie, *Narrative*, 98.

118. See De León, "White Racial Attitudes," 115–116.

119. Matt Field's articles titled "An Arrival," "The Monte Bank," and "A Trader's Shop" closely followed this theme. See Sunder, *Matt Field*, 209–221.

120. See the recollections, for example, of the soldier chroniclers in Albert K. Weinberg, *Manifest Destiny* (Chicago: Quadrangle, 1963), 173.

121. Alloula, *The Colonial Harem*, 120, 122.

122. Ibid., 122. For examples of objectification and ownership of New Mexican women, especially in comments about clothing and breasts, see Drumm, *The Diary of Susan Shelby Magoffin*, 95; David Weber, *The Taos Trappers: The Fur Trade in the Far Southwest, 1540–1846* (Norman: University of Oklahoma Press, 1971), 144, and the sketch by J. W. Abert in Galvin, *J. W. Abert*, 46.

123. For descriptions of a "priest-ridden" populace, see Brewerton, "Incidents of Travel," 588–589; Sunder, *Matt Field*, 213, 253–254; Bieber, *Webb's Adventures*, 102; Pike, *Exploratory Travels*, 340; and Moorhead, *Commerce of the Prairies*, 179–180. On the thieves-and-liars quotation, see Frank S. Edwards, *A Campaign in New Mexico with Colonel Doniphan* (Philadelphia: Carey and Hart, 1848), 50; on Mexican inferiority and brutality, see also John T. Hughes, *Doniphan's Expedition: An Account of the Conquest of New Mexico* (Washington, D.C.: Government Printing Office, 1914), 316; and the work of the historian Francis Parkman, who termed Mexicans "swarthy," "ignoble," and "squalid," in *The Oregon Trail* (Philadelphia: John Winston, 1931), 3, 71, 307. On the origins of some aspects of anti-Mexican fervor and of Hispanophobia, see Philip W. Powell, *Tree of Hate: Propaganda and Prejudices Affecting United States Social Relations with the Hispanic World* (New York: Basic Books, 1971). For a survey of attitudes in the Euro-American literature on the Southwest and its peoples, see Cecil Robinson, *Mexico and the Hispanic Southwest in American Literature* (Tucson: University of Arizona Press, 1977).

124. On the Army of the West, see Hubert Howe Bancroft, *History of Arizona and New Mexico*, vol. 17 (San Francisco, 1889). Also see the diaries of Cooke, *The Conquest*

of New Mexico; of Hughes, *Doniphan's Expedition*; and of Cutts, *The Conquest of California*.

125. Drumm, *The Diary of Susan Shelby Magoffin*, 114. In subsequent pages, Magoffin elaborated on the drinking habits of the officers as well—see 145–146, 148–149.

126. George F. A. Ruxton, *Adventures in Mexico and the Rocky Mountains* (London: John Murray, 1847), 90.

127. On how Kearny coerced the alcaldes and Spanish-Mexican captains to obey him, by use of a public scolding, see the recollections of W. H. Emory, "Notes of a Military Reconnaissance from Fort Leavenworth in Missouri, to San Diego, in California . . . Made in 1846–1847, with the Advanced Guard of the 'Army of the West,'" *House Ex. Doc.* 41, 30th Cong., 1847, 1st sess., 28. for a complete text of the Kearny Code, see Twitchell, *The Military Occupation*, 78–80. On the soldiers' continued revelry, see Ruxton, *Adventures*, 90; and Simmons, *Little Lion*, 97. For a discussion of the extent of local dissatisfaction with the political order and of military rule, see Lamar, *The Far Southwest*, 67–71.

128. Bancroft estimates that Colonel Price, in charge of the New Mexico forces, had two thousand soldiers under his command in December 1846; see Bancroft, *History*, 365.

129. Moorhead, *New Mexico's Royal Road*, 156; Drumm, *The Diary of Susan Shelby Magoffin*, xviii, xix; and Lamar, *The Far Southwest*, 59.

130. Webb, "Memoirs," 43. For other distinctions among the merchant-adventurers and their role in the changing order of business, see Gunther Barth, *Instant Cities: Urbanization and the Rise of San Francisco and Denver* (New York: Oxford University Press, 1975), 71–73. For examples of some of the more well-known mixed marriages, see Lecompte, "The Independent Women," 34; Rebecca McDowell Craver, *The Impact of Intimacy: Mexican-Anglo Intermarriage in New Mexico, 1821–1846*, Southwestern Studies Series, Monograph 66 (El Paso, 1982), 21, 32; and Twitchell, *The Military Occupation*, 282, 376.

131. On intimacy, see Craver, *The Impact of Intimacy*. On upward mobility, see Miller, "Cross-cultural Marriages," 342; for an explanation based on the ratio of single westering men to "available" women, see Richard Griswold del Castillo, *La Familia: Chicano Families in the Urban Southwest, 1848 to the Present* (Notre Dame, Ind.: University of Notre Dame Press, 1984), 69. For intermarriages in Texas in this period, see Jane Dysart, "Mexican Women in San Antonio, 1830–1860: The Assimilation Process," *Western Historical Quarterly* 7 (October 1976), 356–375. On the intermarrying man on a fur-trading frontier, see John M. Faragher, "'Many Tender Ties' in the American West: The Mountain Man as Marrying Man: Cross Cultural Ties and Contact," in Lillian Schlissel, Vicki Ruiz, and Janice Monk, eds., *Western Women: Their Lands, Their Lives* (Albuquerque: University of New Mexico Press, 1988), 199–215; on Native women and Euro-American men on a Canadian frontier, see the important study by Sylvia Van Kirk, *"Many Tender Ties": Women in Fur-Trade Society in Western Canada, 1670–1870* (Winnipeg: Watson and Dwyer, 1980).

132. SFCR, *Probate Court Journal, 1848–1856*, Jury Book (Manuscript Div., NMSRC), 80, 96, 121.

133. For interpretations that focus on social interaction with a positive emphasis, see Miller, "Cross-cultural Marriages"; for an earlier period, see Robert Archibald, "Acculturation and Assimilation in Colonial New Mexico," *New Mexico Historical Review* 53 (July 1978), 205–214. For a general overview that advances the theory of cultural understanding, see Sandra L. Myres, "Mexican Americans and Westering

Anglos: A Feminine Perspective," *New Mexico Historical Review* 57 (October 1982), 310–329.

134. Warren Susman, *Culture as History:The Transformation of American Society in the Twentieth Century* (New York: Pantheon, 1978), 322.

135. Craver's sample, for Santa Fe, consists of seventeen unions spread across the period 1821–1846; see Craver, *The Impact of Intimacy*, appendix 3, 58–60. Miller's sample is more comprehensive, but it also is tentative because of the incomplete documents and scattered sources; like all other studies on this subject, it also does not correlate the unindexed, incomplete marriage certificates in the archdiocese records—see Miller, "Cross-Cultural Marriages." For examples of more comprehensive quantitative work on the subject of Euro-American/Spanish-Mexican intermarriage, and on other frontiers, see Dysart, "Mexican Women in San Antonio"; Alicia Tjarks, "Comparative Demographic Analysis of Texas, 1777–1793," *Southwestern Historical Quarterly* 77 (1974), 291–338; and Barbara Laslett, "Household Structure on an American Frontier: Los Angeles, California, in 1850," *American Journal of Sociology* 81 (1975), 109–128.

136. For examples in other parts of Latin America, see Magnus Morner, *Race Mixture in the History of Latin America* (Boston: Little, Brown, 1967).

137. Castañeda, "Presidarias y Pobladoras," 75–113.

138. For examples of the violence against Natives, see Spicer, *Cycles of Conquest*, chaps. 1–7; and John, *Storms Brewed in Other Men's Worlds*, chaps. 1–6.

139. Sunder, *Matt Field*, 208.

140. On the soldiers attending mass, see Drumm, *The Diary of Susan Shelby Magoffin*, 138.

141. On the 1845 census, see Santa Fe, Census of 1845, Original Schedules of Population (microfilm, NMSRC), Roll 30. For 1850, see USCB, Seventh Census of Population, for Santa Fe, New Mexico (microfilm, NMSRC). Hereafter, the original census schedules are cited according to their number; the 1850 census was the Seventh, the 1860 was the Eighth, the 1870 was the Ninth, and the 1880 was the Tenth.

142. For examples of the practice, see Craver, *The Impact of Intimacy*, 5; her source is Moorhead, *Commerce of the Prairies*, 182.

143. Miller, "Cross-Cultural Marriages."

144. On the origins of the linkages in Spanish law between church and state, see Gutiérrez, *When Jesus Came*, chap. 3; also see J. Lloyd Mecham, *Church and State in Latin America: A History of Politico-Ecclesiastical Relations* (Chapel Hill: University of North Carolina Press, 1966); Wilfred Callcott, *Church and State in Mexico, 1822–1857* (Durham, N.C.: Duke University Press, 1926), and Anne Staples, *La iglesia en la primera república federal mexicana, 1824–1835* (Mexico City: Secretária de Educación Pública, 1976).

145. For additional comments on a "priest-ridden citizenry," see Webb, *Adventures*, 102; and Moorhead, *Commerce of the Prairies*, 141, 173. Apparently, some Euro-Americans set aside their difficulties with dual adjudication when they discovered that their own interests, especially in real estate matters, could be advanced in the ecclesiastical court; for a flagrant example of Spanish-Mexicans losing their land over unpaid bills, and of Euro-Americans purchasing estates for as little as $1.25, see the case against Tomás Valencia in the Papers from the Marshall's Office, n.d., 1852, AASF, LDD.

146. SFCR, *Probate Court Journal*, 1848–1856, Jury Books, 80, 96, 121, 122, 138, 139, 140. Also see the six cases against Samuel Woodhouse in the *Probate Court Journal*, Jury Books, 138–139. For collections of fines against Euro-Americans, see the tax lists in SFCR, Tax Book 5, 1867–1877 (Manuscript Div., NMSRC). For the extent of cultural misunderstanding, see Petition of María Josefa Gallegos regarding obstruction of

a ditch, SFCR, *Probate Court Journal*, 1848–1856, Jury Books, 80–81. Also see Proceedings against Salvador Barceló y Borrego and Diego Martín, for the murder of Andrew Doyle, May 30, 1843, and Testimonies of José Petalán and Alexander Montgomery regarding robberies near Taos, May 19, 1843, JCP, (microfilm, NMSRC), roll 33, by date.

147. On the town and its streets, see Jacob Robinson, "Sketches of the Great West: A Journal of the Santa Fe Expedition under Colonel Doniphan, 1846," *Magazine of History* 32:4, special no. 128 (1927), 230; and Bieber, *The Journal of Marcellus Ball Edwards*, 163. On people and the monte banks, see Ralph Bieber, ed., *George Rutledge Gibson's Journal of a Soldier under Kearny and Doniphan, 1846–1847* (Glendale, Calif.: Arthur H. Clark, 1934), 265, 316. For additional comments about liars, filth, and ignorance and the economy, see Galvin, *J. W. Abert*, 53, 54, 64.

148. Phillips Bradley, ed., *Alexis de Tocqueville's Democracy in America* (New York: Knopf, 1945), vol. 1, 305.

149. In the 1850s and 1860s, the negative commentary heightened; for numerous examples, see Kenneson, "Through the Looking-Glass," chap. 4.

150. Alexander Dyer to Robert Johnston, February 14, 1847 (manuscript, MN-MHL), Box 4, folio 2.

151. Lamar, *The Far Southwest*, 68.

152. Dyer to Johnston, February 14, 1847, 2–3.

153. Dyer, "Mexican War Journal," 97. On how explosive the situation had been earlier, see Drumm, *The Diary of Susan Shelby Magoffin*, 188–189; and Twitchell, *Leading Facts*, vol. 2, 232.

154. Weber, *The Mexican Frontier*, 92–93.

155. Simmons, *Little Lion*, 85; Weber, *The Mexican Frontier*, 93.

156. On Armijo, see Twitchell, *The Spanish Archives*, vol. 1, 62–63; and for his sale of la *cienega* (commons area) of Santa Fe, see Ebright, *Land Grants*, 87–101. On Branch, see Dale Morgan, ed., "The Diary of William H. Ashley, March 25–June 27, 1825," *Bulletin of the Missouri Historical Society* 11 (October 1856), 13. On Kirker, see Moorhead, *New Mexico's Royal Road*, 148; and Ralph Bieber, ed., *Southern Trails to California in 1849* (Glendale, Calif.: Arthur H. Clark, 1937), 357–358.

157. Weber, *The Mexican Frontier*, 271. In the 1850s, Armijo would continue to be hospitable to Euro-American officials, including the territorial governors. William Carr Lane recalled that Armijo received him with "much ceremony and kindness"; see Ralph E. Twitchell, "Historical Sketch of Governor William Carr Lane, Together with Diary of His Journey from St. Louis, Mo., to Santa Fe, N.M., July 31st to Sept. 9, 1852," *Historical Society of New Mexico* 4 (Santa Fe, 1917), 57.

158. Hulbert, *Southwest on the Turquoise Trail*, 178–180; Moorhead, *New Mexico's Royal Road*, 70, 128–129, 143; Lamar, *The Far Southwest*, 55; Webb, "Memoirs," 35.

159. See Cutts, *The Conquest*, 82. The classic work on the topic of manifest destiny is Frederick Merk, *Manifest Destiny and Mission in American History* (New York: Knopf, 1963).

160. See Cutts, *The Conquest*, and Takaki, *Iron Cages*, 154–164.

161. Dyer, "Mexican War Journal," 82.

162. Field's articles for the *New Orleans Picayune* and the popular travelogues were regularly supplemented by articles in the major presses of the southern and eastern United States; see, for example, the *Richmond Enquirer*, 1847, the *St. Louis Republican*, 1846–1848, and the *Missouri Intelligencer*, 1846–1847; also see the *New York Tribune*, January 14, 1847, and the *Washington Union*, April 20 and 27, 1847. For an overview of the impact of negative stereotyping of Mexicans in the press, see Thomas W. Reilly,

"American Reporters and the Mexican War, 1846–1848" (Ph.D. diss., University of Minnesota, 1975). On how earlier events might also have shaped outsiders' perceptions, see Lecompte, *Rebellion in Río Arriba*.

163. See the discussion of the Santa Fe Ring, and of corruption generally, in Lamar, *The Far Southwest*, chap. 6; for examples of the personal worths of the one hundred wealthiest investors, see González, "The Widowed Women of Santa Fe," in Scadron, *On Their Own*, 70, and, in this book, Table 2.2.

164. SFCR, *Probate Court Journals*, Wills and Testaments, Book A-1 (NMSRC), October 1850. The original is filed in the Santa Fe County Probate Court Case File 1005, County Clerk's Office, Santa Fe. See also the deed of trust in Barceló, Baca y Ortiz, and Abreu, Santa Fe, 1844, Roll 1(MANM, NMSRC), frame 1106–1108.

165. For a contemporary look at Santa Fe's shifting demography, see Steve Jones "The Trust Fund Hippies of Santa Fe," *Santa Fe Magazine* 3 (1980).

166. Dana, *Two Years*, 136.

CHAPTER 3

1. The widow's first name was not given; see Official Reports of the Territorial Secretary, summer 1876, Ritch Collection, RI 1731 (MS, HEH).

2. For example, see SFCR, Wills and Testaments, 1856–1897, Index, Books B, C, D, and E (Manuscript Div., NMSRC), as well as the unindexed but prevalent last testaments in the AASF, LDD, 1850–1880.

3. For a demographic breakdown by ethnicity, see González, "The Widowed Women," in Scadron, *On Their Own*, 72, table 3 or, in this book, Table 2.1. The sources are USCB, Seventh, Eighth, Ninth, and Tenth Census of Population, for Santa Fe (microfilm, NMSRC).

4. See Official Reports, Ritch Collection, summer 1876, RI 1731.

5. This point, however, should not be construed to mean that women who are colonized are always victimized, or that woman as the habitually resurrected Other is universally dependent. See Chandra Talpade Mohanty, "Under Western Eyes: Feminist Scholarship and Colonial Discourses," *Boundary* 2:12/13 (Spring/Fall 1984), 333–358, and compare her analysis to Etienne's and Leacock's in their introduction in *Women and Colonization*, 1–24.

6. See, for examples in Latin America, Etienne and Leacock, *Women and Colonization*, introduction. Also see the classic work by Albert Memmi, *The Colonizer and the Colonized* (Boston: Beacon Press, 1965); and the important works of Frantz Fanon: *Black Skin, White Masks* (New York: Grove Weidenfeld, 1991), *The Wretched of the Earth*, (New York: Grove Weidenfeld, 1991), and *On the African Revolution* (New York: Grove Press, 1988).

7. Official Report, Ritch Collection, RI 1731; on the law, see L. Bradford Prince, comp., *General Laws of New Mexico from the "Kearny Code of 1846" to 1880* (Albany: W. C. Little, 1880), 52.

8. See Lamar's excellent descriptions of Ritch's anti-Catholicism, in *The Far Southwest*, 167–168.

9. L. Bradford Prince, *Spanish Mission Churches of New Mexico* (Glorieta, N.M.: Rio Grande Press, 1977), 127–128.

10. John Baptist Lamy to Monseigneur Machebeuf, June 29, 1851, AASF, LDD, and Lamy to Archbishop Purcell, September 2, 1851, AASF, LDD.

11. See SFCR, Tax Book 5, 1867–1877, for fines assessed against many prominent Euro-Americans for drinking and gambling.

12. See SFCR, Tax Book 5, 1867–1877.

13. For example, see "Social Statistics," Eighth Census of Population, for Santa Fe

(microfilm, NMSRC). On the prices of produce and meat, see Sister Blandina Segale, *End of the Santa Fe Trail*, 105–106, and, for other statistics, Sunseri, *Seeds of Discord*, 21–22. On the numbers of orphans, see the problems with the Apaches and Navajos, and the children captured from them, in Sytha Motto, "The Sisters of Charity and St. Vincent's Hospital: An Amplification of Sister Mallon's Journal," *New Mexico Historical Review* 52:2–3 (1977), 230.

14. Motto, "The Sisters of Charity," 52:3 (March 1977), 229–250.

15. Lamy to Purcell, September 2, 1851, AASF, LDD. For an account of how he suspended another priest, see Lamy to Purcell, February 1, 1852, AASF, LDD.

16. See his correspondence to Purcell in the 1850s, beginning with his report on the New Orleans meeting, May 1852, AASF, LDD. On the help Archbishop Purcell of Cincinnati offerred him, see Motto, "The Sisters of Charity," 230.

17. Lamy to Purcell, (no month/day), 1853, AASF, LDD.

18. On Martínez's activities, see Lamar, *The Far Southwest*, 72. On aspects of his legendary influence and concerns about Euro-Americanism, see E. K. Francis, "Padre Martínez: A New Mexico Myth," *New Mexico Historical Review* 31 (October 1956), 265–289. For a short biography, see Pedro Sánchez, "Memorias sobre la vida del presbitero don António José Martínez," in David Weber, ed., *Northern New Mexico on the Eve of the United States Invasion* (New York: Arno Press, 1976); in the same collection, see "Histãria consisa del cura de Taos António José Martínez," *El Historiador*, May 4, 1861.

19. Lamy to Purcell, (no month/day), 1853, AASF, LDD; also see, for his suspension of a priest who drank too much, Lamy to Purcell, February 1, 1852, AASF, LDD.

20. Lamy to Purcell, September 2, 1851, AASF, LDD.

21. Paul Horgan, *Lamy of Santa Fe: His Life and Times* (New York: Farrar, Straus, and Giroux, 1975), 115.

22. Lamy to Purcell, (no month/day), 1853, AASF, LDD.

23. Lamy to Bishop Zubiría, April 15, 1853, AASF, LDD. For the conflict which developed as well between Lamy and Zubiría, see Declaration of Bishop Zubiría y Escalante on Lamy, November 1, 1851, AASF, LDD.

24. Lamy to Zubiría, (no month/day), 1853, AASF, LDD.

25. Lamy to Zubiría, (no month/day), 1853, AASF, LDD; see also, for examples of his orders: Reprimand, Lamy to Cura Tomás Abeyta of San Ildefonso, (no month/day), 1852, AASF, LDD.

26. See the reprimmand to Cura Tomás Abeyta; see also, Lamy to Purcell, (no month/day), 1853, AASF, LDD.

27. List of Priests Who Died, 1852–1868, AASF, LDD.

28. Davis, *El Gringo*, 230.

29. See Craver, *The Impact of Intimacy*, 5; note especially her point that weddings cost, minimally, $20.00 in a period when a carpenter earned $2.00 a day, a bushel of wheat cost $1.00, a large cow was valued at $12.00, and sheep fetched $1.00 each.

30. Richter, "Sister Catherine Mallon's Journal," 141.

31. Lamy to Purcell, September 2, 1851, 2.

32. Segale, *End of the Santa Fe Trail*, 105–106; and Sunseri, *Seeds of Discord*, 21–22. On the changes in the values of currency, see Warner, "Conveyance of Property," *NMHR*, (October 1931), 337.

33. Lamar, *The Far Southwest*, 103.

34. Richter, "Sister Catherine Mallon's Journal," 135.

35. See David Meriwether to Building Commissioners, September, 1853, Ritch Collection, Box 11(MS, HEH).

36. On the masons who helped with the church, see Segale, *At the End of the Santa*

Fe Trail, 81. Construction of the cathedral was halted in 1895, twenty-six years after it had begun, and the project was not completed until the 1970s; see Bruce Ellis, *Bishop Lamy's Santa Fe Cathedral* (Albuquerque: University of New Mexico Press, 1985), xii.

37. *Daily New Mexican*, January 3, 1873.

38. See in this volume Table 2.3; also the chart in González, "The Widowed Women," in Scadron, *On Their Own*, 69, table 1. For data on different periods, but on the same phenomenon in other Mexican communities of the west, see Mario García, "The Chicana in American History: The Mexican Women of El Paso, 1880–1920—A Case Study," *Pacific Historical Review* 49:2 (May 1990), 326, table 2; Camarillo, *Chicanos in a Changing Society*, 91, 99; and De Leon, *The Tejano Community*, 107, 109–110, 189.

39. See in this volume table 2.2; also González, "The Widowed Women," in Scadron, *On Their Own*, 70, table 2. Also see USCB, Eighth and Ninth Censuses of Population, for Santa Fe (microfilm NMSRC).

40. On eggs, see Segale, *End of the Santa Fe Trail*; on mules, see Sunseri, *Seeds of Discord*, 30–31.

41. See the "Productions of Agriculture Schedules," USCB, Seventh and Eighth Censuses of Population, for Santa Fe County (microfilm, NMSRC), 1–7 and 1–8; and Segale, *The End of the Santa Fe Trail*, 104.

42. Sunseri, *Seeds of Discord*, 28, 31.

43. For these statistics, see USCB, Seventh, Eighth, Ninth, and Tenth Censuses of Population, for Santa Fe (microfilm, NMSRC); but examining the original microfilmed or xeroxed copies in the National Archives, Washington, D.C., is necessary because neighborhoods are missing or pages are out of order in some of the microfilm editions, especially in the Schedules' sections of each census that appear at the end of each "precinct"; also, see González, "The Widowed Women of Santa Fe," in Scadron, *On Their Own*, 72, table 3. In this volume, Table 2.1 shows the changing demography and Table 2.3 contains the wage differentials. On the buildings, see Thomas Richter, "Sister Catherine Mallon's Journal," *New Mexico Historical Review* 52:2 (1977), 135, 145, 148. On the role of politicians and lawyers, as well as legislators, see Lamar, *The Far Southwest*, chap. 6.

44. The best sources for tracing this pattern are the wills and testimonials of women, scattered across three major arenas. See the uncatalogued family papers at the State Records Center, Santa Fe; examples include the Mariano Chávez Papers and the María G. Dúran Papers. Also see the County Court Records, NMSRC, especially Books B, C, D, and E. Finally, in the Archives of the Archdiocese of Santa Fe, see the hundreds of testimonials, conveyances, and wills between 1820 and 1880, under LDD; my book-length manuscript, "Chicanas Bequeath," should also prove useful.

45. Official Report, Ritch Collection, RI 1731, 1. For information on Truchard, see Lamar, *The Far Southwest*, 174; and *Santa Fe New Mexican*, July 20, 1877. It is possible that the widow Chaves was Maria (de las) Nieves Chávez; see Will of María Nieves Chávez (inventory), December, 1870, SFCR, Book D, 27–66 (various pages).

46. "Report of the Clerk of the Probate Court," November 10, 1853 (Manuscript, NMSRC), SFCR, *Probate Court Journal*.

47. Lamar, *The Far Southwest*, 138; Catron received fees as high as $25,000 for legal services in some of the grant cases he litigated. See Westphall, *Mercedes Reales*, 191.

48. Lamar, *The Far Southwest*, 140.

49. SFCR, Tax Book 5, Tax List, 1–2, 1867–1877.

50. Ibid., Tax List, 1–2.

51. Papers from the Marshall's Office, (no month/day), 1852, AASF, LDD. For Owens's listing of goods and purchases totaling nearly $25.00, see, in the same papers, the "Richard Owens Listing of Goods," (no month/day), 1852, AASF, LDD.

52. Fitzmaurice's statements quoted here are from SFCR, *Probate Court Journal, 1877–1897*, Book E, Testament of Tomasa Fitzmaurice, February 23, 1882, 140–143.

53. On Carson, see SFCR, "Legitimacy and Adoption Record, 1870–1882," 3–4. On Gallegos, see ibid., 7–8. On Gallegos's marriage to Donaghue, see SFCR, *Probate Court Journal, 1877–1897*, Book E, Inventory of Florence Donaghue, 510.

54. The question about why Euro-American men might sue for custody of children also centers on the matter of inheritance, and usually that of a first or second (Euro-American) wife. In some of the cited cases in this chapter, drawn from the legitimacy and adoption cases appearing in "Legitimacy and Adoption Record, 1870–1882," NM-SRC, the Euro-American men appear to be controlling the passing of an inheritance to "legitimately" acknowledged or claimed children. Does this suggest their humanitarianism, as someone asked me? The question draws us away from the impact of the action on local, Spanish-Mexican mothers whose travail already included the Euro-American invasion and takeover. One or two filed lawsuits do not suggest a trend, and for that reason, I do not tackle the men's incentives here.

55. On the laws, see Capdequí, "Bosquejo histórico," 162–182. On the functions of the dowry, and for an earlier period, see Asunción Lavrin and Edith Couturier, "Dowries and Wills: A View of Women's Socioeconomic Role in Colonial Guadalajara and Puebla, 1640–1790," *Hispanic American Historical Review* 59 (1979), 280–304. On a reading of an eighteenth-century will, see Ahlborn, "The Will of a New Mexico Woman in 1762," *NMHR*, 319–355. Other eighteenth-century readings can be found in Veyna, "It Is My Last Wish," in de la Torre and Pesquera, eds., *Building With Our Hands*, 91–108; and in Gloria Miranda, "Gente de Razón Marriage Patterns in Spanish and Mexican California: A Case Study of Santa Barbara and Los Angeles," *Southern California Quarterly* 63 (Spring 1981), 1–21.

56. For another discussion of the dowry, and of its use among the Mexican nobility in this time period, see Silvia Marina Arrom, *The Women of Mexico City, 1790–1857* (Stanford: Stanford University Press, 1985), 145–146.

57. Will of María Miquela Baca, April 22, 1830, Twitchell Coll. (Manusript Div., NMSRC); Will of María Rafaela Baca, April 26, 1804, Twitchell Coll. (Manuscript Div., NMSRC); and Will of María de la Sur Ortiz, March 6, 1860, SFCR, Wills and Testaments, 1856–1862, Book B, 299–302.

58. See my unpublished manuscript, "Chicanas Bequeath," a volume of the collected wills transcribed and translated, with distinctions drawn between those of the late eighteenth century and of the nineteenth century.

59. On Maria (de las) Nieves Chávez, see SFCR, Book D, 27–66. On Desideria Otero, see ibid., 30, 31.

60. Complaint by Barbará Baca, February 8–9, 1838, JCP, Roll 25 (microfilm, NMSRC), frame 488; and Will of Barbara Baca, Twitchell Coll., Wills and Estates, December 30, 1838 (Manuscript Div., NMSRC).

61. Will of Barbará Baca, December 30, 1838, Twitchell Coll. (Manuscript Div., NMSRC); and the itemization and remonstrances contained in González/Jaramillo Family Papers, a private collection.

62. Will of Barbará Baca, 3.

63. Will of María Josefa Martínez, May 23, 1860, SFCR, Book B, 1856–1862, 318–323.

64. Will of María Josefa Martínez, 318–323.

65. Lamar, *The Far Southwest*, 146–156.

66. Will of María Josefa Martínez, 318–323; many other wills suggest a similar pattern and have been collected and documented in my unpublished manuscript, "Chicanas Bequeath."

67. Will of María Nieves Chaves, 54–55.

68. The extant number of wills examined and collected for the period from 1848 to 1880 is seventy-five; of the thirty-five I have closely examined for this same period, because they are complete and legible (the remainder are not), only three, Ortiz's, Chaves's, and Martínez's, are longer than six pages, and only those detail vast property holdings. "Vast," in this instance, is defined as more than two houses, more than ten acres of land, and more than fifty head of livestock.

69. Will of Juana Terrasas, July 13, 1868, SFCR, Book B, 1856–1862, 392–394.

70. USCB, Tenth Census of Population, for Santa Fe (microfilm, NMSRC), 61, 70.

71. See ibid., 61, 62, 63, 70, 71.

72. USCB, Seventh, Eighth, Ninth, and Tenth Censuses of Population, for Santa Fe (microfilm, NMSRC).

73. USCB, Tenth Census of Population, for Santa Fe (microfilm, NMSRC), 30.

74. See Will of Maria Josefa Martínez, 318. For the names, see SFCR, Book B of the *Probate Court Journals*, 1857–1862.

75. Will of Desideria Otero, December 22, 1870, SFCR, Wills and Testaments, 1869–1877, Book D, 30–31.

76. Will of Desideria Otero, December 22, 1870, 31.

77. See Will of María Jesús Gonzales, Will of María Refugio Gonzales, and Will of Petrona Borrego Gonzales, March 7, 1873; also, Will of Dolores Montoya and Will of María Josefa Montoya, May 21, 1881.

78. Will of María Josefa Prada and Will of María Juana Prada, March 27, 1880; SFCR, 1877–1897, Book E, 155–157, 199–205, 124–127, 158–159, 97–100, 101–102.

79. Will of María Juana Prada, March 27, 1880.

80. For example, see Will of María Guadalupe Martín, n.d., Twitchell Coll. (Manuscript Div., NMSRC); she died in 1850, the year the first U.S. Census was taken in Santa Fe. See "Death Schedules," USCB, Seventh Census of Population, for Santa Fe (microfilm, NMSRC), 1.

81. Will of María Nieves Chaves, 62.

82. Will of Maria Miquela Baca, 1830, frames 1028–1034.

83. Will of María Teresa García, November 24, 1879, SFCR, Wills and Testaments, 1877–1897, Book E, 80–81.

84. See the Tenth Census of Population, for Santa Fe, USCB, (microfilm, NMSRC).

85. On the Santa Fe Ring, see Lamar, *The Far Southwest*, 156–159.

86. By far the clearest explanations about the extent of the territorial issues and of the Maxwell Land Grant are to be found in Lamar, *The Far Southwest*, 146–149. On the capitalization of land, see Ortiz, *Roots of Resistance*.

87. For an example of the changing city codes, ordinances, and the like, see Edward L. Bartlett, Charles W. Greene, Santiago Valdez, Commission, and Ireneo L. Chaves, secretary, *Local and Special Laws of New Mexico: In Accordance with an Act of the Legislature, Approved April 3, 1884* (Santa Fe: New Mexican Printing Company, Printers and Binders, 1885). For examples of associated crimes and punishments, see the work of Robert Torres, New Mexico state historian.

88. See Lebsock, *The Free Women of Petersburg*, introduction.

CHAPTER 4

1. See Montejano, *Anglos and Mexicans*; Gutiérrez, *When Jesus Came*, Castañeda, "Presidarias y Pobladoras"; and Emma M. Pérez, " 'Through Her Love and Sweetness':

Women, Revolution, and Reform in Yucatán, 1916–1930" (Ph.D. diss., UCLA, 1988, and her *The Decolonial Imaginary*. Castañeda is a colonial historian and Pérez is an historian of the twentieth century, but I situate them as Chicana historians because both use that descriptor as well. For just a few of the many works by Native American women and Native scholars, see Gretchen M. Bataille, *American Indian Women: A Guide to Research* (New York: Garland, 1991), as well as Gunn Allen, *The Sacred Hoop*; Albers and Medicine, *The Hidden Half*; and Clara Sue Kidwell, "Indian Women as Cultural Mediators," *Ethnohistory* 39, 2 (1992), 97–107.

2. An exception was the work of Carey McWilliams; see *North from Mexico* (New York, 1968). Chicano historians and scholars of Native societies began several decades ago to address the imbalances. For two examples, see Camarillo, *Chicanos in a Changing Society*, and Forbes, *Apache, Navaho, and Spaniard*. On Asian Americans and African Americans in Mexico's former northern territories, see Ronald Takaki, *Strangers from a Different Shore: A History of Asian Americans*, (New York: Penguin, 1989); Judy Yung, *Unbound Feet*; and the early work of Nell Irvin Painter, *Exodusters* (Kansas City: University of Kansas Press, 1986), and of Lawrence B. DeGraff, "Race, Sex, and Region: Black Women in the American West, 1850–1920," *Pacific Historical Review* (May 1980). For photos, see Katz, *The Black West*.

3. The numerous anthologies produced around conferences held in the far western states suggest the shift. See Armitage and Jameson, *The Women's West*; Schlissel, Ruiz, and Monk, *Western Women: Their Land, Their Lives*; Joan Jensen, Darlis Miller, eds., *New Mexico Women: Intercultural Perspectives* (Albuquerque: University of New Mexico Press, 1986); and Clyde Milner II, ed., *A New Signficance: Re-envisioning the History of the American West* (New York: Oxford University Press, 1996) including the essays of Susan Johnson and David Gutiérrez. See also Susan Johnson, "'A Memory Sweet to Soldiers': The Significance of Gender in the History of the American West," *Western Historical Quarterly* 3(1994), 322–345; and Andrea Yvette Huginnie, "'Strikitos': Race, Class, and Work in the Arizona Copper Industry, 1870–1920" (Ph.D. diss., Yale University, 1991). On western American narratives, see the path-breaking work of Henry Nash Smith, *Virgin Land*; Richard Slotkin, *Regeneration through Violence*; Richard Drinnon, *Facing West*; and Annette Kolodny, *The Lay of the Land* and *The Land before Her*. See the more recent volumes weaving other aspects of ethnicity, gender, and race, including David M. Emmons, *The Butte Irish: Class and Ethnicity in an American Mining Town, 1875–1925* (Champaign: University of Illinois Press, 1989); and Rosaura Sánchez, *Telling Identities: The Californio Testimonios* (Minneapolis: University of Minnesota Press, 1995), as well as the forthcoming book by Susan Johnson on the significance of gender in the U.S. West.

4. In Chicano history, the best textbook on this topic, and on the structural and attitudinal hostilities directed toward Mexicans in the Southwest, is Acuña, *Occupied America*. Also see Sunseri, *Seeds of Discord*, for New Mexico; and Montejano, *Anglos and Mexicans*, for Texas. Newer material can be found in several monographs, including David Gutiérrez, *Walls and Mirrors: Mexican Americans, Mexican Immigrants, and the Politics of Ethnicity in the American Southwest* (Berkeley: University of California Press, 1995), and George J. Sánchez, *Becoming Mexican American: Ethnicity, Culture and Identity in Chicano Los Angeles, 1900–1945* (New York: Oxford University Press, 1993). See the dissertation of Huginnie, "'Strikitos'"; and of Susan Johnson, "'The Gold she Gathered': Difference, Domination, and California's Southern Mines, 1848–1853," (Ph.D. diss., Yale Unviersity, 1993). On the role of nature and history, also a longstanding theme in U.S. western history, see the books by Richard White, including, "*It's Your Misfortune and None of My Own*" and *Roots of Dependency*; see also, Donald

Worster, *Under Western Skies: Nature and History in the American West* (New York: Oxford University Press, 1992), and Donald J. Pisani, *To Reclaim a Divided West: Water, Law, and Public Policy, 1848–1902* (Albuquerque: University of New Mexico Press, 1992).

5. See Limerick, *Legacy of Conquest*, introduction; also, Worster, *Rivers of Empire*. On the role of water in New Mexico, see Ira G. Clark, *Water in New Mexico: A History of its Management and Use* (Albuquerque: University of New Mexico Press, 1987).

6. On sexuality and power, see Michel Foucault, *The History of Sexuality* (New York: Pantheon, 1980). For a hermeneutic argument, see Todorov, *The Conquest of America*; for examples of the range and diversity of topics covered by the new ethnography, see James Clifford, *The Predicament of Culture: Twentieth-Century Ethnography, Literature, and Art* (Cambridge: Harvard University Press, 1988), Fredric Jameson, *Postmodernism: Or, the Cultural Logic of Late Capitalism* (Durham, 1991), Spivak, *In Other Worlds*, and Trinh T. Minh-ha, *Woman, Native, Other: Writing Postcoloniality and Feminism* (Bloomington: Indiana University Press, 1989); for a review of this literature and its specific application to Chicano and Chicana history, see Pérez, *The Decolonial Imaginary*, chap. 1.

7. See the essay by Cornel West, "The New Cultural Politics of Difference," in Russell Ferguson, Martha Gever, Trinh T.Minh-ha, and Cornel West, eds., *Out There: Marginalization and Contemporary Cultures* (Cambridge: MIT Press, 1990); and West, *Race Matters* (Boston: Beacon Press, 1993). The interrogations about intellectual hegemony occur in Chicano Studies as well; see, for example, Angie Chabram and Rosalinda Fregoso, eds., *Cultural Studies*, "Chicana/o Cultural Representations" 4:3 (October 1990).

8. The problems of Latino urban populations and of an "underclass" are well documented, as is poverty in rural areas of the Far West. For contemporary Santa Fe and demographic shifts, see USCB 1980 Census. On Indian reservations and statistics on poverty, see Richard White, *The Roots of Dependency: Subsistence, Environment, and Social Change among the Choctaws, Pawnees, and Navajos* (Lincoln: University of Nebraska Press, 1983), and Michael Dorris, *The Broken Cord* (New York: Harper and Row, 1989).

9. See the works of Roger Daniels, including *Concentration Camps: North America: Japanese in the United States and Canada during World War II* (Malabar, Fla.: R. E. Krieger, 1981), and *The Politics of Prejudice: The Anti-Japanese Movement in California and the Struggle for Japanese Exclusion* (Berkeley: University of California Press, 1977). Also see Roger Daniels, Sandra C. Taylor, and Harry H. L. Kitano, eds., *Japanese Americans: From Relocation to Redress* (Salt Lake City: University of Utah Press, 1986). For a discussion of race and ethnicity, see Paul R. Spickard, *Mixed Blood: Intermarriage and Ethnic Identity in Twentieth-Century America* (Madison: University of Wisconsin Press, 1989).

10. Donald Worster, *Rivers of Empire: Water, Aridity, and the Growth of the American West* (New York: Pantheon, 1985).

11. Castañeda, "Presidarias y Pobladoras," chap. 1; and, by the same author, "Women of Color and the Rewriting of Western History: The Discourse, Politics, and Decolonization of History," *Pacific Historical Review* 61:4 (November, 1992), 501–533.

12. Recent feminist critiques of the assumptions guiding liberal doctrines include Shane Phelan, *Identity Politics: Lesbian Feminism and the Limits of Community* (Philadelphia: Temple University Press, 1989), and Elizabeth V. Spelman, *Inessential Woman: Problems of Exclusion in Feminist Thought* (Boston: Beacon Press, 1988), on the Euro-American women's side, as well as Ruth Frankenberg, *White women, Race matters: The Social Construction of Whiteness,* (Minneapolis: University of Minnesota Press, 1993).

13. Petition of *Rafael Muñiz v. Quirina Montoya*, October 27, 1888 (SFCR, Probate

Court Cases, NMSRC). There is no record of either party in the census that followed later in the century. Did Muñiz leave Santa Fe, or did Montoya? Did she lose her children? Was he successful? This is just one set of questions that remains unanswered. Note, however, that she, even in 1888, sustained the practice of retaining her family-of-origin's name, Montoya.

14. Although the books date from 1893, many of the earliest entries in the first ledger stem from the previous decade. See SFCR, Jail Records, 1893–1928, outsized, 064, Serial Number 15444, 1–64 (NMSRC), and correlated to the Penitentiary Records, Convict Record Books, 1884–1917 (microfilm, NMSRC), 3 reels.

15. See Camarillo, *Chicanos in a Changing Society*; Barrera, *Race and Class in the Southwest*; and Griswold del Castillo, *La Familia*. An exception would be Garcia's "The Chicana in American History," which appeared in 1980, and continues the practice of attempting to fit Chicanas into categories—racial, ethnic, or gendered—established in such mainstream fields as immigrant history, labor history, or ethnic history. I do not criticize the practice because I see that it is as necessary as contribution history; I think, however, that its practice is dated and preliminary. Deploying femaleness or "woman" as a category of analysis signifies rereading all other categories, and feminist analysis is now particularly insistent that mere insertion of Chicanas in articles or chapters is insufficient, for Chicanas clearly had much more to do with, and say about, their situations, and so should we.

16. Recent works that assess and situate gender and women include Ruiz, *From Out of the Shadows* and *Cannery Women, Cannery Lives*, Gutiérrez, *When Jesus Came*; and Mario T. García, *Mexican Americans: Leadership, Ideology, and Identity, 1930–1960* (New Haven: Yale University Press, 1989). In labor history, see the work of Camille Guerin-Gonzales, *Mexican Workers' and American Dreams: Immigration, Repatriation, and California Farm Labor, 1900–1939* (New Brunswick: Rutgers University Press, 1994).

17. See the work of Darlis Miller, for example, who coauthored, with Joan Jensen, an important article, early in the 1980s, calling for multicultural awareness, "The Gentle Tamers Revisited: New Approaches to the History of Women in the American West," *Pacific Historical Review* 59:2 (May 1980); also see Miller and Jensen, *Intercultural Perspectives*. Another group of western frontier historians took the concern for multiculturalism a step further and incorporated issues of race, racism, and interracial relations. See, for example, Pascoe, *Relations of Rescue*; Deutsch, *No Separate Refuge*; and the essay by Susan L. Johnson, "Sharing Bed and Board: Cohabitation and Cultural Difference in Central Arizona Mining Towns, 1863–1873," *The Women's West*, edited by Susan Armitage and Elizabeth Jameson. For an overview of all of these sources, see Castañeda, "Women of Color," *Pacific Historical Review*.

18. For example, see Miller, "The Cross-Cultural Marriages," *New Mexico Historical Review*; Dysart, "Mexican Women in San Antonio," *Western Historical Quarterly*; Craver, *The Impact of Intimacy*; and Myres, "Mexican Americans and Westering Anglos," *New Mexico Historical Review*.

19. For examples of the Hispanicization of Euro-American names, see Craver, *The Impact of Intimacy*, 21, 28, 30, 37, 39, 43. On the Hispanicization of interracial children's first names see Bartlett et al., *Local and Special Laws*, 905, 906, 908, for the petitions of the parents of "Juana Francisca" Collins; "Carlos Serafin," "Maria Paula," and "Dolores Henrietta" Springer. One exception to this pattern can be found in the petition for "Charles Whitlock," heir of John Whitlock and "Margarita Valdés" de Whitlock, cited in ibid., 896–897.

20. See USCB, Eighth Census of Population, for Santa Fe, microfilm (NMSRC).

21. Myres, *Westering Women*, 84–85.

22. The sample was done across two censuses, 1860 and 1870, in the progressive order of the census for the town of Santa Fe. See USCB, Tenth and Eleventh Censuses. Another worthwile sample might be drawn from the "Acts of Legitimation," published in 1885 and derived from special petitions working their way through the territorial legislature. Here again, petitioners displayed a range of patterns, from adoption of interracial children by interracial couples, to the standard ones in which Spanish-Mexican women continue retaining their family, or Spanish, surnames, but sustain the practice of giving their non-Spanish-surnamed children Spanish first names. See Bartlett et al., *Local and Special Laws*, 896–913.

23. An example of the notion of "conquest as destiny" is suggested in the subtitle of one historian's recent book on this same period, Weber, *The Mexican Frontier, 1821– 1846: The American Southwest Under Mexico.*

24. Myres, *Westering Women*, 84–85. Also see Miller, "The Cross-Cultural Marriages," *New Mexico Historical Review*, 57:4 (Oct. 1982), 352, which states that "marriage to an Anglo started the process of assimilation for Spanish-speaking women and their offspring." For Texas, see Dysart, "Mexican Women in San Antonio," the *Western Historical Quarterly*, 372, which states that "marriage to an Anglo after 1830 initiated a process of assimilation and acculturation which in the vast majority of cases led to the Americanization of their children."

25. See Craver's *The Impact of Intimacy*, for example. In another vein and, conceptually, a newer direction, see Richard White's work on "the middle ground," used to examine Native-European relations, in *The Middle Ground: Indians, Empires, and Republics in the Great Lakes Region, 1650–1815* (New York: Cambridge University Press, 1991), and his *'It's Your Misfortune and None of My Own': A History of the American West*, (Norman: University of Oklahoma Press, 1991). For an earlier example, because it examines the social milieu in which Asian-westering/Euro-American interracial relations existed, see Pascoe, *Relations of Rescue*, and Pascoe, "Western Women at the Cultural Crossroads," in Patricia Limerick, ed., *Trails: Toward a New Western History* (Kansas City: University of Kansas Press, 1991), as well as her "Race, Gender, and Intercultural Relations: The Case of Interracial Marriage," *Frontiers* 12:1 (1991), 16–32. For a review of mixed marriages in U.S. history, see Spickard, *Mixed Blood*, 6–17. For an analysis from a Chicano/mixed-blood perspective, see the fascinating work of Arturo Aldama, "Disrupting Savagism in the Borderlands of Identity: Subjectification and Resistance in Mexican Immigrant, Native American, and Chicana/o Signifying Practices" (Ph.D. diss., University of California, Berkeley 1996).

26. For an example of the logic even in the popular folklore, see Craver, *The Impact of Intimacy*, 25–27. For a discussion of the correlation between intermarriage and Euro-American acquisitions of Spanish-Mexican land grants, see ibid., 32.

27. The question was raised on two separate occasions after I had delivered papers detailing conclusions based on the evidence from the marriage and legitimacy records, NMSRC; from the University of New Mexico, Albuquerque, February, 1989; and from the Huntington Library, San Marino, Calif., May 1985.

28. Sources where statistical information is available abound; see the SFCR, Probate Court Records, on legitimacy and adoption. Also see Bartlett al., *Local and Special Laws*, especially 896–912; and the censuses for 1870, 1880, and at the turn of the century. The secondary literature has yet to cultivate this material.

29. See Glenda Riley, *Women and Indians on the Frontier, 1825–1915*, for an example of a work which distinguishes the two categories only superficially, "women" and "Indians." For my criticisms of such tendencies, see my commentary on John Mack Faragher's "The Custom of the Country," in Schlissel, Ruiz, and Monk, *Western Women*,

217–220. Also see, for a classic example of this sort of leveling tendency, Walter O'Meara, *Daughters of the Country: The Women of the Fur Trappers and Mountain Men* (New York: Harcourt, Brace, and World, 1968).

30. The literature on this topic is rich, across disciplines. On African American/ Euro-American relationships, begin with Winthrop Jordan's *White over Black: American Attitudes toward the Negro, 1550–1812* (Chapel Hill: University of North Carolina Press, 1968); on miscegenation laws, applied against interracial relationships, see Takaki, *Iron Cages,* 49, 59, 60, 114–115, 134, 142, 209–210. On Chicano/Euro-American relationships, for a different perspective from the viewpoint of a psychologist, see Nellie Salgado de Synder and Amado M. Padilla, "Interethnic Marriages of Mexican Americans after Nearly Two Decades," Spanish Speaking Mental Health Research Center, UCLA, Occasional Paper 15, 1981. On mixed marriages in general, see Spickard, *Mixed Blood,* introduction. For an evaluation of the "logic of racial thinking," see the commentary of Tessie P. Liu, "Race and Gender in the Politics of Group Formation: A comment on Notions of Multiculturalism," paper delivered at the University of Arizona, March 1991, and her "Teaching the Differences Among Women from a Historical Perspective: Rethinking Race and Gender as Social Categories," in DuBois and Ruiz, *Unequal Sisters,* 571–583.

31. The scholarship the "proves" institutionalized racism is rich and varied. See Jordan, *White Over Black;* Ringer, *We, the People;* and Takaki, *Iron Cages.*

32. For an example of the middle-ground concept, but one based on evidence and research, see White, *The Middle Ground;* the concepts have long been in use, especially in ethnography. For the Southwest, see Spicer, *Cycles of Conquest,* and John, *Storms Brewed in Other Men's Worlds.* My question remains: Exactly what middle ground does a contemporary reservation or an inner-city barrio provide?

33. An excellent example occurred in a Los Angeles courtroom in *Acuña v. U.C. Board of Regents* in 1995. As his lawyers presented the case and evidence, letters revealed that Professor Acuña's critics thought him to be "ideological," despite my letter of evaluation and those of such senior scholars as Professors Ramón Ruiz, Juan Gómez-Quiñones, and Carlos Vélez-Ibañez, who documented Professor Acuña's numerous analytical contributions to the field of Chicano History. The attorneys and officers of the University of California thought the contrary and suggested in closing arguments that even some of us thought he was a scholar "with an ax to grind." From my letter of evaluation—revealed in court by the lawsuit and now part of the public record—they failed to read to the jury the entire paragraph, which continued, "But none have ever proven him wrong in his conclusions." The jury found for Acuña and against U.C. Santa Barbara's denial of his appointment; the university continued to appeal the decision, quibbling over the amount of money Acuña's lawyers were charging. Asked to review every case for promotion at UCSB (the site of the lawsuit) over the past decade, as part of Acuña's challenge to the university, the university lawyers sent his legal team literally thousands of file folders, causing them more extensive, costly work. The university next argued against the bills for services.

34. One recommendation is to distinguish, of course, from among the different practitioners of history, and from among PBS filmmakers, the oft-quoted "new western" historians, ethnic history surveyors, and the like, as not all are similar or can be so easily lumped into their respective orientations. The repetitive and serviceable refrain Native American scholars and indigenous philosophers lend is equally important, and explains why, as they say, the best knowledge is reserved for internal use, and not for popular consumption. See the PBS series "The Native Americans," and, in sharp contrast, "Surviving Columbus: The Story of the Pueblo People."

35. The friars were Bernardino Sahagún and Bartolomé de las Casas. On the Aztec

codices, see Miguel Leon-Portilla, ed., *The Broken Spears: The Aztec Account of the Conquest of Mexico* (Boston: Beacon Press, 1962).

36. Many of the debates surrounding these issues have been published in professional journals. See *American Historical Review* 94:3 (June 1989), and *Journal of American History* 76:2 (1989), 393–478. Also see Joan Scott, *Gender and the Politics of History* (New York: Columbia University Press, 1988), and Lynn Hunt, ed., *The New Cultural History* (Berkeley: University of California Press, 1989). On the question of objectivity, see Peter Novick, *That Noble Dream: History and the Question of Objectivity* (Cambridge: Cambridge University Press, 1988). For the implications surrounding historians' writings, also see Hayden White, *Metahistory*, (Baltimore: Johns Hopkins University Press, 1973).

37. Historians can be said to be of two minds on these issues; some say that, for example, women's history and ethnic history do not revolutionize the field because they simply "fill a gap," while others are more concerned about the implications of this approach in what is perceived to be more than "contribution." See Lebsock, *The Free Women of Petersburg*, introduction, and the special issues of *American Historical Review*, 94:3 (1989), and *Journal of American History*, 76:2 (1988), for some examples of the contours of the debate. For recent work in Chicano/a Studies documenting some of the same issues, but influenced by work in popular cultural studies, especially on gender, see the first monograph published in Chicano/a art criticism, Alicia Gaspar de Alba, *Chicano Art Inside/Outside the Master's House: Cultural Politics and the CARA Exhibition* (Austin: University of Texas Press, 1998).

38. See, for example, Myres, *Westering Women*, who, in chapter 4 on Mexican women, cites only one set of sources in Spanish, and none for the Spanish-Mexican women of New Mexico. Miller's sources in "Cross-Cultural Marriages" are also drawn from English-based documents. Several new monographs suffer from the same problem. See, for example, Limerick, *Legacy of Conquest*, and Deutsch, *No Separate Refuge*.

39. Some noticeable exceptions exist. See the work of David Weber, beginning with *The Spanish Frontier in North America* (New Haven: Yale University Press, 1992), *The Mexican Frontier*, and including *Foreigners in their Native Land: Historical Roots of the Mexican-Americans* (Albuquerque: University of New Mexico Press, 1973). Also see Gutiérrez, *When Jesus Came*. Another problem for scholars of the Spanish-Mexican experience is that few of us read or understand the indigenous, and surviving, languages of the regions we study. Because so much of what interests historians about colonization revolves as much around linguistics as it does around politics, this deficiency in our graduate and research institutions plagues our discipline.

40. Richard Griswold del Castillo had, in his work on Chicano families, provided guidelines and some figures, but these focus mostly on the later period. See del Castillo, *La Familia: Chicano Families in the Urban Southwest, 1848 to the Present* (Notre Dame, Ind.: University of Notre Dame Press, 1984).

41. Mrs. Henry Wetter, letter to her sister, April 3, 1877, mss., NMHL.

42. Elizabeth Perry, "On Virgins and Martyrs," Spaulding Lecture, Pomona College, February 3, 1987; also see, for some refinements of the categorization based on research on prostitutes in London, Ruth Mazo Karras, public lecture delivered at the Scripps Humanities Institute, February 28, 1991: "Common Women: Prostitution and Sexuality in Medieval Culture." The work of Latin American historian Asunción Lavrin on convents counters many stereotypes of Mexican women; see her "Values and Meanings of Monastic Life," *Catholic Historical Review* 58:3 (1972–1973), 367–387.

43. For a different interpretation, using an Oedipal reading, see Emma Pérez, "Speaking from the Margin: Uninvited Discourse on Sexuality and Power," in de la

Torre and Pesquera, eds., *Building With Our Own Hands*, 57–71; and, in a slightly different form, the same article appearing in Carla Trujillo, ed., *Chicana Lesbians: The Girls Our Mothers Warned Us About* (Berkeley: Third Women Press, 1991), 159–184. For a traditional culturalist reading, see Octavio Paz, Diane Marting, trans., "Juana Ramírez," *Signs: Journal of Women in Culture and Society* (Autumn 1979), 80–97. On Sor Juana, see the feminist and lesbian historical novel by Alicia Gaspar de Alba, *Sor Juana's Second Dream* (Albuquerque: University of New Mexico Press, 1999).

44. Scholars who have been especially helpful in outlining such processes include liberation theologians of Latin America and some living in the United States. See the cycle and pattern of identification and disidentification embodied in the reflections of Ernesto Cardenal, *The Gospel in Solentiname*, vol. 1 (New York: Orbis Books, 1975), and in Paulo Freire, *Pedagogy of the Oppressed* (New York: Herder and Herder, 1970). For texts addressing women's responses, and a mujerista-constructed theology guided by notions of recovery and reconstruction, see Isasi-Diaz, *Hispanic Women*.

45. On the problematic characteristics of some new work, see, on prostitution and Mexican women, Marion Goldman, *Gold Diggers and Silver Miners: Prostitution and Social Life on the Comstock Lode* (Ann Arbor: University of Michigan Press, 1981).

46. The Turnerians were especially fond of writing around traditional themes. Trappers, miners, crooks, and vigilantes were the standard players, but there were also the accompanying discussions about the fur trade, gold rushes, bank robberies or frontier justice. See Ray Allen Billington, *The Far Western Frontier*. For books about women from the same period, see O'Meara, *Daughters of the Country*, and Ross, *Westward the Women*. These can be compared to Jeffrey, *Frontier Women*; Schlissel, *Women's Diaries of the Westward Journey*; Pascoe, *Relations of Rescue*; Albers and Medicine, *The Hidden Half*; Allen, *The Sacred Hoop*; Yung, *Unbound Feet*.

47. An example is the number of Chicanas with Ph.D.'s in the entire historical profession—nineteen, with three more in the pipeline for the 1990s. At the current rate, parity will be reached at the end of the next millenium.

48. See the American Historical Association's newsletter, *Perspectives*, February 1991, and March 1994, for a recent summary of the statistics.

BIBLIOGRAPHY

ABBREVIATIONS

AASF   Archives of the Archdiocese of Santa Fe, Coronado Collection, University of New Mexico, Albuquerque; New Mexico State Records Center, Santa Fe, microfilm

GONZ   González and Jaramillo Family Papers, Private Collection, Garfield, New Mexico, and Denver.

HEH   Henry E. Huntington Library, San Marino, California

JCP   Judicial Court Proceedings, State Records Center, Santa Fe, microfilm

LDD   Loose Documents, Diocesan

MANM   Mexican Archives of New Mexico, New Mexico State Records Center, Santa Fe, microfilm

MNMHL   Museum of New Mexico, History Library

NMHR   New Mexico Historical Review

NMSRC   New Mexico State Records Center, Santa Fe

SANM   Spanish Archives of New Mexico, New Mexico State Records Center, Santa Fe, microfilm

SENA   Sena Family Papers, Private Collection, Denver and Pueblo, Colorado

SFCR   Santa Fe County Records, New Mexico State Records Center, Santa Fe

Twitchell   Twitchell Collection, Manuscript Division, New Mexico State Records
Coll.   Center, Santa Fe, copies (originals in the Coronado Collection, University of New Mexico, Albuquerque)

UNM   Coronado Collection at the University of New Mexico

USCB   United States Census Bureau, Original Schedules, New Mexico State Records Center, Santa Fe, microfilm; originals in the National Archives, Washington, D.C.

PRIMARY SOURCES

Manuscripts and Manuscript Collections

Abert, J. W. *Western America in 1846–1847: The Original Travel Diary of Lieutenant J. W. Abert, Who Mapped New Mexico for the United States Army.* Ed. John Galvin. San Francisco: J. Howell, 1966.

Aldama, Arturo. "Disrupting Savagism in the Borderlands of Identity: Subjectification and Resistance in Mexican Immigrant, Native American, and Chicana/o Signifying Practices." Ph.D. diss., University of California, Berkeley, 1996.

Archives of the Archdiocese of Santa Fe. Coronado Collection, University of New Mexico.

Archives of the Archdiocese of Santa Fe. New Mexico State Records Center, Santa Fe.

Bartlett, Edward, Charles W. Greene, Santiago Valdes, Commission, and Ireneo L. Chaves, secretary, "Local and Special Laws of New Mexico: In Accordance with an Act of the Legislature, Approved April 3, 1884." Santa Fe, 1885.

Beckwourth, James P. *The Life and Adventures of James P. Beckwourth, Mountaineer, Scout, Pioneer, and the Chief of the Crow Indians.* Ed. T. D. Bonner. New York: Macmillan, 1892.

Bieber, Ralph, ed. *Adventures in the Santa Fe Trade, 1844–1847 by James Josiah Webb.* Glendale: Arthur H. Clark, 1931.

Bradley, Phillips, ed. *Alexis de Tocqueville's Democracy in America.* New York: Knopf, 1945.

Brewerton, George. "Incidents of Travel in New Mexico." *Harper's* 47 (April 1854).

Calderón de la Barca, Frances. *Life in Mexico.* New York: E.P. Dutton, 1954.

Castañeda, Antonia I. "Presidarias y Pobladoras: Spanish-Mexican Women in Frontier Monterey, Alta California, 1770–1821." Ph.D. diss., Stanford University, 1990.

Congressional Globe, 28th Cong., 2d sess.

Congressional Globe, 29th Cong., 1st sess.

Cooke, Philip St. George. *The Conquest of New Mexico and California: An Historical and Personal Narrative.* New York: Putnam's, 1878. (Reprint, New York: Arno Press, 1976.)

Cutts, James Madison. *The Conquest of California and New Mexico by the Forces of the United States in the Years 1846 and 1847.* Philadelphia: Carey and Hart, 1847. (Reprint, Albuquerque: Horn and Wallace, 1965.)

Dana, Richard Henry. *Two Years before the Mast.* New York: Modern Library, 1964.

Davis, W. W. H. *El Gringo: or New Mexico and Her People.* New York: Harper and Brothers, 1857. (Reprint, Lincoln: University of Nebraska Press, 1982.)

Duflot de Mofras, Eugene. *Duflot de Mofras' Travels on the Pacific Coast.* Trans., ed., and annot. Marguerite Eyer Wilbur. Santa Ana, Calif.: Fine Arts Press, 1937.

Dyer, Alexander B. "Mexican War Journal, 1846–1848." Museum of New Mexico, History Library, Santa Fe.

de las Casas, Bartolomé. *In Defense of the Indians; The Defense of the Most Reverend Lord, Don Fray Bartolome de las Casas, of the Order of Preachers, Late Bishop of Chiapa, against the Persecutors and Slanderers of the Peoples of the New World Discovered across the Seas.* Trans., ed., and annot. Stafford Poole. DeKalb: Northern Illinois University Press, 1974. (Reprint, 1992.)

De León, Arnoldo. "White Racial Attitudes towards Mexicanos in Texas, 1821–1900." Ph.D. diss., Texas Christian University, 1974.

Edwards, Frank S. *A Campaign in New Mexico with Colonel Doniphan.* Philadelphia: Carey and Hart, 1847.

Emory, W. H. "General Kearny and the Army of the West: Extracts from the Journal of Lieutenant Emory." *Niles National Register* 71 (November 7, 1846): 158.

Emory, W. H., "Notes of a Military Reconnaissance from Fort Leavenworth, in Missouri, to San Diego, in California. Made in 1846–7, with the advanced guard of the Army of the West," *House Ex. Doc.* 41, 30th Cong., 1st sess. *House Ex. Doc.*. 41, 30th Cong., 1st sess. *House Ex. Doc.* 2, 29th Cong., 1st sess.

Field, Matthew C. *Matt Field on the Santa Fe Trial.* Ed. John E. Sunder. Norman: University of Oklahoma Press, 1960.

Franco, Bernardo Vásquez. Papers, Otero Collection, 1840–1845. New Mexico State Records Center, Santa Fe.

Gaspar de Alba, Alicia. "'Mi Casa [No] Es Su Casa': The Cultural Politics of the *Chicano Art: Resistance and Affirmation, 1965–1985 Exhibition*." Ph.D. diss., University of New Mexico, 1994.

Gregg, Josiah. Correspondence and Memoirs, 1831–1840. Museum of New Mexico, History Library, Santa Fe.

Gregg, Josiah. *The Commerce of the Prairies.* Ed. Milo M. Quaife. Chicago: R. R. Donnelley, 1926. (Reprint, Lincoln: University of Nebraska Press, 1967.)

Gregg, Josiah L. *The Commerce of the Prairies.* Ed. Max Moorhead. Norman: University of Oklahoma Press, 1958.

Gutiérrez, Ramón Arturo. "Marriage, Sex, and the Family: Social Change in Colonial New Mexico, 1690–1846." Ph.D. diss., University of Wisconsin, 1980.

Harper's Monthly (title varies), April, 1854.

Hernández, Philip Anthony. "The Other Americans: The American Image of Mexico and Mexicans, 1550–1850." Ph.D. diss., University of California, Berkeley, 1974.

Hickok, Jane. *Calamity Jane's Letters to Her Daughter.* San Lorenzo, Calif.: Shameless Hussy Press, 1976.

Holley, Mary Austin. *Observations Historical, Geographical and Descriptive.* Austin, Tex.: Overland Press, 1981 (Orig. ed., Baltimore: Armstrong and Plaskitt, 1833.)

Hughes, John Taylor. *Doniphan's Expedition Containing An Account of the Conquest of New Mexico.* New York: Arno Press, 1973. (Orig. ed., Washington, D.C.: Government Printing Office, 1914.)

Huginnie, Andrea Yvette. "'Strikitos': Race, Class, and Work in the Arizona Copper Industry, 1870–1920." Ph.D. diss., Yale University, 1991.

Hulbert, Archer B., ed. *Southwest on the Turquoise Trail: The First Diaries on the Road to Santa Fe.* Colorado Springs: Stewart Commission of Colorado College; and Denver: Denver Public Library, 1933.

James, Thomas. *Three Years among the Indians and Mexicans.* Philadelphia: Lippincott, 1962.

Johnson, Susan. "'The Gold She Gathered': Difference, Domination, and California's Southern Mines, 1848–1853." Ph.D. diss., Yale University, 1993.

Journal of the House of Representatives of the State of Missouri. Jefferson City, March 1875.

Kennerly, William Clark, as told to Elizabeth Russell. *Persimmon Hill: A Narrative of Old St. Louis and the Far West.* Norman: University of Oklahoma Press, 1948.

Kenneson, Susan Reyner. "Through the Looking-Glass: A History of Anglo-American Attitudes towards the Spanish-American and Indians of New Mexico." Ph.D. diss., Yale University, 1978.

Livermore, Abiel Abbot. *The War with Mexico Reviewed.* New York: Arno Press, 1976. (Orig. ed., Boston: American Peace Society, 1850.)

Magoffin, Susan Shelby. *The Diary of Susan Shelby Magoffin, 1846–1847: Down the*

Santa Fe Trail and into Mexico. Ed. Stella Drumm. Lincoln: University of Nebraska Press, 1982.

Mayer, Brantz. *Mexico as It Was and as It Is.* Philadelphia: G. B. Zieber, 1847.

McDermott, John Francis, ed. *Travels in Search of an Elephant: The Wanderings of Alfred S. Waugh, Artist, in Louisiana, Missouri, and Santa Fe, in 1845–1846.* St. Louis: Missouri Historical Society, 1951.

Mexican Archives of New Mexico, 1821–1846. New Mexico State Records Center, Santa Fe.

Olmsted, Virginia Langham, trans. and comp. *Spanish and Mexican Colonial Census of New Mexico, 1790, 1823, 1845.* Albuquerque: New Mexico Genealogical Society, 1975. Coronado Collection, Zimmerman Library.

Pattie, James Ohio. *The Personal Narrative of James O. Pattie, of Kentucky: 1831 edition unabridged.* Ed. Timothy Flint. Lincoln: University of Nebraska Press, 1984.

Pattie, James O. *The Personal Narrative of James O. Pattie.* Ed. William H. Goetzmann. Philadelphia: Lippincott, 1962; 1831 ed., unabridged.

Pérez, Emma M. "'Through Her Love and Sweetness': Women, Revolution, and Reform in Yucatán, 1916–1930." Ph.D. diss., University of California, Los Angeles, 1988.

Pike, Albert. *Prose Sketches and Poems, Written in the Western Country with Additional Stories.* Ed. David J. Weber. College Station: Texas A & M University Press, 1987. (Orig. ed., Boston: Light and Horton, 1843.)

Pike, Zebulon Montgomery. *Exploratory Travels through the Western Territories of North America.* Denver: W. H. Lawrence, 1889.

Pino, Pedro Bautista. *Three New Mexico Chronicles: The Exposición of Don Pedro Bautista Pino 1812; The Ojeada of Lic. Antonio Barreiro 1832; and the Additions by Don José Augustin de Escudero.* Trans. H. Bailey Carrol and J. Villasana Haggard. Albuquerque: Quivira Society, 1942. (Reprint, New York: Arno Press, 1967.)

Poinsett, Joel Roberts. *Notes on Mexico, Made in the Autumn of 1822.* New York: Praeger, 1969.

Prince, L. Bradford, comp. *General Laws of New Mexico from the "Kearny Code of 1846" to 1880.* Albany, New York: W. C. Little, 1880.

Probate Court Journals, 1856–1897. New Mexico State Records Center, Santa Fe.

Quaife, Milo M., ed. *George Wilkins Kendall Narrative of the Texas–Santa Fe Expedition.* Chicago: R. R. Donnelley, 1929.

Reilly, Thomas W. "American Reporters and the Mexican War, 1846–1848." Ph.D. diss., University of Minnesota, 1975.

Ritch, William G., Papers, 1846–1896. The Henry E. Huntington Library, San Marino, Calif.

Robinson, Alfred. *Life in California: During a Residence of Several Years in That Territory.* New York: De Capo Press, 1969. (Orig. ed., New York: Wiley and Putnam, 1846.)

Ruxton, George F. A. *Adventures in Mexico and the Rocky Mountains.* London: John Murray, 1847. (Rev. ed., with new preface, new introduction, new bibliography, new map, and new index. Glorieta, N.M.: Rio Grande Press, 1973.)

Sánchez, Pedro. "Memórias sobre la vida del presbitero don António José Martínez," in David Weber, ed., *Northern New Mexico on the Eve of the United States Invasion.* New York: Arno Press, 1976.

Sánchez, Pedro. "Historia consisa del cura de Taos António José Martínez." *El Historiador,* May 4, 1861.

Santa Fe County Records, 1856–1897. New Mexico State Records Center, Santa Fe.

Santa Fe County Records, Jail and Penitentiary Records, 1893–1928.

Segale, Sister Blandina. *At the End of the Santa Fe Trail.* Milwaukee: Bruce Publishing, 1948. (Orig. ed., Columbus, Ohio: Columbian Press, 1932.)

Senate Ex. Doc. 23, 29th Cong., 1st sess.

Spanish Archives of New Mexico, 1621–1821. New Mexico State Records Center, Santa Fe.

Territorial Archives of New Mexico, 1846–1912. New Mexico State Records Center, Santa Fe.

Thompson, Waddy. *Recollections of Mexico.* New York and London: Wiley and Putnam, 1846.

Twitchell, Ralph Emerson, Papers (copies), 1727–1929. Manuscripts Division, New Mexico State Records Center, Santa Fe.

Twitchell, Ralph Emerson, Papers, 1727–1929. Manuscripts Division, Coronado Collection, University of New Mexico, Albuquerque.

Ulibarrí, Richard Onofre. "American Interest in the Spanish Mexican Southwest, 1803–1848." Ph.D. diss., University of Utah, 1963.

United States, Census Bureau, Original Schedule of the Seventh Census of Population, for Santa Fe.

United States, Census Bureau, Original Schedule of the Eighth Census of Population, for Santa Fe.

United States, Census Bureau, Original Schedule of the Ninth Census of Population, for Santa Fe.

United States, Census Bureau, Original Schedule of the Tenth Census of Population, for Santa Fe.

United States, Census Bureau, Original Schedule of the Twelfth Census of Population, for Santa Fe.

United States, Census Bureau, Original Schedule of the Twentieth Census of Population, for Santa Fe.

Webb, James Josiah. *Adventures in the Santa Fe Trade 1844–1847.* Ralph Bieber, ed. Glendale, Calif.: Arthur H. Clark, 1931.

Webb, James Josiah, Memoirs, 1844–1889. Museum of New Mexico, History Library, Santa Fe.

Webb, James Josiah, Papers, 1852–1864. New Mexico State Records Center, Santa Fe.

Weber, David, ed. *Northern Mexico on the Eve of the United States Invasion.* New York, Arno Press, 1976.

Wetter, Henry, Collection, 1860–1872. Museum of New Mexico, History Library, Santa Fe.

Wislizenus, Dr. Adolphus, "Memoir of a Tour to Northern Mexico," *Senate* [Misc.] *Doc.* 30th Cong., 1st sess.

Yung, Judy. "Unbinding the Feet, Unbinding Their Lives: Social Change for Chinese Women in San Francisco, 1902–1945." Ph.D. diss., University of California, Berkeley, 1990.

Newspapers

Missouri Intelligencer, 1846–1847.

New Orleans Daily Picayune, 1840–1848.

New York Tribune, 1847.

Richmond Enquirer, Va., 1847.

Richmond Daily Union, 1847.

Santa Fe New Mexican, 1865–1883.

Santa Fe Republican, 1848.

St. Louis Republican, 1846–1848.

Washington Union, 1847.

Niles Weekly Register (title varies). Baltimore, Washington, D.C., Philadelphia, 1811–1849.

SECONDARY SOURCES

Abu-Lughod, Lila. *Veiled Sentiments: Honor and Poetry in a Bedouin Society.* Berkeley: University of California Press, 1986.

Acuña, Rodolfo. *Occupied America: A History of Chicanos.* New York: Harper and Row, 1981.

Adams, Alexander. *Geronimo: A Biography.* New York: Putnam, 1971.

Ahlborn, Richard Eighme. "The Will of a New Mexico Woman in 1762." *New Mexico Historical Review* 65 (July 1990), 319–355.

Albers, Patricia, and Beatrice Medicine. *The Hidden Half: Studies of Plains Indian Women.* Washington, D.C.: University Press of America, 1983.

Alloula, Malek. *The Colonial Harem.* Minneapolis: University of Minnesota Press, 1986.

Almaguer, Tomas. *Racial Fault Lines: The Historical Origins of White Supremacy in California.* Berkeley: University of California Press, 1994.

Anonymous (Sena Family Spokesperson), Denver. Interview, July 30, 1991.

Anzaldúa, Gloria. *Borderlands/La Frontera: The New Mestiza.* San Francisco: Spinsters/Aunt Lute, 1987.

Archibald, Robert. "Acculturation and Assimilation in Colonial New Mexico." *New Mexico Historical Review* 53 (July 1978), 205–214.

Armitage, Susan, and Elizabeth Jameson, eds. *The Women's West.* Norman: University of Oklahoma Press, 1987.

Arrom, Silvia M. *La Mujer Mexicana ante el Divórcio Eclesiástico, 1800–1857.* Mexico City: Secretária de Educación Pública, Dirección General de Divulgación, 1976.

Arrom, Silvia M. *The Women of Mexico City, 1790–1857.* Stanford, Calif.: Stanford University Press, 1985.

Bancroft, Hubert Howe. *History of Arizona and New Mexico, 1530–1888.* San Francisco: History Co., 1889. (Reprint, Albuquerque: Horn and Wallace, 1962.)

Barrera, Mario. *Race and Class in the Southwest: A Theory of Racial Inequality.* Notre Dame, Ind.: University of Notre Dame Press, 1979.

Barth, Gunther. *Instant Cities: Urbanization and the Rise of San Francisco and Denver.* New York: Oxford University Press, 1975.

Bash, Harry H. *Sociology, Race, and Ethnicity: A Critique of American Ideological Intrusions Upon Sociological Theory.* New York: Gordon and Breach, 1979.

Bataille, Gretchen M. *American Indian Women: A Guide to Research.* New York: Garland, 1991.

Bauer, Arnold. *Chilean Rural Society from the Spanish Conquest to 1930.* Cambridge: Cambridge University Press, 1975.

Bauman, Richard, Roger Abrahams, and Susan Kalcik. "American Folklore and American Studies." *American Quarterly* 38 (1976), 360–377.

Beck, Warren A. and Ynez D. Haase. *Historical Atlas of New Mexico.* Norman: University of Oklahoma Press, 1969.

Beers, George A. *The California Outlaw: Tiburcio Vásquez.* Comp. Robert Greenwood. Los Gatos, Calif.: Talisman Press, 1960. (Reprint, New York: Arno Press, 1974.)

Bernal, Ignacio. *Mexico before Cortez: Art, History, and Legend.* Garden City, N.Y.: Doubleday, 1963.

Bieber, Ralph P., ed. *Southern Trails to California in 1849*. Glendale: Arthur H. Clark, 1937.

Bieber, Ralph P., ed. *The Journal of Marcellus Ball Edwards*. Glendale: Arthur H. Clark, 1932.

Billington, Ray Allen. *The Protestant Crusade, 1800–1860: A Study of the Origins of American Nativism*. Gloucester, Mass.: Peter Smith, 1963.

Billington, Ray Allen. *The Far Western Frontier, 1830–1860*, New York: Harper, 1956.

Blackburn, George, and Sherman L. Richards. "The Prostitutes and Gamblers of Virginia City, Nevada: 1870." *Pacific Historical Review* 47 (May 1979), No. 2, 239–258.

Bolton, Herbert Eugene, ed. *Spanish Exploration in the Southwest, 1542–1706*. New York: Barnes and Noble, 1963.

Brack, Gene M. "Mexican Opinion, American Racism, and the War of 1846." *Western Historical Quarterly* 1 (1970), 161–174.

Braudel, Fernand. *The Mediterranean and the Mediterranean World in the Age of Philip II*, vol. I, II. Trans. Sian Reynolds. New York: Harper and Row, 1972–1973.

Briggs, Charles L., and John R. Van Ness, eds. *Land, Water, and Culture: New Perspectives on Hispanic Land Grants*. Albuquerque: University of New Mexico Press, 1987.

Briggs, Walter. "The Lady They Called Tules." *New Mexico Magazine* 44 (1971), 9–16.

Brown, Dee A. *Bury My Heart at Wounded Knee: An Indian History of the American West*. New York: Holt, Rinehart and Winston, 1971.

Burr, Anna Robeson. *The Golden Quicksand: A Novel of Santa Fé*. New York: D. Appleton-Century, 1936.

Bustamante, Antonio Rios. "New Mexico in the Eighteenth Century: Life, Labor and Trade in La Villa de San Felipe de Albuquerque, 1706–1790," *Aztlan: A Journal of Chicano Studies* 7:3 (Fall 1976), 357–389.

Butler, Anne M. *Daughters of Joy, Sisters of Mercy: Prostitutes in the American West, 1865–1890*. Champaign: University of Illinois Press, 1985.

Butler, Anne M. *Gendered Justice in the American West: Women Prisoners in Men's Penitentiaries*. Champaign: University of Illinois Press, 1997.

Callcott, Wilfred H. *Church and State in Mexico, 1822–1857*. Durham, N.C.: Duke University Press, 1926.

Camarillo, Albert. *Chicanos in a Changing Society: From Mexican Pueblos to American Barrios in Santa Barbara and Southern California. 1848–1930*. Cambridge: Harvard University Press, 1979.

Campbell, John. K. *Honour, Family and Patronage: A Study of Institutions and Moral Values in a Greek Mountain Community*. Oxford: Clarendon, 1964.

Capdégui, José Maria Ots. "Bosquejo histórico de los derechos de la mujer casada en la legislación de Indias." *Revista General de legislación y jurisprudencia* 132 (1918), 162–182.

Cardenal, Ernesto. *The Gospel in Solentiname*, vol. I. Trans. Donald D. Walsh. Maryknoll, N.Y.: Orbis Books, 1976.

Castañeda, Antonia. "Gender, Race, and Culture: Spanish-Mexican Women in the Historiography of Frontier California." *Frontiers: A Journal of Women's Studies* 11 (1990), 8–20.

Castañeda, Antonia. "Women of Color and the Rewriting of Western History: The Discourse, Politics, and Decolonization of History." *Pacific Historical Review* 61:4 (November 1992), 501–533.

Cather, Willa. *Death Comes for the Archbishop*. New York: Knopf, 1927. (Reprint, New York: Vintage Books, 1971.)

Chabram, Angie, and Rosalinda Fregoso, eds. *Special Issue:* "Chicana/o Cultural Representations: Reframing Alternative Critical Discourses." *Cultural Studies* 4:3 (October 1990).

Chabram-Dernersesian, Angie. "I Throw Punches for my Race, but I Don't Want to Be a Man: Writing US—Chica-nos (Girl, Us)/Chicanas—into the Movement Script," in Lawrence Grossberg, Cary Nelson, and Paula Treichler, eds., *Cultural Studies* (New York: Routledge, 1992).

Chacón, Rafael. *Legacy of Honor: The Life of Rafael Chacón, a Nineteenth-Century New Mexican*. Ed. Jacqueline Dorgan Meketa. Albuquerque: University of New Mexico Press, 1986.

Chávez, Fray Angélico. "Doña Tules, Her Fame and Her Funeral." *El Palacio* 57 (August 1950), 227–234.

Chené, Roberto (College of Santa Fe, invited speaker). Santa Fe. Interview, November 15, 1978.

Christian, Barbara. "The Race for Theory." *Cultural Critique*, no. 6 (Spring 1987). (Special Issue: "The Nature and Context of Minority Discourse," ed. Abdul R. JanMohamed and David Lloyd).

Clark, Ira. *Water in New Mexico: A History of Its Management and Use*. Albuquerque: University of New Mexico Press, 1987.

Clarke, Dwight L. *Stephen Watts Kearny, Soldier of the West*. Norman: University of Oklahoma Press, 1961.

Clifford, James. *The Predicament of Culture: Twentieth-Century Ethnography, Literature, and Art*. Cambridge: Harvard University Press, 1988.

Cluett, Ron. "Roman Women in the Second Triumviral." Lecture delivered at Pomona College, January 24, 1997.

Coates, Jennifer, and Deborah Cameron, eds. *Women in Their Speech Communities: New Perspectives on Language and Sex*. London: Longman, 1988.

Cohen, Robin. "Resistance and Hidden Forms of Consciousness amongst African Workers." *Review of African Political Economy* (July 1981).

Collier, Jane F. *Marriage and Inequality in Classless Societies*. Stanford: Stanford University Press, 1988.

Coontz, Stephanie. *The Social Origins of Private Life: A History of American Families, 1600–1900*. London: Verso, 1988.

Córdova, Teresa, ed. *Chicano Studies: Critical Connections between Research and Community*. Albuquerque: University of New Mexico Press, 1992.

Craver, Rebecca McDowell. *The Impact of Intimacy: Mexican-Anglo Intermarriage in New Mexico, 1821–1846*. El Paso: Texas Western Press, 1982.

Crisp, Jeff. *The Story of an African Working Class: Ghanaian Miners' Struggles 1870–1980*. London: Zed Books, 1984.

Croy, Homer. *Jesse James Was My Neighbor*. New York: Duell, Sloane and Pearce, 1949.

Daniels, Roger. *The Politics of Prejudice: The Anti-Japanese Movement in California and the Struggle for Japanese Exclusion*. Berkeley: University of California Press, 1977.

Daniels, Roger. *Concentration Camps: North America: Japanese in the United States and Canada During World War II*. Malabar, Fla.: R.E. Krieger Publishing, 1981.

Daniels, Roger, Sandra C. Taylor, and Harry H. L. Kitano, eds. *Japanese Americans: From Relocation to Redress*. Salt Lake City: University of Utah Press, 1986.

De Graff, Lawrence B. "Race, Sex, and Region: Black Women in the American West, 1850–1920." *Pacific Historical Review* 49 (May 1980), 285–313.

Del Castillo, Adelaida. "Malintzin Tenepal: A Preliminary Look into a New Perspective," in Rosaura Sánchez and Rosa Martínez Cruz, eds., *Essays on La Mujer*. Los Angeles: Chicano Studies Publications, University of California, Los Angeles, 1978.

Del Castillo, Adelaida, ed. *Between Borders: Essays on Mexicana/Chicana History*. Encino, Calif.: Floricanto Press, 1990.

De León, Arnoldo. *The Tejano Community, 1836–1900*. Albuquerque: University of New Mexico Press, 1982.

Deutsch, Sarah. *No Separate Refuge: Culture, Class and Gender on an Anglo-Hispanic Frontier in the American Southwest 1880–1940*. New York: Oxford University Press, 1987.

Dorris, Michael. *The Broken Cord*. New York: Harper and Row, 1989.

Drinnon, Richard. *Facing West: The Metaphysics of Indian-Hating and Empire-Building*. Minneapolis: University of Minnesota Press, 1980.

Dundes, Alan. "North American Folklore Studies." *Journal de la Société des Américanistes* 56 (1967), 53–79.

Dundes, Alan. "Folk Ideas as Units of Worldview." *Journal of American Folklore* 82 (January–March 1971), 93–103.

Dysart, Jane. "Mexican Women in San Antonio, 1830–1860: The Assimilation Process." *Western Historical Quarterly* 7 (October 1976), 365–375.

Ebright, Malcolm. *Land Grants and Lawsuits in Northern New Mexico*. Albuquerque: University of New Mexico Press, 1994.

Ellis, Bruce T. *Bishop Lamy's Santa Fe Cathedral*. Albuquerque: University of New Mexico Press, 1985.

Emmons, David M., *The Butte Irish: Class and Ethnicity in an American Mining Town, 1875–1925*. Champaign: University of Illinois Press, 1989.

Etienne, Mona, and Eleanor Leacock, eds. *Women and Colonization: Anthropological Perspectives*. New York: Praeger, 1980.

Fanon, Frantz. *Black Skin, White Masks*. Trans. Charles Lam Markmann. New York: Grove Weidenfeld, 1991.

Fanon, Frantz. *The Wretched of the Earth*. Trans. Constance Farrington. New York: Grove Weidenfeld, 1991.

Fanon, Frantz. *Toward the African Revolution: Political Essays*. Trans. Haakan Chevalier. New York: Monthly Review Press, 1967. (Reprint, New York: Grove Press, 1988.)

Faragher, John M. "The Custom of the Country: Cross-Cultural Marriage in the Far Western Fur Trade," in Lillian Schlissel, Vicki Ruiz, and Janice Monk, eds. *Western Women: Their Lands Their Lives*. Albuquerque: University of New Mexico Press, 1988, 199–215.

Ferguson, Russell, et al., eds. *Out There: Marginalization and Contemporary Cultures*. New York: New Museum of Contemporary Art; Cambridge: MIT Press, 1990.

Findlay, John. *People of Chance: Gambling in American Society from Jamestown to Las Vegas*. New York: Oxford University Press, 1986.

Foote, Cheryl J., and Sandra K. Schackel, "Indian Women of New Mexico, 1535–1680," in Joan M. Jensen and Darlis A. Miller, eds., *New Mexico Women: Intercultural Perspectives*. Albuquerque: University of New Mexico Press, 1986.

Forbes, Jack D. *Apache, Navaho, and Spaniard*. Norman: University of Oklahoma Press, 1960.

Foucault, Michel. *The History of Sexuality*. New York: Pantheon, 1980.

Francis, E. K. "Padre Martínez: A New Mexico Myth." *New Mexico Historical Review* 31 (October 1956), 265–289.

Frankenberg, Ruth. *White Women, Race Matters: The Social Construction of Whiteness.* Minneapolis: University of Minnesota Press, 1993.

Freire, Paulo. *Pedagogy of the Oppressed.* Trans. Myra Bergman Ramos. New York: Herder and Herder, 1970.

García, Mario. "The Chicana in American History: The Mexican Women of El Paso, 1880–1920—A Case Study." *Pacific Historical Review* 49:2 (May 1980), 315–338.

García, Mario T. *Desert Immigrants: The Mexicans of El Paso, 1880–1920.* New Haven: Yale University Press, 1981.

García, Mario T. *Mexican Americans: Leadership, Ideology, and Identity, 1930–1960.* New Haven: Yale University Press, 1989.

Gaspar de Alba, Alicia. *Chicano Art Inside/Outside the Master's House: Cultural Politics and the CARA Exhibition.* Austin: University of Texas Press, 1998.

Gaspar de Alba, Alicia. *Sor Juana's Second Dream.* Albuquerque: University of New Mexico Press, 1999.

Gibson, George Rutledge. *George Rutledge Gibson's Journal of a Soldier under Kearny and Doniphan: 1846–1847.* Ed. Ralph P. Bieber. Glendale: Clark, 1935.

Gilmore, David D., ed. *Honor and Shame and the Unity of the Mediterranean.* Washington, D.C.: American Anthropological Association, 1987.

Goldman, Marion. "Western Women, Their Lands, Their Lives." Paper presented at the Southwest Institute for Research on Women, Tucson, April 1984.

Goldman, Marion S. *Gold Diggers and Silver Miners: Prostitution and Social Life on the Comstock Lode.* Ann Arbor: University of Michigan Press, 1981.

González, Deena J. "Chicana Identity Matters," in Antonia Darder, *Culture and Difference: Critical Perspectives on the Bicultural Experience in the United States.* Westport, Conn.: Bergin and Garvey, 1995. (Reprinted in *Aztlán: A Journal of Chicano Studies* 22 [Fall 1997].)

González, Deena J. "La Tules of Image and Reality: Euro-American Attitudes and Legend Formation on a Spanish-Mexican Frontier," in Adela de la Torre and Beatríz M. Pesquera, *Building with Our Hands: New Directions in Chicana Studies.* Berkeley: University of California Press, 1993. (Reprinted in Ellen DuBois and Vicki Ruiz, eds., *Unequal Sisters: A Multicultural Reader in U.S. Women's History.* New York: Routledge, 1995.)

González, Deena J. "The Widowed Women of Santa Fe: Assessments on the Lives of an Unmarried Population, 1850–1880," in Arlene Scadron, ed., *On Their Own: Widows and Widowhood in the American Southwest. 1848–1939.* Champaign: University of Illinois Press, 1989. (Reprinted in Ellen DuBois and Vicki Ruiz, eds., *Unequal Sisters: A Multicultural Reader in U.S. Women's History.* New York: Routledge, 1990.)

González, Deena J. "Chicano Studies and La Chicana," Background paper, in Alfredo Gonzalez and David Sandoval, eds., *Symposium on Chicano Studies* (1988).

Goodfriend, Joyce D. "The Struggle for Survival: Widows in Denver, 1880–1912," in Arlene Scadron, ed., *On Their Own: Widows and Widowhood in the American Southwest, 1848–1939.* Champaign: University of Illinois Press, 1989.

Gordon, Milton M. *Assimilation in American Life: The Role of Race, Religion, and National Origins.* New York: Oxford University Press, 1964.

Gordon, Milton M., ed. *America as a Multicultural Society.* Philadelphia: Annals of the American Academy of Political and Social Science, 1981.

Grant, Blanche C. *Doña Lona: A Story of Old Taos and Santa Fe.* New York: Wilfred Funk, 1941.

Griswold Del Castillo, Richard. *La Familia: Chicano Families in the Urban Southwest, 1848 to the Present.* Notre Dame, Ind.: University of Notre Dame Press, 1984.

Griswold Del Castillo, Richard. *The Los Angeles Barrio, 1850–1890: A Social History.* Berkeley: University of California Press, 1979.

Guerin-Gonzales, Camille. *Mexican Workers and American Dreams: Immigration, Repatriation, and California Farm Labor, 1900–1939.* New Brunswick, N.J.: Rutgers University Press, 1994.

Gunn Allen, Paula. *The Sacred Hoop: Recovering the Feminine in American Indian Traditions.* Boston: Beacon Press, 1986.

Gutiérrez, David. *Walls and Mirrors: Mexican Americans, Mexican Immigrants, and the Politics of Ethnicity in the American Southwest.* Berkeley: University of California Press, 1995.

Gutiérrez, Ramón A. "Honor Ideology, Marriage Negotiation, and Class-Gender Domination in New Mexico, 1690–1846." *Latin American Perspectives* 12 (Winter 1985), 81–104.

Gutiérrez, Ramón A. "Honor, Witchcraft, and Sexual Inversion in Colonial New Mexico." Paper presented at Western Historical Association Annual Meeting, Salt Lake City, Utah, October 12, 1984.

Gutiérrez, Ramón A. *When Jesus Came, the Corn Mothers Went Away: Marriage, Sexuality and Power in New Mexico, 1800–1846.* Stanford, Calif.: Stanford University Press, 1991.

Gutiérrez, Ramón, and Genaro Padilla, eds. *Recovering the U.S. Literary Hispanic Heritage.* Houston: Arte Publico Press, 1993.

Gutman, Herbert. *The Black Family in Slavery and Freedom, 1750–1925.* New York: Pantheon, 1976.

Haas, Lizbeth. *Conquests and Historical Identities in California, 1769–1936.* Berkeley: University of California Press, 1995.

Hall, Emlen, and David J. Weber. "Mexican Liberals and the Pueblo Indians, 1821–1829." *New Mexico Historical Review* 59:1 (1984), 5–32.

Hall, Thomas D. *Social Change in the Southwest, 1350–1880.* Lawrence: University Press of Kansas, 1989.

Hernández, Salomé. "Nueva Mexicanas as Refugees and Reconquest Settlers," in Joan M. Jensen and Darlis A. Miller, eds. *New Mexico Women: Intercultural Perspectives.* Albuquerque: University of New Mexico Press, 1986.

Herzfeld, Michael. "Honor and Shame: Problems in the Comparative Analysis of Moral Systems." *Man* 15.

Hirata, Lucie Cheng. "Free, Indentured, Enslaved: Chinese Prostitutes in Nineteenth Century America." *Signs: Journal of Women in Culture and Society* 5 (Autumn, 1979), 3–29.

Hobsbawm, Eric J. *Primitive Rebels: Studies in Archaic Forms of Social Movement in the l9th and 20th Centuries.* Manchester, Eng.: Manchester University Press, 1959.

Horgan, Paul. *Lamy of Santa Fe: His Life and Times.* New York: Farrar, Straus and Giroux, 1975.

Horgan, Paul. *Centuries of Santa Fe.* New York: E. P. Dutton, 1965.

Horgan, Paul F. *Great River: The Rio Grande in North American History.* 2 vols. New York: Holt, Rinehart and Winston, 1954.

Horn, Calvin. *New Mexico's Troubled Years: The Story of the Early Territorial Governors.* Albuquerque: Horn and Wallace, 1963.

Horvath, Steven M. Jr. "The Genízaros of Eighteenth Century New Mexico: A Reexamination." *Discovery* 12 (Fall 1977), 3.

Hunt, Lynn, ed. *The New Cultural History*. Berkeley: University of California Press, 1989.

Hurtado, Albert. *Indian Survival on the California Frontier*. New Haven: Yale University Press, 1988.

I Shot Jesse James. Director: Samuel Fuller, 1949.

Isasi-Díaz, Ada María. *In the Struggle: A Hispanic Women's Liberation Theology*. Minneapolis: Fortress Press, 1993.

Isasi-Díaz, Ada María. *Hispanic Women, Prophetic Voice in the Church: Toward a Hispanic Women's Liberation Theology*. San Francisco: Harper and Row, 1988.

Jameson, Frederic. *Postmodernism: Or, the Cultural Logic of Late Capitalism*. Durham, N.C.: Duke University Press, 1991.

Jeffrey, Julie Roy. *Frontier Women: The Trans-Mississippi West, 1840–1880*. New York: Hill and Wang, 1979.

Jesse James at Bay. Director: Joseph Kane, 1941.

John, Elizabeth A. H. *Storms Brewed in Other Men's Worlds: The Confrontation of Indians, Spanish, and French in the Southwest, 1540–1795*. College Station: Texas A & M University Press, 1975.

Johnson, Allen. *The Dictionary of American Biography*. New York: Scribner, 1936.

Johnson, Susan L. "Sharing Bed and Board: Cohabitation and Cultural Difference in Central Arizona Mining Towns, 1863–1873," in Susan Armitage and Elizabeth Jameson, eds., *The Women's West*. Norman: University of Oklahoma Press, 1987.

Johnson, Susan. "'A Memory Sweet to Soldiers': The Significance of Gender in the History of the American West." *Western Historical Quarterly* 3 (1994), 322–345.

Jones, Hester. "The Spiegelbergs and Early Trade in New Mexico." *El Palacio* 38 (April 1935), 81–89.

Jones, Steve. "The Trust Fund Hippies of Santa Fe." *Santa Fe Magazine* 3 (1980).

Jordan, Winthrop D. *White over Black: American Attitudes toward the Negro*. Published for the Institute of Early American History and Culture, Williamsburg, Va. Chapel Hill: University of North Carolina Press, 1968.

Josephy, Alvin M. *The Nez Percé Indians and the Opening of the Northwest*. New Haven: Yale University Press 1965.

Karras, Ruth Mazo. "Common Women: Prostitution and Sexuality in Medieval Culture." Lecture delivered at Scripps College Humanities Institute, February 28, 1991.

Katz, William Loren. *The Black West: A Documentary and Pictorial History of the African-American Role in the Westward Expansion of the United States*. New York: Oxford University Press, 1996.

Kay, Geoffrey. *Development and Underdevelopment: A Marxist Analysis*. London: Macmillan, 1975.

Kidwell, Clara Sue, "Indian Women as Cultural Mediators." *Ethnohistory* 39:2 (1992), 97–107.

Kolodny, Annette. *The Lay of the Land: Metaphor As Experience and History in American Life and Letters*. Chapel Hill: University of North Carolina Press, 1975.

Kolodny, Annette. *The Land before Her: Fantasy and Experience of the American Frontiers, 1630–1860*. Chapel Hill: University of North Carolina Press, 1984.

La Farge, Oliver. *Santa Fe: The Autobiography of a Southwestern Town*. Norman: University of Oklahoma Press, 1959.

Lamar, Howard Roberts. *The Far Southwest, 1846–1912: A Territorial History*. New York: Norton, 1970.

Laslett, Barbara. "Household Structure on an American Frontier: Los Angeles, California, in 1850." *American Journal of Sociology* 81 (July 1975), 109–128.

Laughlin, Ruth. *The Wind Leaves No Shadow*. Caldwell, Idaho: Caxton Printers, 1978.

Lavrin, Asunción. "Values and Meaning of Monastic Life for Nuns in Colonial Mexico." *Catholic Historical Review* 57 (October 1972), 367–387.

Lavrin, Asunción, ed. *Latin American Women: Historical Perspectives*. Westport, Conn.: Greenwood Press, 1978.

Lavrin, Asunción, and Couturier, Edith. "Dowries and Wills: A View of Women's Socioeconomic Role in Colonial Guadalajara and Puebla, 1640–1790." *Hispanic American Historical Review* 59 (1979), 280–304.

Lawrence, Eleanor. "Mexican Trade between Santa Fe and Los Angeles, 1830–1848." *California Historical Society Quarterly* 10 (March 1931), 27–39.

Lebsock, Suzanne. *The Free Women of Petersburg: Status and Culture in a Southern Town, 1784–1860*. New York: Norton, 1984.

Lecompte, Janet. "La Tules and the Americans." *Arizona and the West*, (Autumn 1978), 228.

Lecompte, Janet. "The Independent Women of Hispanic New Mexico, 1821–1846." *Western Historical Quarterly* 22 (January 1981), 17–35.

Lecompte, Janet. *Rebellion in Rio Arriba, 1837*. Albuquerque: University of New Mexico Press, 1985.

Leon-Portilla, Miguel, ed. *The Broken Spears: The Aztec Account of the Conquest of Mexico*. Boston: Beacon Press, 1962; rev. ed., 1992.

Levine, Robert A., and Donald T. Campbell. *Ethnocentrism: Theories of Conflict, Ethnic Attitudes, and Group Behavior*. New York: Wiley, 1971.

Limerick, Patricia Nelson. *The Legacy of Conquest: The Unbroken Past of the American West*. New York: Norton, 1987.

Limerick, Patricia Nelson, et al., eds. *Trails: Toward a New Western History*. Lawrence: University Press of Kansas, 1991.

Limón, Jose E. "La Llorona, The Third Legend of Greater Mexico: Cultural Symbols, Women, and the Political Unconscious," in Adelaida del Castillo, ed., *Between Borders: Essays on Mexicana/Chicana History*. Encino, Calif.: Floricanto Press, 1990, 399–432.

Little Injustices: Laura Nader Looks at the Law. Public Broadcasting Associates. Boston: PBS Video, 1981.

Liu, Tessie P. "Race and Gender in the Politics of Group Formation: A Comment on Notions of Multiculturalism." Paper delivered at the University of Arizona, March 1991.

Lucero-White, Aurora, ed. *The Folklore of New Mexico*. Santa Fe: Seton Village Press, 1941.

Major, Mabel, Rebecca W. Smith, and T. M. Pearce. *Southwest Heritage: A Literary History with Bibliography*. Albuquerque: University of New Mexico Press, 1938.

Mani, Lata. Multiple Mediations: Feminist Scholarship in the Age of Multicultural Reception. *Feminist Review*, no. 35 (Summer 1990), 24–41.

Markovitz, Irving Leonard, ed. *Studies in Power and Class in Africa*. New York: Oxford University Press, 1987.

Matsumoto, Valerie J. *Farming the Home Place: A Japanese American Community in California, 1919–1982*. Ithaca, N.Y.: Cornell University Press, 1993.

McCurdy, Ed. *Songs of the Old West*. New York: Elektra Records, 1957.

McGrath, Roger D. *Gunfighters, Highwaymen and Vigilantes: Violence on the Frontier*. Berkeley: University of California Press, 1984.

McNitt, Frank. *Navajo Wars: Military Campaigns, Slave Raids, and Reprisals*. Albuquerque: University of New Mexico Press, 1972.

McWilliams, Carey. *North From Mexico: The Spanish-Speaking People of the United States*. New York: Greenwood Press, 1968.

Mecham, J. Lloyd. *Church and State in Latin America: A History of Politico-Ecclesiastical Relations*. Rev. ed. Chapel Hill: University of North Carolina Press, 1966.

Melville, Herman. *The Confidence-Man: His Masquerade*. New York: New American Library, 1964.

Memmi, Albert. *The Colonizer and the Colonized*. Trans. Howard Greenfeld. Boston: Beacon Press, 1967.

Merk, Frederick. *Manifest Destiny and Mission in American History: A Reinterpretation*. New York: Knopf, 1963.

Miller, Darlis A. "Cross-Cultural Marriages in the Southwest: The New Mexico Experience, 1846–1900." *New Mexico Historical Review* 57 (October 1982), 335–359.

Miller, Darlis A., and Jensen, Joan M. "The Gentle Tamers Revisited: New Approaches to the History of Women in the American West." *Pacific Historical Review* 49:2 (May 1980), 173–214.

Miller, Darlis A., and Joan M. Jensen, eds. *New Mexico Women: Intercultural Perspectives*. Albuquerque: University of New Mexico Press, 1986.

Milner, Clyde II, ed., *A New Significance: Re-envisioning the History of the American West*. New York: Oxford University Press, 1996.

Minh-ha, Trinh T. *Woman, Native, Other: Writing Postcoloniality and Feminism*. Bloomington: Indiana University Press, 1989.

Miranda, Gloria. "Gente de Razón Marriage Patterns in Spanish and Mexican California: A Case Study of Santa Barbara and Los Angeles." *Southern California Quarterly* 63 (Spring 1981), 1–21.

Mirandé, Alfred, and Evangelina Enríquez. *La Chicana: The Mexican-American Woman*. Chicago: University of Chicago Press, 1979.

Mitchell, Juliet. *Woman's Estate*. New York: Vintage Books, 1973.

Mohanty, Chandra Talpade. "Under Western Eyes: Feminist Scholarship and Colonial Discourse." *Boundary II*, vol. 12, no. 3/vol. 13, no. 1 (Spring/Fall 1984), 333–358.

Mohanty, Chandra Talpade, Ann Russo, and Lourdes Torres, eds., *Third World Women and the Politics of Feminism*. Bloomington: Indiana University Press, 1991.

Montejano, David. *Anglos and Mexicans in the Making of Texas, 1836–1986*. Austin: University of Texas Press, 1987.

Moorhead, Max. *New Mexico's Royal Road: Trade and Travel on the Chihuahua Trail*. Norman: University of Oklahoma Press, 1958.

Moraga, Cherrie, and Gloria Anzaldúa, eds. *This Bridge Called My Back: Writings by Radical Women of Color*. Watertown, Mass.: Persephone Press, 1981.

Morgan, Dale. "The Diary of William H. Ashley, March 25-June 27, 1825." *Bulletin of the Missouri Historical Society* 11 (October 1856), 13.

Mörner, Magnus. *Race Mixture in the History of Latin America*. Boston: Little, Brown, 1967.

Motto, Sytha. "The Sisters of Charity and St. Vincent's Hospital: An Amplification of Sister Mallon's Journal." *New Mexico Historical Review* 52 (March 1977), 229–250.

Myers, Joan, and Marc Simmons. *Along the Santa Fe Trail*. Albuquerque: University of New Mexico Press, 1986.

Myres, Sandra L. "Mexican Americans and Westering Anglos: A Feminine Perspective." *New Mexico Historical Review* 57 (October 1982), 310–329.

Myres, Sandra L. *Westering Women and the Frontier Experience, 1800–1915.* Albuquerque: University of New Mexico Press, 1982.

Nash, June. "Aztec Women: The Transition from Status to Class in Empire and Colony," in Mona Etienne and Eleanor Leacock, eds., *Women and Colonization.* New York: Praeger, 1980.

Novick, Peter. *That Noble Dream: The "Objectivity Question" and the American Historical Profession.* Cambridge: Cambridge University Press, 1988.

O'Meara, Walter. *Daughters of the Country: The Women of the Fur Traders and Mountain Men.* New York: Harcourt, Brace and World, 1968.

Omi, Michael, and Howard Winant. *Racial Formation in the U.S.: From the 1960s to the 1980s.* New York: Routledge and Kegan Paul, 1987.

Ortiz, Roxanne Dunbar. *Roots of Resistance: Land Tenure in New Mexico, 1680–1980.* Los Angeles: Chicano Studies Research Center Publications, University of California, Los Angeles; and American Indian Studies Center, University of California, Los Angeles, 1980.

Painter, Nell. *Exodusters: Black Migration to Kansas after Reconstruction.* New York: Norton, 1976.

Paredes, Raymond A. "The Mexican Image in American Travel Literature, 1831–1869." *New Mexico Historical Quarterly* 1 (1977), 5–29.

Parkman, Francis. *Prairie and Rocky Mountain Life, Or the California and Oregon Trail.* Columbus: J. Miller, 1857.

Pascoe, Peggy. *Relations of Rescue: The Search for Female Moral Authority in the American West, 1874–1939.* New York: Oxford University Press, 1990.

Pascoe, Peggy, "Race, Gender, and Intercultural Relations: The Case of Interracial Marriage," *Frontiers* 12:1 (1991), 16–32.

Paz, Octavio. "Juana Ramirez." Trans. Diane Marting. *Signs: Journal of Women in Culture and Society* (Autumn 1979), 80–97.

Paz, Octavio. *Labyrinth of Solitude: Life and Thought in Mexico.* Trans. Lysander Kemp. New York: Grove Press, 1962.

Pearce, Roy Harvey. "Melville's Indian Hater: A Note on the Meaning of the Confidence-Man." *Publications of the Modern Language Association* 57 (1952), 942–948.

Pérez, Emma M. "Speaking from the Margin: Uninvited Discourse on Sexuality and Power," in Beatríz Pesquera and Adela de la Torre, eds., *Building with Our Hands: New Directions in Chicana Scholarship.* Berkeley: University of California Press, 1991, 57–71.

Pérez, Emma M. *The Decolonial Imaginary: Writing Chicanas into History.* Bloomington: Indiana University Press, 1999.

Peristiany, John George. *Honour and Shame: The Values of Mediterranean Society.* Chicago: University of Chicago Press, 1966.

Perry, Elizabeth. "On Virgins and Martyrs." Phoebe Estelle Spaulding Lecture at Pomona College, February 3, 1987.

Pessen, Edward. *Jacksonian American: Society Personality and Politics.* Homewood, Ill.: Dorsey Press, 1969; rev. ed., 1978.

Petrik, Paula. *No Step Backward: Women and Family on the Rocky Mountain Mining Frontier, Helena, Montana, 1865–1900.* Helena: Montana Historical Society Press, 1987.

Phelan, Shane. *Identity Politics: Lesbian Feminism and the Limits of Community.* Philadelphia: Temple University Press, 1989.

Pisani, Donald J. *To Reclaim a Divided West: Water, Law, and Public Policy, 1848–1902.* Albuquerque: University of New Mexico Press, 1992.

Pitt, Leonard. *The Decline of the Californios: A Social History of the Spanish-Speaking Californians, 1846–1890.* Berkeley: University of California Press, 1966.

Powell, Philip Wayne. *Tree of Hate: Propaganda and Prejudices Affecting United States Social Relations with the Hispanic World.* New York: Basic Books, 1971.

Priest, Loring Benson. *Uncle Sam's Stepchildren: The Reformation of United States Indian Policy, 1865–1887.* New Brunswick, N.J.: Octagon, 1942. (Reprint, Lincoln: University of Nebraska Press, 1978.)

Prince, L. Bradford. *Old Fort Marcy, Santa Fe. New Mexico: Historical Sketch and Panoramic View of Santa Fe and Its Vicinity.* Santa Fe: New Mexican Printing, 1912.

Prince, L. Bradford. *Spanish Mission Churches of New Mexico.* Glorieta, N.M.: Rio Grande Press, 1977.

Prucha, Francis Paul. *American Indian Policy in the Formative Years: The Indian Trade and Intercourse Acts, 1790–1834.* New Brunswick, N.J.: Rutgers University Press, 1942.

Reilly, Tom. "Jane McManus Storms: Letters from the Mexican War, 1846–1848." *Southwestern Historical Quarterly* 85 (July/April 1981–1982), 21–44.

Reiter, Rayna. *Toward an Anthropology of Women.* New York: Monthly Review Press, 1975.

Richter, Thomas. "Sister Catherine Mallon's Journal (Part One)." *New Mexico Historical Review* 52 (April 1977), 135–155.

Riley, Glenda. *Women and Indians on the Frontier, 1825–1915.* Albuquerque: University of New Mexico Press, 1984.

Ringer, Benjamin B. *"We the People" and Others: Duality and America's Treatment of Its Racial Minorities.* New York: Tavistock Publications, 1983.

Robinson, Cecil. *Mexico and the Hispanic Southwest in American Literature.* Tucson: University of Arizona Press, 1977.

Robinson, Jacob, "Sketches of the Great West: A Journal of the Santa Fe Expedition under Colonel Doniphan, 1846." *Magazine of History* 32:4, Special Issue no. 128 (1927).

Rock, Rosalind Z. "'Pido y Suplico': Women and the Law in Spanish New Mexico, 1697–1763." *New Mexico Historical Review* 65 (April 1990), 145–159.

Rosaldo, Michelle Zimbalist, and Louise Lamphere, eds. *Woman, Culture, and Society.* Stanford: Stanford University Press, 1974.

Rosen, Ruth. *The Lost Sisterhood: Prostitution in America, 1900–1918.* Baltimore: Johns Hopkins University Press, 1982.

Ross, Nancy W. *Westward the Women.* New York: Random House, 1958. (Reprint, San Francisco: North Point Press, 1985.)

Rothman, David J. *The Discovery of the Asylum: Social Order and Disorder in the New Republic.* Boston: Little, Brown, 1971; rev. ed., 1990.

Rubin, Gayle. "The Traffic in Women: Notes toward a Political Economy of Sex," in Rayna Reiter, ed., *Toward an Anthropology of Women.* New York: Monthly Review Press, 1975.

Ruiz, Vicki L. *Cannery Women, Cannery Lives: Mexican Women, Unionization and the California Food Processing Industry, 1930–1950.* Albuquerque: University of New Mexico Press, 1987.

Ruiz, Vicki L. *From Out of the Shadows: Mexican Women in Twentieth-Century America.* New York: Oxford University Press, 1998.

Said, Edward W. *Orientalism.* New York: Pantheon Books, 1978.

Salgado de Synder, Nellie Padilla, and Amado M. Padilla. "Interethnic Marriages of Mexican Americans after Nearly Two Decades." Spanish- Speaking Mental Health Research Center, UCLA, Occasional Paper 15, 1981.

Sánchez, George J. *Becoming Mexican American: Ethnicity, Culture, and Identity in Chicano Los Angeles, 1900–1945*. New York: Oxford University Press, 1993.

Sánchez, Rosaura. *Telling Identities: The Californio Testimonios*. Minneapolis: University of Minnesota Press, 1995.

Sánchez, Rosaura, and Rosa Martínez Cruz. *Essays on La Mujer*. Los Angeles: Chicano Studies Center Publications, University of California, Los Angeles, 1978.

Schlissel, Lillian. *Women's Diaries of the Westward Journey*. New York: Schocken Books, 1982.

Schlissel, Lillian, Vicki L. Ruiz, and Janice Monk. *Western Women: Their Land, Their Lives*. Albuquerque: University of New Mexico Press, 1988.

Scholes, Frances V. "Church and State in New Mexico, 1610–1650." *New Mexico Historical Review* 11 (1936), 9–76.

Scott, Joan W. *Gender and the Politics of History*. New York: Columbia University Press, 1988.

Seed, Patricia. *To Love, Honor, and Obey in Colonial Mexico: Conflicts over Marriage Choice, 1574–1821*. Stanford, Calif.: Stanford University Press, 1988.

Simmons, Marc. *The Little Lion of the Southwest: The Life of Manuel Antonio Chaves*. Chicago: Sage Books, 1973.

Simmons, Marc. *Witchcraft in the Southwest: Spanish and Indian Supernaturalism on the Rio Grande*. Flagstaff: Northland Press, 1974. (Reprint, Lincoln: University of Nebraska Press, 1980.)

Simpson, Lesley Byrd. *Many Mexicos*. 4th ed. rev. Berkeley: University of California Press, 1966.

Slotkin, Richard. *Regeneration through Violence: The Mythology of the American Frontier, 1600–1860*. Middletown, Conn.: Wesleyan University Press, 1973.

Smith, Henry Nash. *Virgin Land: The American West as Symbol and Myth*. Cambridge: Harvard University Press, 1978.

Spelman, Elisabeth V. *Inessential Woman: Problems of Exclusion in Feminist Thought*. Boston: Beacon Press, 1988.

Spicer, Edward H. *Cycles of Conquest: The Impact of Spain, Mexico, and the United States on the Indians of the Southwest, 1533–1960*. Tucson: University of Arizona Press, 1962.

Spickard, Paul R. *Mixed Blood: Intermarriage and Ethnic Identity in Twentieth-Century America*. Madison: University of Wisconsin Press, 1989.

Spivak, Gayatri Chakravorty. *In Other Worlds: Essays in Cultural Politics*. New York: Routledge, 1988.

Staples, Anne. *La iglésia en la Primera República Federal Mexicana, 1824–1835*. Mexico: Secretaria de Educación Pública, 1976.

Staudt, Kathleen. "Women's Politics, the State, and Capitalist Transformation in Africa," in Irving Leonard Markovitz, *Studies in Power and Class in Africa*. New York: Oxford University Press, 1987.

Staudt, Kathleen. *Free Trade?: Informal Economies at the U.S.-Mexico Border*. Philadelphia: Temple University Press, 1998.

Steinberg, Stephen. *The Ethnic Myth: Race, Ethnicity, and Class in America*. Boston: Beacon Press, 1989.

Sunseri, Alvin. *Seeds of Discord: New Mexico in the Aftermath of the American Conquest, 1846–1861*. Chicago: Nelson-Hall, 1979.

Surviving Columbus: The Story of the Pueblo People. New York: Public Broadcasting System, 1992.

Susman, Warren. *Culture as History: The Transformation of American Society in the Twentieth Century*. New York: Pantheon Books, 1984.

Swadesh, Frances Leon. *Los Primeros Pobladores: Hispanic Americans on the Ute Frontier.* Notre Dame, Ind.: University of Notre Dame Press, 1974.

Takaki, Ronald T. *Iron Cages: Race and Culture in 19th-Century America.* Seattle: University of Washington Press, 1982. (Reprint, New York: Oxford University Press, 1990.)

Takaki, Ronald T. *Strangers from a Different Shore: A History of Asian Americans.* New York: Penguin Books, 1989.

Taylor, Quintard. *The Forging of a Black Community: Seattle's Central District from 1870 through the Civil Rights Era.* Seattle: University of Washington Press, 1994.

Titus, N. C. "The Last Stand of the Nez Perces." *Washington Historical Quarterly* 6 (July 1915), 145–153.

Tjarks, Alicia. "Comparative Demographic Analysis of Texas, 1777–1793." *Southwestern Historical Quarterly* 77 (1974), 291–338.

Todorov, Tzvetan. *The Conquest of America: The Question of the Other.* New York: Harper and Row, 1984. (Reprint, New York: Harper Perennial, 1992).

The Life and Times of Jesse James. New York: ABC Television, 1965.

The Native Americans, Parts I, II, III. New York: Turner Broadcasting System, 1994.

The Return of Jesse James. Director: Arthur David Hilton, Los Angeles, 1950.

The True Story of Jesse James. Director: Nicholas Ray, 20th Century Fox, Los Angeles, 1957.

Trujillo, Carla, ed. *Chicana Lesbians: The Girls Our Mothers Warned Us About.* Berkeley: Third Woman Press, 1991.

Trulio, Beverly. "Anglo-American Attitudes toward New Mexican Women." *Journal of the West* 12 (1973), 229–239.

Twitchell, Ralph Emerson. *The Spanish Archives of New Mexico.* Cedar Rapids, Iowa: Torch Press, 1914.

Twitchell, Ralph Emerson. "The Historical Sketch of Governor William Carr Lane, Together with the Diary of His Journey from St. Louis, Mo., to Santa Fe, N.M. July 31st to September 9, 1852." *Historical Society of New Mexico* 4 (Santa Fe, 1917).

Twitchell, Ralph Emerson. *The Story of the Conquest of Santa Fe, New Mexico and the Building of Old Fort Marcy,* A.D. 1846. Santa Fe: Historical Society of New Mexico, 1923.

Twitchell, Ralph Emerson. *Leading Facts of New Mexico History,* vol. 2. Cedar Rapids, Iowa: Torch Press, 1911–1917.

Twitchell, Ralph Emerson. *The History of the Military Occupation of the Territory of New Mexico from 1846 to 1851 by the Government of the United States.* Denver: Smith-Brooks, 1909. (Reprint, New York: Arno Press, 1976.)

Tyler, Daniel. "Mexican Indian Policy in New Mexico." *New Mexico Historical Review* 55 (March 1980), 101–102.

Van Kirk, Sylvia. *"Many Tender Ties": Women in Fur-Trade Society in Western Canada, 1670–1870.* Winnipeg, Man.: Watson and Dwyer, 1980.

Vansina, Jan. *Oral Tradition: A Study in Historical Methodology.* Trans. H. M. Wright. Chicago: Aldine, 1965.

Veyna, Angelina, "'It is my Last Wish That . . .': A Look at Colonial Nuevo Mexicanas through Their Testaments," in Adela de la Torre and Beatríz Pesquera, eds., *Building with Our Hands: New Directions in Chicana Scholarship.* Berkeley: University of California Press, 1993, 91–108.

Wall, Helena M. *Fierce Communion: Family and Community in Early America.* Cambridge: Harvard University Press, 1990.

Wardhaugh, Ronald. *Languages in Competition: Dominance, Diversity, and Decline.* Oxford: B. Blackwell, 1987.

Warner, Louis H. "Conveyance of Property." *New Mexico Historical Review* 6 (October 1931), 327–359.

Warner, Louis H. "Wills and Hijuelas." *New Mexico Historical Review* 7 (January 1932), 75–89.

Warner, Marina. *Joan of Arc: The Image of Female Heroism.* New York: Knopf, 1981.

Waugh, Alfred S. *Travels in Search of the Elephant: The Wanderings of Alfred S. Waugh, Artist in Louisiana, Missouri, and Santa Fe in 1845–1846.* Ed. John Francis McDermott. St. Louis: Missouri Historical Society, 1951.

Weber, David J., ed. *Prose Sketches and Poems: Written in the Western Country with Additional Stories.* Albuquerque: C. Horn, 1967.

Weber, David J. *The Taos Trappers: The Fur Trade in the Far Southwest, 1540–1846.* Norman: University of Oklahoma Press, 1971.

Weber, David J. *The Mexican Frontier, 1821–1846: The American Southwest under Mexico.* Albuquerque: University of New Mexico Press, 1982.

Weber, David. *Foreigners in Their Own Land: Historical Roots of the Mexican Americans.* Albuquerque: University of New Mexico Press, 1973.

Weber, David. *The Spanish Frontier in North America.* New Haven: Yale University Press, 1992.

Weigle, Marta. *Brothers of Light. Brothers of Blood: The Penitents of the Southwest.* Albuquerque: University of New Mexico Press, 1976. (Reprint, Santa Fe: Ancient City Press, 1989.)

Weinberg, Albert K. *Manifest Destiny: A Study of Nationalist Expansionism in American History.* Chicago: Quadrangle Books, 1963. (Reprint, New York: AMS Press, 1979.)

West, Cornel. "The New Cultural Politics of Difference," in Russell Ferguson et al., eds., *Out There: Marginalization and Contemporary Cultures.* New York: New Museum of Contemporary Art, and Cambridge: MIT Press, 1990, 19–36.

West, Cornel. *Race Matters.* Boston: Beacon Press, 1993.

Westphall, Victor. *Mercedes Reales: Hispanic Land Grants of the Upper Rio Grande Region.* Albuquerque: University of New Mexico, 1983.

White, Hayden. *Metahistory.* Baltimore: Johns Hopkins University Press, 1973.

White, Richard. *Roots of Dependency: Subsistence, Environment, and Social Change among the Choctaws, Pawnees, and Navajos.* Lincoln: University of Nebraska Press, 1983.

White, Richard. *The Middle Ground: Indians, Empires, and Republics in the Great Lakes Region, 1650–1815.* New York: Cambridge University Press, 1991.

White, Richard. *"It's Your Misfortune and None of My Own": A New History of the American West.* Norman: University of Oklahoma Press, 1991.

Williams, Stanley T. *The Spanish Background of American Literature.* Hamden, Conn.: Archon Books, 1968.

Worster, Donald. *Rivers of Empire: Water, Aridity, and the Growth of the American West.* New York: Pantheon, 1985.

Worster, Donald. *Under Western Skies: Nature and History in the American West.* Oxford University Press, 1992.

Yung, Judy. *Unbound Feet: A Social History of Chinese Women in San Francisco.* Berkeley: University of California Press, 1995.

INDEX